ON DEATH ROW

Edited by Mike James

True Crime Library — No. 6
A Forum Press Book
by the Paperback Division of
Forum Design,
P.O. Box 158, London SE 20 7QA.

An Imprint of True Crime Library
© 1993 by Mike James
All rights reserved

Typeset by Techniset,
1 Back Cross Lane, Newton-le-Willows, Merseyside WA12 9YE.
Printed and bound in Great Britain by
Harper Collins Manufacturing, Glasgow.

ISBN 1 874358 05 2

For David Edwards,
a friend and colleague
for many years

In the True Crime Library series:

CONTENTS

PREFACE

To wake in the morning and realise that this is your last day alive is something straight out of a nightmare. Some men* understandably break under the strain and have to be carried screaming to their death. Ray Anderson was grinning until he saw the electric chair before him. Then his mouth fell open as if to utter a cry, but no sound came out. Paralysed with fear he was led reeling and whimpering to the chair.

But a surprising number find the strength to die with style. Caryl Chessman walked unhesitatingly into the gas chamber, sat in the chair and smiled at the warden. "I'm all right," he said.

Others show a quiet dignity that they didn't possess in earlier days. They remain outwardly quite composed, seemingly more concerned about the effect this will have upon their loved ones than themselves. On the morning of her execution, Irene Schroeder's thoughts were centred upon her lover Glenn Dague, who was also due to die that day. When the matron asked Irene whether there was anything she could do for her, she replied, "Please tell them in the kitchen to fry Glenn's eggs on both sides. He likes them that way."

I have used the masculine pronoun to refer to a condemned prisoner, because less than one per cent of those executed in America are women.

Prison officials try hard to create the illusion that an execution is just part of the job. But even the coldest heart must find it difficult not to feel some sympathy for the condemned man on such a day. The warden has perhaps the hardest task of all ... that of comforting and being kind to the man he is about to kill ...

Death Row is a sad and lonely place peopled by the legion of the doomed. Most of its inhabitants begin by dreaming the impossible dream, clinging to hope long after hope has gone. Some accept the reality, finding their own peace and a certain tranquillity. Others have their appeals upheld, and exchange death by execution for life behind bars — not always a good swap. But many more sink into a pit of dark despair. Death Row is truly a ghastly place.

Yet due to their very nature, the Death Rows of America provide a glimpse of human behaviour which is quite unique. Emotions run the entire spectrum. To be suddenly isolated from the world, to have nothing else to do but think and reflect, can do strange and wondrous things to the mind.

Life on Death Row can be guaranteed to change a man. If we can assume that Caryl Chessman, despite his denials, really was the Red Light Bandit, he came into Death Row as a monster ... and died 12 years later as a civilised, urbane human being.

This transformation has been echoed by many other long-term prisoners as the clock ticked their lives away. The character of the man sentenced to death and the character of the man who eventually dies are often light years apart. To the unbiased eye, they appear as two totally different people.

This is doubtless why the subject has come to fascinate sociologists and writers alike ... why men such as Truman Capote and Norman Mailer have become so involved ... and why so many movies have featured that last walk towards eternity with the audience (including yours truly) hoping that the telephone will ring.

But despite all those thousands of words written on the

subject, very few of us have a true picture of Death Row or any clear understanding of the issues involved. And yet for the sake of justice, it seems important that we should. This book isn't setting out to pose an argument for or against the death penalty. However we do wish to question the merits of Death Row itself. For in this grim fortress of the doomed, justice leaves much to be desired.

You won't find any millionaires on Death Row and very few Harvard men. The common badge shared by its inhabitants is poverty. It is a simple matter of getting what you pay for; and the poor have no access to the expensive and oh-so-effective lawyers who defended the likes of Leopold and Loeb.

The US Supreme Court has decreed that anyone wishing to appeal against a death sentence has no constitutional rights to state-funded counsel. Bear in mind that the 10 levels of appeal are a legal maze; and that a recent survey stated that 40 per cent of the men on Death Row are retarded; and you see the extent of the problem.

For most of the condemned, the only hope must lie in securing the help of one of that small band of lawyers prepared to forego financial reward for the sake of an ideal.

It would be comforting to believe that Death Row is reserved for murderers of the most monstrous kind, the torturers of children, the cruellest of the cruel, men who kill for killing's sake. But this just isn't so. The death sentence in the United States is a matter of chance and caprice. The lightning bolt of electrocution strikes at random. The satanic Charles Manson is spared. Troy Dugar, 15 at the time of the crime and with a mental age of nine, is sentenced to die on his 16th birthday.

When sentencing, judges in the United States have a wider licence than their counterparts in the United Kingdom. Most of them are doubtless honest, caring men who wish to preserve both the spirit and the letter of the law. But down in the Deep South, the great bastion of capital punishment, prejudice all too often plays its part.

When on trial for murder in those cotton-picking states,

it doesn't pay to be black. Prosecuting counsel, with their rights of challenge, traditionally set out to ensure that juries are predominantly white (all-white, if possible); and judges, usually from an older generation, frequently operate from the inherited tenets of another less tolerant, less under-standing, less compassionate age.

Geography comes into the equation too. Of the 50 states in the Union, 38 have retained the death penalty; and of those 38, only a handful still practice it with conviction. So if you have murder in mind, you will be wise to pick your state. New York is a better bet than Florida; while if you're black, mayhem in Mississippi is not to be recommended.

The notion of permitting a series of appeals against sentence of death is, in theory, eminently democratic and humane. It's just that in practice it doesn't work out that way; for it's the length of stay which makes Death Row so horrendous. At times, it must seem as though society is playing a game of cat and mouse with the condemned, constantly raising and dashing their hopes.

In the end when all hope has gone, the condemned man finds himself living by the clock, counting down the months, the days, the hours and finally the minutes that separate him from his doom. This time of waiting won't be made any easier by the knowledge that he won't be receiving any sympathy from the vast majority of his fellow-Americans.

At the latest count, four out of every five Americans polled were in favour of the death penalty; and it isn't difficult to understand why. The murder rate of the USA is one of the highest in the so-called civilised world.

Every year, the best part of 20,000 Americans come to a violent end. The citizens know that their lives and those of their loved ones are in greater danger than ever before; and so find the death penalty a comfort of a kind.

They see it variously as a way of striking back against the forces of evil ... rightly or wrongly, as a deterrent ... and as a definitive method of ensuring that the murderer can never stalk the streets to kill again. A few see it simply as a form of revenge, the Biblical eye-for-an-eye, tooth-for-a-tooth.

So for this last band at least, the condemned man remains a monster right up to and beyond his dying day. The crime for which he stands condemned may well have been monstrous, and probably was. But if we were all to be judged as human beings solely on the worst act we ever committed, none of us would look too good in the spotlight's glare.

However, capital punishment still remains a grim and grisly ritual — not helped in the past by the hangmen of America, a careless crew, and the vagaries of Old Sparky, an unpredictable beast. Mercifully, death by lethal injection is fast becoming the norm.

Today it isn't just the thousands of men, women and children on Death Rows who are left to wait and wonder.

Death Row itself is in the spotlight and facing an uncertain future.

1

INVITE TO AN EXECUTION

Allan Rankin

*"Want to go to a barbecue?" An editor's words to
a cub reporter.*

It was a bright moonlight night. I was twenty-two, and as I
cruised along in the new family car, I clicked on the radio.
Somebody was singing *Stardust*. I had a heavy date — to see
four men die.

"Want to go to a barbecue?" my editor had asked me that
morning. "If nobody else wants to," I'd said, trying to look
as grave and reluctant as possible, but inside I was elated.
By "barbecue" the editor meant an electrocution at Kilby
Prison a few miles from Montgomery — and this one was
going to be the second largest execution in the history of
Alabama.

Millions of people would like to see an execution if given
the chance — or they think they would. This was my
chance. The assignment meant I had arrived as a fully
fledged reporter, no longer to be considered a cub, but
driving out to Kilby on the night of June 8th, 1939, I was
worried about how I would react to the legal, scientific
killing of four men. Some reporters got sick at electrocutions;
some fainted.

"This your first barbecue?" asked George Meeker, the
police reporter for the opposition paper, who was riding out
with me. It was an embarrassing and unfair question, I
thought, but I had to answer, "Yes."

"Then you'd better have a slug of this," said Meeker as

6

we parked beside Kilby's high white wall. He held out half a pint of bourbon. "You'll probably need it."

I declined, but watching Meeker, two years older than I, take several long belts of raw whisky to fortify himself made me more uneasy. I began to wish our midnight party was over.

Electrocutions are very exclusive affairs, and only the few guests who "belong" are invited, but at the flash of a press card, many locked doors swing open.

Meeker and I walked in about 11.50 p.m., ten minutes before the scheduled hour. What struck me most was that nobody seemed to look or act as if anything out the ordinary were happening.

In the starkly lit lobby with the red tiled floor, twenty or thirty people stood around like people at a convention waiting to be called into a hotel dining-room. Warden Earl Wilson was acting as a kind of host, quietly greeting people, shaking hands. A good-looking, deeply suntanned man with blue eyes, he might have been — except for his informal sports shirt — the chairman and the master of ceremonies at a manufacturers' convention.

Wilson looked at his watch. "All right," he said, "I guess we'd better start up."

The second the double gates of the main cell-block clanged shut behind us, we were in a different world. The corridors were almost dark, lit only by dim bulbs at the end. I felt the usual discomfort of being locked in with convicts, dangerous men. It was three hours after they'd been locked up, but they were all awake. I could sense it. Some of them moved around in their cells like caged shadows as we passed. I asked the warden about it.

"They're always nervous on the night of an execution," he said. "They wouldn't think of trying to sleep until it's over."

Our heels rang on the steel stairs as we started up. The staircase to the death chamber looked like a wide fire escape. I thought about the four men who had climbed it to Death Row a few weeks or months before, and how they would never find their way back down again — alive. I knew they could hear us coming up to get them — our feet ringing on the steel — our little group, chatting of the weather and the price of cotton and tomorrow, the probabilities of tomorrow. What did the men at the top of the stairs feel? What did men whose tomorrows had run out think as they heard death approaching?

Cut that out, I warned myself. Don't think of that. Don't think of anything.

The stairs were over the kitchen, and the smells of vegetables, grease and close packed humanity, still hung there, heavy and warm. I felt a little sick.

Suddenly, we left the dark and came into a bright, white, sterile-looking room arranged like a theatre. The electric chair itself stood to the front and centre on a kind of stage of bare white concrete. It was made of wood and painted yellow. It had surprisingly appealing arms and a graceful, curving back. The grey restraining harness lay as slackly and as innocently as the straps and catches of an unused garter belt. In the middle of the room was a railing, and behind it perhaps forty theatre type seats. The seats were there to afford us, the selected guests, maximum comfort and the best possible view. Near the chair was an American flag.

The room was, in a way, like a little arena in which four gladiators would meet the tiger of high voltage, but these gladiators had already done all possible fighting for their lives. Here they wouldn't be able to fight back. The hopeless, one-sided nature of the forthcoming show was unappealing, slightly nauseating.

It was small comfort to realise just then that my emotions were standard. I noticed that large paper cups had been stacked on the railing for any onlookers who might become upset enough to need them. I wondered uneasily if I was already as pale as Meeker beside me.

The hands of the electric clock on the wall reached midnight. In the soundless room, I remembered I had forgotten something. "The condemned man ate a hearty last meal..." Readers of newspapers always wanted to know that, for some reason.

I tapped the chaplain on the shoulder and asked him. Yes, he said, all four men had eaten hearty last suppers. One had ordered steak, two fried chicken, and one fried fish. All had topped it with ice cream. I jotted the information down.

It began at 12.09. It was now June 9th, 1939.

"Ray Anderson," the warden announced, in a tone like a college dean calling the first student on stage to receive a diploma. The green steel door swung open. A skinny little man was led into the white concrete area. I glanced at my notes. This would be Ray Anderson, 26-year-old handyman, rapist, assaulter of a Birmingham matron.

He moved towards us, a nervous, almost jaunty grin on his face. He looked as if he might be bringing us some cheerful announcement.

This is the kind of nerve you read about, I thought. He was grey with fright, but he was well-braced inside. You could see he was determined to die by his own code of toughness — die grinning.

But a man is not always the master of himself, even in such a small thing as choosing to die with a grin.

It was clear now, as Anderson came waddling out grinning, that he thought he had one more room to go before he reached the chair. He was looking for it just ahead of him, and he was ready for it just ahead of him, but, suddenly glancing around, he saw it already behind him. He had not meant to reach it, certainly not to pass it yet. His mouth fell open as if to utter a cry that did not come. By this little accident of timing, his smile crumbled, collapsed into terror and panic. He had to be led, reeling and muttering, to the yellow wooden chair and be lifted into it.

He shook uncontrollably as they strapped him in, rolled up his clean white prison trousers, dampened and scrubbed his ankles with a special solution so that the metal electrodes they buckled on would make a perfect contact. They did the same thing to his wrist.

At this point, four men brought in a pine coffin. Walking two on each side of it, as formal as pall-bearers, they set it down just in front of the chair, in full view of the man strapped in it. Anderson's eyes, already wide, dilated in protest as an attendant took off his shoes and tossed them into the pine box. He now realised that, within a minute or so he would be lying in the box on top of the shoes, not hearing them nail the pine lid over him. In the morning, they would take the box and its contents and bury it in the cold red clay of the Kilby potter's field, which received the bodies of the executed who were unclaimed by their families.

"Have mercy, Lord!" Anderson cried, his eyes glued to the bottom of the coffin. "I think I'm living to meet my fate!"

In the South I had heard both expressions uttered a thousand times as exclamations — light, laughing jokes. The way Anderson said them was different.

Out of consideration for the executioner, the room in which he pulls the switch is usually separated from the chair by a wall or partition. This is supposed to make the puller of the death lever feel more clinical and impersonal about it — less guilty.

The warden raised his hand. The executioner in the next room closed the circuit. There was a hum like a diesel train getting under way; an unreal bluish light filled the room. The man in the chair rose as if to get up quickly and run out, but he was stopped abruptly, joltingly, in mid-air by the restraining straps. His body, straining against the straps, seemed about to burst them and take flight. His hair sparked and sizzled with bluish flame for an instant. Then the humming sound stopped; 2200 volts dropped out from under him and he slumped back into the chair, no longer a man but a body.

Despite the sponge helmet that had been rammed on his head at the last minute to keep down the stench of burning hair, the sweetish smell of it filled the room, but it was not this that seemed suddenly unbearable. It was the full realisation of how easily one man can separate another from his life. I had seen a man die screaming, trapped, burning alive in a car, but the simple, sudden, deliberate snuffing out of a man's life in the electric chair was, in a way, more terrible. This was not something the victim had done to himself, but something that had been done to him — and it was so ordered, systematic and dispassionate. Here the great thumb of justice and the forefinger of majority will closed upon one weak, fluttering life and snuffed it out.

I felt nausea, and acute need to reach for one of the paper cups. I avoided it by thinking of the tune *Stardust* on the car radio and the date I would have on my next night off. Still, the thought crept in: how did the next man feel, waiting his turn in the hall, watching that unpainted pine box being carried past him?

I needn't have worried about that. The next man to enter was Charles White, who, a glance at my notes told me, was a fortune teller convicted of raping a young woman.

He was a physical giant of a man, quietly composed, and, as far as anyone will ever know, ignorant of the meaning of fear.

"Do you realise you are about to die?" Warden Wilson asked him.

"Do I realise it!" said White. He was actually joking. It would have been a funny crack in vaudeville, but here nobody laughed, or even smiled, except White. He grinned and climbed up into the chair as nonchalantly as if he were about to get a haircut.

"Do you have anything to say before you die?"

"Yes." White pulled off the electrode that was being buckled to his head. "This thing is entirely too tight."

"Your head's too big for it," said the attendant. "It has to be a tight fit."

"All right," said White. "Now I have something else to say if everybody's listening." His big, calm voice filled the little execution room. "I know that I'm an innocent man. I know that a lot of people here tonight know I'm an innocent man. I am glad that I can go up to Jesus an innocent man."

Was he telling the truth? Was he innocent, as some men who die in the chair undoubtedly are? Had his case been investigated thoroughly enough? Had every one of the twelve good men and true on the jury been sure of his guilt? Was each juror's judgment perfect? Is any man's? If he was guilty was he any more so than the rest of us in various ways?

These are the most uncomfortable kinds of questions that can occur to the observer of an execution, and they usually do occur. But White himself did not linger upon them or dramatise them. At the moment, he was interested in showing that a man can face one of the worst things that can come to him — death by execution — without the sign or shadow of fear — and that he did.

White was spared the long look into his own coffin that the first man had got. Outside, his family was waiting to do his remains the honour of tears and a good silk-lined coffin placed in a family plot.

But the 2200 volts lifted his massive frame as easily as it had lifted the smaller man's. The few seconds of lightning converted him into the same worthless, lifeless doll of clay.

Officials felt his pulse, found none, but gave him a second jolt anyway, as they always do in order to be on the safe side. Some men miraculously have survived hangings; none survive electric chairs or gas chambers.

12.38. By now I felt anything but good, and there were still two to go. This was all necessary, I told myself; something that had to be done "as an example to other criminals," but I had read enough to know there was no real basis for such reasoning. History proves that the most terrible penalties do not prevent crime. As a rule, the more severe a society's punishment has become, the greater the increase in the crime rate.

I remembered reading how, in old England, pickpockets had thrived, operating in crowds assembled to watch the execution of pickpockets, and in defiance of the beheading of killers, the murder toll had risen.

The last thought brought me back with a start to where I was — at just such an execution — in a room in the middle of a grim prison. We were surrounded on all sides by desperate and rebellious men. What were they doing now?

What was that noise? For some minutes, I realized, I had been half aware of a low murmur beginning to spread through the prison. Now it was rising to a discordant babble, now a clamour!

Were the men rioting?

For a moment my imagination went wild. The sound was now definitely a great racket, rising in waves from every wing and cell and niche of the prison.

Then I realized it. The other prisoners were singing *Silent Night, Holy Night*.

It was weird and off key in the hot June night, but it must have been the only song all of them knew, and upon some prearranged signal they had burst out with it in ragged unison. It pushed back the muggy stale smell of turnip greens and burning flesh. It floated into the white, sterile room of the chair and out across the fields heavy with the scent of cotton blooms and honeysuckle.

All is calm, all is bright...

These were the criminals who were all around us, and this was their answer, their plot, their rebellion against what we were doing. This song:

Round yon Virgin, mother and child,
Holy Infant, so tender and mild...

This and the rest of the song came up louder and louder as twenty-one-year-old Grady Tubbs, convicted of the roadside murder of Horace J. Nash, was escorted to the chair and taken limp from it — as twenty-two-year-old Joseph Frazier received his two jolts for the shooting of his grandmother.

With the song going, the attendants somehow forgot to present the last two men with a preview of their coffins.

It was over! I had got through the whole ordeal without once having to reach for one of the paper cups, as had a few older and perhaps more sensitive onlookers. I had stood the test, and there would be no jokes back at the paper about my having a weak stomach or being chicken-hearted.

As we descended the steel stairway, every light in the

prison went off and the escape siren screamed out. It was later explained there had been some short-circuit at the powerhouse. Ordinarily, I would have been frightened to be plunged into darkness in the middle of a prison, but the singing of the inmates went on in the blackness:

Sleep in heavenly peace.

Sleep in heavenly peace.:.

When the lights came on again, Meeker and I looked at each other sheepishly, unhappily.

"We'll get used to this one day," he said. "These electrocutions, I mean. We'll get used to them and then we won't feel dirty and guilty and afraid any more from watching them..."

But we never did. We never did get used to them or feel right in ourselves about any of them.

After that night I was never again in favour of capital punishment. Since then, I have often wondered if there would be any executions if judges and jurymen personally had to pull the death switch, or even had to watch the results of its pulling.

2
SATAN'S DISCIPLE
Philip Madigan

"Lee is still playing. Will probably wait until morning to kill him. That way his body will still be fairly fresh for experiments after work."
Extract from the diary of Westley Dodd.

At five minutes after midnight on January 5th, 1993, Westley Allan Dodd became the first man to be hanged in America for 28 years when he plummeted to his death through the trap-door at the Washington State Penitentiary in Walla Walla.

The 31-year-old sex murderer had insisted that he be hanged, declaring: "I don't believe I deserve anything better than what those kids got. They didn't get a nice, neat, painless, easy death. Why should I?"

Dodd had never spoken a truer word. He had raped and tortured those poor children before killing them.

It was September 4th, 1989, Labor Day in America, when the reign of terror began in Vancouver, Washington. A few minutes before 7 p.m. a man we will call Dave Miller was walking along the Andiesen Road that runs beside David Douglas Park, when he spotted an injured child.

The boy appeared to be of Asian descent and lay motionless in a ditch beside a bicycle trail.

Miller noticed at once that there was a lot of blood on the lad's upper torso, and his first impression was that the boy had been struck by a car. The child, who appeared to be about nine or 10, was unconscious but still breathing, which gave Miller hope that he could be saved...

Without moving the boy, Miller ran to a store about a quarter of a mile from the park and called the emergency services. When officers from the Vancouver police department arrived they could tell immediately that the lad was a victim, but certainly not an accident victim. It was obvious to them that he had been stabbed repeatedly in the upper chest!

Incredibly the boy was still alive, and the emergency helicopter was summoned from Emanuel Hospital just across the Columbia River in Portland, Oregon.

The boy was barely breathing as a nurse and paramedic feverishly treated his wounds during the short flight to Portland. However, despite all their efforts, his injuries were too extensive and he had lost far too much blood. The child, who had no identification on him, was pronounced dead on arrival at the hospital at 7.37 p.m.

Duane Bigoni, a deputy Oregon state medical examiner, was assigned to the case because the victim had died in Oregon, even though the attack was believed to have occurred in Washington state.

Meanwhile, a few minutes before 8 p.m., a worried father began searching the neighbourhood adjacent to David Douglas Park for his two young sons who had not yet returned home from a bicycle ride.

At about 4 p.m. that day 10-year-old William Neer and his 11-year-old brother Cole had informed their father that they were going to a nearby driving range. They planned to scavenge for lost golf balls, for which they were regularly paid one cent each by the golf course's manager. They promised their father that they would be home by 6.30 p.m., but they had not yet returned.

Around 9 p.m., following a frantic street-by-street search that yielded no trace of the boys or their bikes, and after being unable to find anyone who had seen them, the boys' alarmed father called the Vancouver police to report his two children missing.

When word of the missing boys reached the lawmen investigating the David Douglas Park homicide the officers tried to determine if the victim was one of the Neer brothers. Meanwhile, at the park, one group of searchers armed with torches proceeded carefully along the narrow trails, while another group beat the bushes in search of evidence and possibly another victim.

It was slow going in the dark, but a short time later searchers found not one but two children's BMX bicycles about 45 yards from where the stabbing victim had been found.

Fearing that the discovery meant there might be another victim somewhere, the officers decided to call in extra help and expand the search.

Some seven hours later, at about 2 a.m., a volunteer found what all those concerned hoped they wouldn't find — another victim. Like the first, it was a little boy and this one was already dead at the scene. Appearing to be more than 10 or 11 years-old, his body was lying in heavy brush about 25 yards from where the bicycles had been found earlier in the evening.

Like the first body, the second victim had been stabbed numerous times in the chest and abdomen. Both had defence wounds on their hands and legs, indications that they had attempted to fight off their attacker before succumbing.

A short time later there was no longer any doubt who the boys were. They were identified as William and Cole Neer. William had been found first, police said, and both had probably been attacked about the same time, between 6.15 and 6.45 p.m. There was no apparent motive for the murders, which had occurred less than a mile from their home.

A police spokesman said that both lads were fully clothed when found, but that did not necessarily mean they had not been sexually assaulted. Investigators sent the victims' clothes and other evidence from the crime scene to the lab. in Washington for analysis. However, little of significance was learned.

In their efforts to understand every aspect of the tragedy,

detectives looked at the Neer family's background. They learned that they had moved to the Vancouver area in 1986 from North Dakota, settling in the suburb of Hazel Dell. Because of employment difficulties, however, the family was forced to move in July, 1989, into local authority housing in the McLoughlin Heights area of Vancouver.

Neighbours told detectives that the Neer family were quiet and generally kept to themselves.

As the days passed only a few leads of any significance trickled into police headquarters. With little else they could do unless something substantial turned up, detectives, aided by numerous volunteers, returned to the scene of the murders. Unfortunately, by mid-September the probers were still at square one.

Despite their efforts, all the investigators had been able to do was retrace the victims' activities up to about 6.10 p.m. on the day they were murdered. They were without clues as to the boys' movements from then on until the time William's body was discovered by the passer-by.

At the request of the Vancouver police, the FBI in Washington provided a psychological profile of the killer. It suggested that the murderer most likely lived in the community and was probably familiar with David Douglas Park and the surrounding area.

The profile also suggested that the killer could have known the two boys and was most likely physically strong enough easily to overpower them both together. The nature of the deaths indicated that he was comfortable with knives and might have used a knife in a previous assault or killing.

The senselessness of the crime, the profile said, suggested that the killer could have been "acting in response to a significant traumatic experience that happened to him in a close time frame" with the murders.

Vancouver investigators were grateful for the FBI's psychological profile, but it really didn't bring them any closer to collaring a suspect. All it did was give them an insight into the mind of the type of killer they were dealing with. But by the end of September the case seemed destined for the unsolved files.

In late October, tragedy struck again. Across the river from Vancouver, in Portland, Oregon, four-year-old Lee Joseph Iseli was reported missing.

According to the report taken by the Portland police, Lee had gone with his nine-year-old brother to a school playground on Sunday afternoon, October 29th. The playground was near the boys' home, and both played there regularly.

The older boy told detectives that at about 1 p.m. that afternoon Lee had been playing on a concrete climbing knoll known as the volcano and had been talking to a man. The older boy carried on playing, but when he looked towards the volcano a few minutes later, Lee had gone. Unable to find him, the boy rushed home and told his family about the disappearance.

Lee's nine-year-old brother told police that the man he had seen talking to Lee was in his early 30s, about six feet tall, and thin in build. He was wearing a T-shirt and blue jeans.

The police immediately began searching throughout the neighbourhood. Dog-handlers brought in bloodhounds, and they picked up Lee's scent in the school playground, but lost it at the kerb. This strongly suggested that the boy had been picked up by someone in a car.

Police fanned out in the neighbourhood, knocking on doors and visiting local businesses. At one point assistants at a nearby grocery store told police that Lee Iseli had been seen inside the store just after 1 p.m., wandering around the aisles alone.

That he was seen alone in the store prompted police to consider the possibility that Lee might have wandered away from the school playground after he was seen talking to the stranger. Store employees insisted they were certain of the time because it had been at the beginning of the 1 p.m. lunch break.

However, as the day wore on and no further trace of Lee Iseli was found, relatives and police began to fear the worst.

As darkness approached, a full-scale alert was broadcast describing Lee as four years old, three foot eight inches tall, and weighting just over two stone. The alert also described the boy's hair as blond. He was wearing a grey jacket with red stripes on its sleeves, a white T-shirt with writing on the front, and blue trousers. He might also have been carrying a jumper with him.

Frantic relatives waited by the telephone, but no trace of Lee Iseli had been found by Sunday night. Because temperatures were only a few degrees above freezing, there was added concern about the possibility of the boy having to spend the night outdoors.

By the time Halloween crept around there was still no sign of little Lee, and the police reluctantly began to scale down their search for him.

In Vancouver, Washington, early the following morning, November 1st, a pheasant hunter parked his car near Vancouver Lake's south shore and unloaded his gun and backpack. It was a few minutes short of 8 a.m. when he began beating the brush for his quarry in the Washington State Game Reserve.

The Washington State Department of Wildlife stocks the reserve — sited well away from the city and residential area — twice weekly with pheasant during the hunting season, and hunting is allowed to begin after 8 a.m.

Half an hour later, however, the hunter decided to return to his car. He had walked only a few yards when he noticed the lily-white object lying in the brush just ahead of him. Curious, he walked towards it, only to stop dead in his tracks after a few paces. To his horror and surprise, the man could see that the object was a little boy, naked and dead!

The hunter ran back to his car and drove quickly to the nearest telephone. Although nearly incoherent from distress, he managed to report his discovery to the dispatcher at the sheriff's department.

Minutes later, Clark County Sheriff Frank Kanekoa and

Under-sheriff Robert Songer arrived at the remote site situated at the end of a two mile dead-end road, where they met the hunter.

The distraught man led Kanekoa and Songer to the boy's body, which lay face up in the brush about 50 yards from a boat ramp and 50 feet from the edge of a gravel car park. It was obvious that no attempt had been made to conceal the body, and there was no clothing on or near the ice-cold corpse.

The probers noted signs of strangulation, but they found nothing at the scene that could have been used to throttle the boy. Aware of Lee Iseli's disappearance, Kanekoa and Songer strongly suspected that the child had now been found, for the young victim matched the physical description of the Iseli boy.

Before noon the search for Lee Iseli was officially over. Through his fingerprints, experts positively identified the body found at Vancouver Lake as that of the missing boy. Lee Iseli had been fingerprinted a few months earlier at a children's fair in Portland, and a set of those prints was used to make the identification.

An autopsy conducted later that day confirmed that Lee had died as a result of strangulation, but it did not conclusively determine how long he had been dead. Authorities declined to say whether or not the boy had been sexually assaulted.

As a community began to talk and rumours began to circulate, the authorities initially attempted to play down any possible connection between Lee Iseli's murder and the stabbing deaths of the Neer brothers two months earlier.

Detectives said the killer's method of operation was different in the Iseli case, particularly in that Lee had been strangled and the Neer brothers stabbed repeatedly.

Meanwhile, psychologist Don Adamski, who specialised in sexual abuse and homicide cases, provided investigators with a profile of Lee Iseli's killer. He told probers that the murderer was probably a middle-class or blue-collar man who had often fantasised about killing a child. Adamski said he was also probably living a normal life, but harbouring a tremendous amount of hostility.

"I would say the killer had been having thoughts like this for a long time," said Adamski. "The other possibility is that this could be a drug-crazed individual, but that would be unusual. The person probably leads a passive life and finally had to act out his fantasy."

Despite a telephone hotline and a $10,000 reward fund, a childkiller continued to walk the streets while frustrated detectives quickly ran out of leads.

Barely two weeks later, on Wednesday, November 15th, a six-year-old boy went with his family and friends to see the film —*Honey, I Shrunk The Kids!* at the New Liberty cinema in Camas, Washington, about 15 miles east of Vancouver.

At 7.45 p.m. the boy, whom we shall call Tommy Staley, told his mother that he had to go to the toilet. After sliding through a row of crowded seats, Tommy walked up the aisle, passed through double doors that led to the lobby, and entered the rest-room. On the way he passed a young, harmless-looking, dark-haired man in the foyer that separates the rest-room from the lobby.

Tommy was alone in the rest-room and about to wash his hands when the dark-haired man approached him. To Tommy's horror and surprise the man suddenly punched him in the stomach. When Tommy doubled over in pain, the man hoisted him over his left shoulder.

Thinking he'd knocked the air out of the boy, the man carried Tommy out of the toilet and through the lobby.

As he approached the front doors leading to the outside, Tommy began kicking and screaming as loud as he could.

Cinema employees didn't like what they were seeing. Although the man appeared unruffled, the altercation smelled of an abduction. As a result, one of them quickly called the police as two others followed the man and boy into the street.

Across the road, Les Wilson was opening the door of his

truck when he spotted the man carrying the boy out of the cinema. He was still watching as the man carried the screaming boy around the corner and approached an old yellow estate car. As the suspect reached into his pocket for the keys, the abductor put the boy down.

Sensing his chance, Tommy Staley bolted back towards the cinema. Crying, he ran headlong into the arms of cinema employees and embraced one of them.

By this time Pete Mann, a friend of the Staley family, had heard some of the commotion and begun to wonder what was keeping Tommy so long in the toilet. Pete went to look for the boy. When he reached the lobby he noticed all the turmoil and saw the cinema staff walking back inside with Tommy. After he was told what had happened, Pete Mann ran outside in pursuit of Tommy's abductor.

He looked up and down the street, but the only person he saw was Les Wilson, who had witnessed the kidnapper drive away in the old yellow estate car. After giving Mann a description of the suspect and his vehicle, the latter jumped into his own car and went after him.

Mann soon found the old estate car. By a twist of fate, it had broken down not far from the entrance to the motorway that leads back to Vancouver. The car's driver was trying to get it started again.

Mann parked his vehicle in the car park of a nearby paper mill, then walked over to the old yellow vehicle. He approached cautiously and asked the driver if he needed any help.

"Looks like you're having car trouble here," said Mann, speaking to the unsuspecting abductor through the side window.

When the driver said he was, Mann explained that he could probably fix it, but suggested that they first get the vehicle into the paper mill's car park. As they pushed the car, Mann continued to ask "innocent" questions until he was satisfied that the yellow vehicle's driver was the one who had tried to abduct the boy.

That's when Mann, a burly labourer, made his move. He

wrapped his right arm around the abductor's neck in a tight choke hold and seized the suspect's left wrist with his left hand. Mann then marched the suspect all the way back to the cinema, where he pinned him against a wall while he waited for the police to arrive.

When the officers got there they took a statement from each person concerned about what had happened. The only person not talking was the suspect, who sat quietly on the floor in the cinema lobby. After getting enough preliminary information, the officers took the man into custody.

At the police station, officers identified the suspect as Westley Allan Dodd, 28, from Vancouver. At first Dodd didn't provide much information: just his name, address and the fact that he was at the cinema to see the film. However, after further questions, Dodd told the officers that he worked at a paper factory in Vancouver. They noted that the work address Dodd gave was not far from the site where little Lee Iseli's nude body was found. Moreover, his home address was less than a mile from David Douglas Park!

It was at that point that Westley Dodd became a suspect in the murders of the Neer brothers and Lee Iseli. Although he was advised of his statutory rights, Dodd continued to talk.

To everyone's astonishment, Dodd confessed to all three murders and provided information to the police regarding the slayings that only the killer could know.

The authorities now revealed that a list of 50 possible suspects — all of whom were known sex offenders — had been compiled, but Dodd's name was not on it.

After being transferred to the Clark County jail, Dodd was interviewed by Detective David Trimble. In a bombshell statement, Dodd explained how he had killed William and Cole Neer on Labor Day. He also told in graphic detail how he'd abducted, killed and then had sex with four-year-old Lee Iseli.

Dodd explained that he'd moved to Vancouver from Seattle during the summer and lived with relatives until he had saved enough money to rent his own place. Two days after moving into an apartment near David Douglas Park, Dodd said he began looking for victims.

"I was getting bored — I didn't have a TV," said Dodd during taped interviews with detectives. He said he drove to David Douglas Park because he thought "it might be a place where I could find a boy and get something going."

He described how he discovered the Neer brothers along the dirt bike path on the western edge of the park. He said he ordered them to go with him, but William asked why they should. Dodd told the detectives that he replied, "Because I told you to."

Dodd said that he tied the boys' hands with shoelaces, after which he ordered Cole Neer to pull down his trousers. When Cole complied, Dodd said he performed oral sex on the boy in front of his brother. Then he ordered William to do the same thing, but the boy began crying so much that he was unable to comply.

When he was finished, Dodd told the children, "Okay, there's one more thing." He then raised his trouser leg and revealed a six-inch fish-filleting knife. Dodd said that the boys, sensing they were in great danger, cried even harder and begged him not to hurt them.

"I pulled the knife out from under my trouser leg," Dodd told detectives. "Billy was over to my right, about a foot away, Cole on my left. I reached over and stabbed Billy with the knife. Then I turned to Cole and stabbed him two or three times.

"While I was stabbing Cole, Billy got up and started to run back down the trail towards the road, so I ran after him. I didn't wait to see if Cole was dead or anything, I just wanted to get Billy before he got to the road.

"I caught him and grabbed him by his right arm, stopped him and spun him around. Then as Billy said, 'I'm sorry' I stabbed him again."

At that point Billy ran away again, but Dodd did not chase after him. Dodd explained that he was more concerned with returning to Cole's body to make certain that he hadn't left behind any incriminating evidence.

A short time after murdering the Neer brothers, Dodd said he began planning his next attack. He said he used a map of Portland and marked off several parks where he thought he could find children playing alone. The day before he abducted Lee Iseli, Dodd said he went to several of the parks where he contemplated abducting and killing a number of children. His plans had been unsuccessful, however, and he drove home.

He became lost along the way and happened to drive by the school. Although there were children there, none were playing alone, so he left in an agitated state, frustrated and disappointed. However, Dodd said he returned the following day and found Lee Iseli playing by himself.

"I went up to the little boy and said, 'Hi! How are you doing?' I asked him if he wanted to make some money and play some games. He was a little hesitant, but I put out my hand and he took it."

Dodd said he told Lee that his dad had sent him to pick Lee up and that sealed it. They drove off together in Dodd's car.

After driving a short distance Dodd said Lee began protesting that he didn't live in the direction they were heading. "I said, 'Well, we're going to my house.' " Dodd said the child began to cry on the way to Vancouver, but he was able to calm him down.

"When we got to my apartment I told him he had to be very quiet because a lady neighbour didn't like kids." Once inside, Dodd ordered the boy to remove all his clothing, and he said he spent the next several hours molesting Lee and taking Polaroid pictures of him.

"I asked him if he'd like to stay the night and he said no, that his brother would miss him. I said, 'Nah, your brother is probably having fun too.' "

Dodd said he told Lee that he was sorry he didn't have any toys for him to play with, but he promised to take him to a toy shop and buy him a He-Man toy and to McDonald's for dinner if he would agree to stay. The child eventually said that he would stay.

Dodd said he molested the little boy throughout the night, and at one point told him he was going to kill him. When the boy began to cry Dodd said he tried to reassure Lee by telling him he wouldn't harm him. However, Dodd then graphically described how he killed Lee Iseli at 5.30 on the morning of October 30th before he left for work.

"I took a piece of rope and wrapped it around his neck and pulled it tight," said Dodd in a chilling, matter-of-fact tone. "I figured I'd probably been trying to choke him for two minutes or so already, and didn't know how much longer it was going to take. So, using the rope, I carried him over to the wardrobe and tied the end of the rope around the clothes rack in the wardrobe and left him hanging there. Then I took a picture of it."

Because he didn't want to "hurt the boy or cause him any pain," Dodd said he waited until after the boy was dead before engaging in anal intercourse.

What did he do with the corpse when he went to work? Dodd calmly explained that he put the corpse on a shelf in the wardrobe and concealed it by placing pillows and other items in front of it "just in case the landlady decided to come in and have a nose around."

When he returned home that evening, Dodd wrapped the boy's body in a plastic rubbish bag and took it to where it was found near Vancouver Lake. He said he then burned the child's clothing in a barrel outside his apartment, but retained his underpants as a "trophy" of his kill.

Armed with search warrants, homicide probers converged on Westley Dodd's apartment in Vancouver. During the lengthy search, they found a briefcase containing photographs in a pink album. Many of the photos showed Dodd engaging in sex acts with Lee Iseli before and after the boy's death. And one of the pictures depicted the boy hanging from a rope inside the wardrobe.

Officers also seized a pair of boy's underpants, a diary, plastic dustbin bags, a Polaroid camera, a roll of undeveloped but exposed 35 mm film, several volumes of "Parent-

Child" books, a section of Dodd's bed frame with pieces of rope attached and numerous newspaper cuttings regarding the murders of the Neer brothers and Lee Iseli.

A short time later, Westley Dodd was charged with three counts of aggravated first-degree murder in connection with the deaths of the three boys. Prosecutor Art Curtis said he would seek the death penalty in two separate trials. One trial would be for the death of Lee Iseli, the other for the deaths of William and Cole Neer. That way, explained Curtis, he would have two attempts at obtaining the death penalty.

Dodd was also charged with one count each of first-degree attempted kidnapping and first-degree attempted murder in the cinema case involving Tommy Staley. Despite his confession, Dodd pleaded not guilty to all the charges. Vancouver attorney Darrell Lee was appointed to represent him.

When the detectives made enquiries in Dodd's neighbourhood in their attempt to build a stronger case against him, they found a woman who told them that she recalled seeing Dodd arrive home with a small blond boy at about the time Lee Iseli disappeared.

When officers began checking Westley Dodd's background, they were told by the owner of the paper company where he worked as a shipping clerk that he was a model employee. He was conscientious about his work, and had never missed a day since he started.

However, Westley Dodd had an ominous past, the detectives soon learned, and he had somehow managed to slip between the cracks in the system that was supposed to protect citizens from such predatory animals. Dodd, it seemed, had a long trail of sex offences behind him, all involving children. He was no stranger to the law in the state of Washington.

He had been born in Toppenish, Washington, on July 3rd, 1961, and his family moved to Kennewick when he was three years old. The rest of his life was marked by frequent family moves and the eventual divorce of his parents.

Although Dodd was bright and had an avid interest in music, he held mostly low-paying jobs throughout his life.

By the time he reached the age of 12 he began to develop a sexual attraction towards young boys. By 16, he began seeking frequent sexual contacts with children, mostly boys. Police had reason to talk to him on a number of occasions, but there was never enough evidence to bring formal charges.

Dodd graduated from Columbia High School in Richland, Washington, in 1979 and went to work as a stock boy for a local grocery shop. The following year he was arrested for soliciting sex from a minor, but the case was dismissed.

Looking for a change, Dodd enlisted in the US Navy during the summer of 1981. He was sent to Groton, Connecticut, where he was trained for submarine duty. After training, he was stationed at the Bangor Naval Station in Bangor, Washington, where he began spending a lot of his free time at local arcades propositioning seven to 10-year-old boys.

In June, 1982, Dodd went AWOL and attempted to solicit a sexual act from a nine-year-old boy at a Richland playground. In August of that same year, the navy found and arrested him on charges of child molestation stemming from the June incident. He received a less than honourable discharge from the navy.

A few months later, in December, Dodd lured a young Benton City, Washington, boy from a playground and persuaded him to undress. He was arrested, pleaded guilty the following month, and was ordered to participate in a counselling programme.

Failing to meet the conditions of his court-ordered counselling, Dodd served just 23 days in jail. After his release, he moved to Lewiston, Idaho, where he engaged in sexual acts with a nine-year-old boy on at least two occasions.

Nearly a year later, the boy's parents reported the incidents to police, and Dodd was convicted of lewd conduct with a minor. He was sentenced to 10 years in jail.

Although he served time in the county jail, Dodd's sentence was reduced to time served and he was released after he agreed to attend an outpatient programme for sex offenders under the jurisdiction of the state of Idaho.

In 1986, Dodd moved back to Richland, Washington, where he sexually abused a neighbour's four-year-old boy over a period of five months. Again, Dodd escaped receiving any significant punishment for his actions.

By the autumn of 1986, Dodd was living and working as a lorry driver in Seattle. In June of the following year he attempted to lure a young boy into a vacant building. Luckily, the boy escaped, but Dodd was arrested and convicted of attempted unlawful imprisonment — a misdemeanour. He was incarcerated until October, at which time he was put on probation and ordered to undergo treatment again.

When his probation expired in the autumn of 1988, Dodd quit the treatment programme, despite objections from officials who said he was far from being cured. Dodd was employed for the next several months at a petrol station/store, a job he had held while on probation, and where he was trusted and well liked by co-workers who knew nothing about his sexual habits.

Alone and strapped for money, Dodd moved in with relatives in Vancouver in July, 1989. On September 1st, he moved into his own apartment. Within days, children began turning up dead.

During a jailhouse interview with your author after his arrest, Westley Dodd admitted that he would have killed the Seattle boy had he not escaped. He explained that this had been the first incident where he intended to commit murder. Unfortunately, it had not been his last.

On Monday, June 11th, 1990, Dodd appeared in Clark County Superior Court for a hearing before Judge Robert Harris. In a move that took authorities by surprise, Dodd — against the vigorous objections of his attorney — announced that he wanted to change his plea to guilty. In low tones, Westley Dodd confessed his crimes in court.

"On September 4th, 1989, I went to David Douglas Park with the premeditated intent to cause the death of a human being," he said, reading from a prepared statement. "I met Cole Neer and I raped Cole Neer. Then I killed him. Also about the same time I murdered William Neer."

He told the judge that he took a knife with him to the park with the intention of raping and murdering a child. He said he committed the murders to conceal his identity from the police.

"Afterwards I was very nervous. I was afraid that I was going to get caught. Then as I read the papers I realised that the police didn't have any clues. I started feeling a little bit more confident and it dawned on me that I could do it and get away with it. The next step would be to actually kidnap a boy.

"On October 29th, 1989, I kidnapped Lee Iseli from Portland and drove him to my apartment in Vancouver. There I raped him, and on the morning of October 30th, I murdered him."

Judge Harris asked Dodd if the killing had occurred on the spur of the moment; on a whim.

"No, sir," Dodd replied. "It was premeditated."

Dodd also admitted that when he attempted to kidnap Tommy Staley from the cinema it was his intention to rape and murder him.

Although Dodd's admission of guilt made it unnecessary for the state to continue with a trial, it was necessary to empower a jury to decide whether Dodd should be sentenced to death or life in prison. By pleading guilty, Dodd had relinquished the right to appeal against many of the legal issues of the case, including whether the warrant used to search his apartment was legal and whether the confessions he made to police were valid.

The following month, before a jury of six men and six women, Chief Prosecutor Roger Bennett began presenting his case. He took the jurors through the evidence step by step, from the heinous killings to Dodd's confessions to his lurid past. He showed them grisly photographs of the victims and a 20-minute video made by police at the scene where Lee Iseli's body was found.

But perhaps the most chilling part of the proceedings was Westley Dodd's diary, which detailed the killings, his future plans to kill children, and a pact he had made with Satan in which he described him as a "Love God" who would help him achieve his murderous goals.

Bennett said Dodd's diary showed a desire to torture children before he killed them. The prosecutor also produced drawings from the diary that depicted a rack which he could use to tie up his victims so that he could perform "experimental surgery" and dismember them while they were still alive.

Dodd's diary told of numerous ways in which he would murder children. Some he planned to strangle, others he intended to suffocate. Still others would be drowned or poisoned — and he referred to the planned deaths as his "experiments."

"Cole and William Neer died in David Douglas Park as victims of 'the hunt,' " said co-prosecutor Art Curtis, his voice often cracking with emotion. "At least twenty other children avoided death through fate that weekend alone. They were the lucky ones."

Curtis then read a passage from the diary: "6.30 p.m. Lee is still playing. Will probably wait until morning to kill him. He suspects nothing now. That way his body will still be fairly fresh for experiments after work."

Arguing against leniency for Dodd, Curtis told jurors there was absolutely no evidence for them to consider that warranted leniency.

Dodd's attorney argued that the defendant should be sentenced to life in prison without parole. He argued that Dodd would not pose a future threat to society because he killed only children and none would be available to him if he was sentenced to life in prison.

On Sunday, July 15th, 1990, following 14 hours of deliberations over three days, the jury concluded that

Westley Allan Dodd must die for his crimes.

Dodd subsequently asked that his death sentence be carried out expeditiously.

Writing to the Washington State Supreme Court from his cell on Death Row at the state penitentiary in Walla Walla, he requested that they quickly conclude the one mandatory appeal afforded all death penalty cases, urging the justices to uphold his conviction and sentence.

Having hanged a four-year-old boy, he said he deserved to die the same way. This posed a problem for penitentiary officials, who had to study the most recent US Army manual to learn how to carry out such an execution. Nobody had been hanged in the United States since 1965. Now the prison took the opportunity to update its hanging procedure. Reference to the army manual ensured that all the apparatus was improved, from the design of the hood to be placed over the condemned man's head to the length of Manila hemp rope required to break his neck.

"Death is the only way out for me against my uncontrollable urges to kill," Dodd told his captors. "I must be executed before I have an opportunity to escape. If I do escape, I promise you I will kill and rape again, and I will enjoy every minute of it."

Earlier, when he refused to let his attorney appeal against his sentence, he had declared: "I don't believe I deserve anything better than what those kids got. They didn't get a nice, neat, painless, easy death. Why should I?"

He was reported to have chosen the noose rather than "the easy way out" by lethal injection, although his lawyer claimed hanging was the least painful form of execution: "It can result in unconsciousness in one second and death in seventeen seconds. So it can be quite humane when properly done."

As he lay in his cell awaiting a decision, Dodd was reported to masturbate night and day, apparently reliving his sex-driven killings.

His death wish was granted on January 5th, 1993. Just before the day began, at 11.50 p.m., 12 reporters climbed two flights of stairs in the prison's two-storey death chamber and filed into a small room to witness the execution. Already present were the father of the Neer brothers and the mother of Lee Iseli, together with Dodd's lawyer, Darrell Lee, three prison officials and a representative of the American Civil Liberties Union.

Facing the witnesses were two windows. One of these, above the observers, looked onto the room from which Dodd would say his last words. Leaning against a wall of the room was a board with straps, to be used to prop up and secure the prisoner if he fainted. Immediately in front of the witnesses was the window through which they would see the conclusion of the killer's last journey. The reporters learned that he had refused the offer of a special last meal, preferring to eat the salmon being dished up for the rest of the prisoners.

At 11.55 p.m., Dodd appeared at the top window, wearing the orange uniform of a prison inmate. Through an indistinct public address system, he said: "I was once asked by somebody, I don't remember who, if there was any way sex offenders could be stopped.

"I said no. I was wrong when I said 'There is no hope, no peace.' There is hope, there is peace. I found both in the Lord Jesus Christ. I urge everyone: look to the Lord and you will find peace."

The Neer boys' father hissed when the name of the Lord was invoked. Lee Iseli's mother gave what sounded like a sigh of disgust.

A blind was then drawn down over the top window. Against it, the witnesses saw the silhouettes of one of the executioners placing the hood over Dodd's head, while another, apparently chewing gum, put the noose around his neck.

At 12.05 a.m., a red button was pushed, springing open the trap-door on which Dodd stood. As he dropped, the hangman's knot behind his left ear tightened, fracturing his neck.

Slowly, his black-hooded body spun anti-clockwise at

the end of the rope, his legs bound, his hands strapped in front of him.

"I will never forget the bang of the trap-door and the sight of his body plunging seven feet towards the floor," one of the observers reported. "It appeared lifeless from the moment it fell into view. There was no dancing at the end of a rope, no gruesome display."

"There was no violent movement or noticeable twitching," another reporter confirmed.

Although some of the witnesses thought they detected an almost imperceptible movement in the body's abdomen as the figure swayed before them, most put this down to involuntary muscle contractions and agreed Dodd could not have been conscious at that time.

A curtain was then drawn across the window. The Neer boys' father shook the hand of Dodd's lawyer, who had followed his client's instructions in striving to hasten the execution. Now he had tears in his eyes. Lee Iseli's mother patted him on the back, and the trio departed. At 12.09, Dodd's death was confirmed by a physician.

The child-killer had become the first person to be hanged in the United States for 28 years, and the 185th person to be executed in America since the resumption there of capital punishment in 1977.

Keeping vigil in the snow outside the prison had been anti-death-penalty campaigners. Their last appeal against the hanging had been rejected by Washington State Court, the justices ruling that this was not "cruel and unusual punishment".

Also objecting to the execution, but for a different reason, was Nancy Gibbs, who noted in *Time* magazine that the prospect of what amounted to "a glamorous public suicide was vastly more appealing" to Westley Dodd "than a life spent alone in a cell the size of a parking space, crushed by boredom, without the least chance of freedom.

"For him, perhaps justice would have been better served by denying him his death wish and letting him wait, for a very long time, for death to come to him."

3

BLOODY BABS

Seymour Ettman

"Life is so short. Why does mine have to be even shorter?" Barbara Graham's lament while on Death Row.

When the ghosts of Barbara Graham, Big Jack Santo and Emmett Perkins were resurrected before a special committee appointed by the California State Legislature, the spotlight once-again centred on the much-belaboured question of whether or not "Bloody Babs" was really guilty of the murder of crippled Mabel Monahan, for which she had been executed in the San Quentin gas chamber some years before.

Debate was spurred by the controversial film *I Want To Live,* which won Susan Hayward an Oscar for her emotional and dramatic, but not entirely factual, portrayal of the doomed murderess.

More or less overlooked in the sentimental hubbub over what has come to be known as the "Graham Case" is the fact that the single murder of which shapely Barbara was convicted, revolting though it was, marked only the climax of the most atrocious multiple-murder series in California's modern crime annals — an appalling record of at least seven violent deaths.

To make a detailed study of the Barbara Graham case, we have to go back to 1951, four years before the triple executions at San Quentin.

First-time readers may wonder why Barbara Graham does not figure in most of this part of the story. Has the author got the name wrong? Does he actually mean Harriet Henson? No! But to paint a picture of the case — and to show the type of murderous guys Barbara Graham became mixed up with and accompanied to the gas chamber — we must return to the backwoods of the gold-mining country and the Christmas night of 1951, when mine-owner Edward Hansen was murdered. Then to 10 months later, on the quiet autumn Saturday morning of October 11th, 1952, when the ghastly chronicle of slaughter exploded in headlines. That was the day pure horror burst on the sparsely settled logging country of Plumas County, high up in the rugged Cascade Mountains of north-eastern California.

The bloody nightmare had begun to unfold at 6 o'clock the previous evening — Friday — when Mrs. Christal Young, wife of Guard Young, a supermarket proprietor in the tiny lumber town of Chester on the shore of Lake Almanor, telephoned a family friend. "I'm worried about Guard," she said. "He should have been back from Westwood a long time ago. He drove over to the bank, you know, like he always does on Friday. He has the three girls and the little Saile boy with him — and all that money for the payroll cheques."

"Don't get upset," the friend reassured her. "Maybe he was delayed on some business in Westwood. Or maybe his car broke down and he can't get to a phone. We'll take a run out along the highway and find him. I'll pick you up in a few minutes."

The friend's voice conveyed more assurance than he felt. He too was gravely concerned.

The small community of Chester, numbering only about 2,000 people, had no banking facilities of its own. Businessmen had to drive 12 miles east to the slightly larger town of Westwood, just over the Lassen County line, where the Bank of America maintains a branch. It was common knowledge that Guard Young, proprietor of the principal store in Chester, drove over to the Westwood bank regularly every Friday afternoon and brought back several thousand dollars in cash to accommodate the lumber mill workers and loggers who came in with their pay-cheques on that day.

Friends and fellow shopkeepers had often cautioned Young to beware of bandits on the lonely mountain highway. But the 43-year-old supermarket owner, a deeply religious man descended from hardy Mormon pioneers, smiled at their warnings. He refused to carry a gun or take a bodyguard on his trips to the bank.

That Friday afternoon, a crisp autumn day, Guard Young had left his supermarket at 2.15 p.m. Calling at his home on the outskirts of town, he had smilingly yielded to the entreaties of his three little daughters, Jean, aged 7, Judy, 6, and Sondra Gay, 4, who clamoured to go with him. Young bundled them into his car along with their playmate, little Michael Saile, 4, whose mother rented an apartment from the Youngs. "We'll be back before four o'clock, dear," the affable grocer told his pretty wife, who stayed at home with their baby, Wayne, aged five months.

Now it was after 6 p.m., almost dark, and there was no sign of Young and the children, or any word from him.

The family friend picked up worried Mrs. Young, who had to bring the baby along with her for lack of a sitter. They drove on State Route 36, along the north shore of Lake Almanor, towards Westwood. Cruising slowly, they scanned the ditches and the narrow entrances to the logging roads where a broken-down car might be parked. They saw no sign of Guard Young's green 1951 Chrysler convertible, or of its five occupants.

The miles ticked by. "I'm scared," Christal Young shivered when they reached Westwood as dusk settled over the forest. Her escort now fully shared her alarm. He telephoned the bank teller's home to learn that Young had left the bank at 2.50 p.m., after depositing his week's bundle of cheques and withdrawing $7,128 in cash, mostly in 20-dollar bills. He carried the money, as usual, in a canvas bank bag.

Further inquiries established that the grocer had bought ice-cream for the four children across the street from the bank. Several people had seen them start back towards Chester at about 3 o'clock.

Young's friend telephoned the resident deputy sheriff. As soon as they heard the facts, the authorities took a most serious view of the disappearances. Sheriff Melvin Schooler of Plumas County and Sheriff Olin Johnson of Lassen County joined forces. That night, a hastily assembled volunteer posse of more than 100 mill-workers, loggers and businessmen from the two towns beat through the woods along the 12-mile stretch of mountain highway, but the near-freezing night passed without any development.

Soon after daybreak on Saturday, two local pilots took off in small planes from the Chester landing strip to skim low over the towering pines and firs. A little after 7 a.m., one of the pilots came circling back to report to Sheriff Schooler. He had seen a green car parked in the brush off an abandoned logging road near Bailey Creek, some four miles east of Chester.

At that same moment, a Chester mill-worker who had just heard of the search was telling Highway Patrolman Jeff Cooley about a green Chrysler which he and his deer-hunting companions had seen parked at Bailey Creek at about 5.30 on Friday afternoon. There was no one around the car, and they had assumed that it belonged to some other hunters.

Cooley, with the mill-worker and a couple of loggers, sped along the highway and turned up the rutted track into the dense forest. The Chester man directed them to the spot, about half a mile from Route 36, where a shiny green car stood half hidden in the tangled undergrowth at the very lip of the creek. It was Guard Young's car.

"Looks like it's abandoned," Patrolman Cooley said as the four men approached the car. Then he noticed the blood on the rear bumper. The boot was open a crack. Cooley jerked the lid up and reeled back with a choked exclamation.

His companions, craning to look, gasped in horror, "Young and the four kids — all dead! God!"

The battered, bloodstained face of Guard Young stared sightlessly up at them. A white cloth blindfold had slipped down from his eyes. One arm was twisted behind him, a length of a white sashcord dangling from it. The grocer's corpse, clad in trousers and green sports shirt, was high in the boot, jammed in on top of the four tiny forms. Crumpled far back in the boot were the bludgeoned, lifeless bodies of little Jean and Judy Young and Mike Saile. Three-year-old Sondra Gay, tiniest of all, lay pinned and crushed under the others, almost hidden at the bottom of that ghastly tangle of dead flesh.

Patrolman Cooley and the other men stood white-faced and shaken. Then, as the highway patrolman fumbled for a cigarette, he suddenly tensed and made a dive for the boot. "Hey! This one's alive! I saw her move!"

It was true. Little Sondra Gay was stirring feebly, the sole moving thing in that charnel heap. Tenderly, the men lifted her out. They smoothed back the blood-matted golden curls. As the sunlight struck her, the little girl's eyes flicked open for a moment, then closed again. There was an ugly gash on the back of her head and blood was oozing from her right ear. She was barely breathing.

Swift examination of the other four bodies confirmed that they were cold in death. Leaving their companions to await the arrival of other officers, Cooley and one of the loggers rushed the unconscious child to a doctor's office in Chester — and then to the hospital in Westwood.

Sheriffs Schooler and Johnson, who had already departed on hearing the flash from the pilot, were at the scene a few minutes after the bodies were found. Other officers were close on their heels. Schooler and a hastily-summoned physician supervised the removal of the four victims, who were laid in a pathetic row on the sunlit forest ground. The skulls of all four had been crushed by savage blows from behind. Guard Young's hands had evidently been tied when he was killed, then one hand was freed to make it easier to jam him into the boot on top of the slaughtered children.

Young's bag of money and his wallet were missing. The motive for the massacre was obvious. Cold-blooded, inhuman highway robbers, for the sake of Guard Young's $7,000, had bludgeoned the four innocent children, along with the grocer, to ensure that no one would live to identify them.

While patrolmen blocked off the logging road pending the arrival of state crime technicians from Sacramento, the two sheriffs and their deputies studied the scene. It was evident that an attempt had been made to push the car over the bank into the creek. Only the heavy undergrowth had stopped it from rolling over. If it had gone down, it might have remained hidden for weeks.

There was no sign of any struggle among the pine needles at the spot where the car stood. "That means the murders took place somewhere else," Schooler decided. "At least two people were involved. They stuffed the bodies in the boot, then one of them drove Young's car here and abandoned it after trying to push it into the creek. His partner followed in their getaway car. Let's look around. They wouldn't have dared to drive this load very far."

The only item found near the car was Guard Young's ring of keys, lying on the ground. The investigators noted that the grocer's hat was missing. Silent teams of taut-faced deputies searched the creek bank and back-tracked down the rutted logging road. They noted faint tracks of a car with one bald tyre, in addition to those of Young's Chrysler. Soon, at a rubbish dump in a forest clearing near where the dirt road joined Route 36, they came upon sinister and eloquent evidence.

A deputy picked up a couple of strips of adding machine tape, recording the dead grocer's bank transaction. Also found were Young's comb, a torn piece of white cloth that matched the blindfold, a length of sashcord and some bloodstained tissue paper. There were bits of matted hair and flecks of blood on the scuffed ground. This secluded spot, within shouting distance of the state highway but hidden from it, was the murder scene beyond a doubt.

At the hospital, little Sondra Gay Young was found to be suffering from a skull fracture and extreme shock. She was still unconscious, but the doctors believed she would pull through.

All cars were stopped on mountain highways and back roads and their occupants questioned. Fourteen potential suspects — ex-convicts with records of sadistic violence — were picked up for investigation in various parts of northern California. But Saturday's widespread police activity came to nothing. On Sunday morning, a deputy found the murder weapon, a blood-spattered 18-inch length of gas pipe under the bushes at the rubbish dump. It yielded only fragmentary finger smudges, as had the death car. The state crime lab. men concentrated on efforts to trace the pipe and the sashcord, a slim hope at best.

"A piece of lead pipe isn't a mountain man's usual weapon," Sheriff Schooler commented. "My guess is that these killers are outsiders. But they must have had some local contact — somebody who knew about Young's Friday trip to the bank and set up the job for them."

Earl Warren, then California's governor, announced a $1,000 reward for information leading to the arrest of the killers, the first such reward posted by the Golden State since pioneer days. Rewards eventually totalled more than $6,000.

The hunt spread across the West. Tips poured in from all directions. An urgent alarm was broadcast for a black Buick with Arkansas plates carrying two or three rough-looking strangers, reportedly seen driving out of Westwood just about the time Guard Young started for home with the children.

Also sought was a tan Chevrolet seen parked at the mouth of the logging road on Friday afternoon. A young man wearing a hunter's red cap was standing by it, peering up the forest road. There were also several reports of a mystery woman seen in the vicinity — a brunette wearing red jeans. A Chester businessman, who had been on bad terms with Guard Young, was questioned at length when some pipe resembling the lethal bludgeon was found on his premises. But all these promising leads fizzled out.

On October 14th, the fourth day after the massacre, the doctors finally allowed Sheriff Schooler and District Attorney Bertram Jane to interview little Sondra Young, while her anguished mother cradled the wide-eyed three-year-old in her arms. Sondra said she went for a ride with Daddy and ate an ice-cream.

"What happened then, honey?" the sheriff asked gently.

"Two bad men," the child answered, lowering her eyes. "I didn't want to go up the road."

Piecing together little Sondra's halting story, the sheriff gathered that two men in a "big blue car" had forced Young to stop on the lonely highway. One man "with no hair in front" wore a white mask over the lower part of his face. The other, unmasked, was a tall man with curly black hair who brandished a "short, shiny gun." Sondra didn't know either of the men, both of whom wore "pretty shirts." She related how the pair had forced the children to lie down in the back seat. Then the tall man took the wheel and drove up the logging road, while his masked companion followed in the blue car.

It was obvious that Guard Young had submitted without resistance for the sake of the children — never dreaming that they would be bludgeoned anyway. Perhaps the calculating robbers had counted on that very thing.

Sondra described one further scene — her father lying in the middle of the dirt road, face down, while the masked man tied his hands behind him.

At that point, the child's memory faltered. Nature had drawn a merciful curtain. Later, when driven out to the scene, Sondra clung in terror to her mother as they approached the logging road. "No, no!" she sobbed, "I don't want to go up there!"

The tiny survivor of the horror was not particularly interested when shown "mug-shots" of suspects — until the lower halves of the faces were masked. Then she would point gleefully and cry, "That's the bad man!" as though it

were a game. The lawmen were doubtful as to whether
Sondra would actually be able to identify the killers if she
ever saw them. Still, her sketchy information was vital.

Late in October came a tip, just one among many others,
but rating special attention because of its source. It was
relayed to Schooler by his old friend Dewey Johnson, sheriff
of neighbouring Sierra County.

The information came from the wife of one of Johnson's
deputies, Percy Watters. Mrs. Watters worked as a waitress
in a restaurant at Grass Valley, in the Mother Lode country,
some 150 miles south of Chester. She had thought to tell
her husband about a conversation she had had over the
restaurant counter that day with a woman acquaintance.

The woman involved was a shapely 32-year-old blonde
divorcee named Beverly Winter. She worked as a stenogra-
pher at Beale Air Force Base, near Marysville, and was
known as something of a playgirl.

Beverly had confided to Mrs. Watters that she recently
went on a wonderful weekend spree in Reno with her latest
boy friend, a tall, handsome man named Jack Santo, who
lived in nearby Auburn. Santo was something of a mystery
figure — a man who never worked and was rumoured to
have his fingers in various rackets.

That weekend, said Beverly, Jack was loaded with money.
He bought her a complete new outfit in Reno — and they
really lived it up around the Nevada fun city's bars and
casinos. Not only that, Beverly bragged, but Jack had
ditched his regular girl friend, Harriet Henson, to go
partying over the weekend with her. Another couple, Gene
Faris and his wife, friends of Jack's from Chester, had been
along with them. Jack footed the bill for all.

The deputy's wife pricked up her ears when she heard
mention of the northern lumber town. She learned that the
big Reno party had started on Friday night, October 10th
— the date of the Guard Young massacre.

Discreetly, she pressed the talkative blonde for further
details. Big Jack had been deer-hunting, staying with his
friends up in Chester. Harriet was with him, but they

quarrelled. So, on Friday afternoon, Jack telephoned Beverly from Chester, inviting her to drive up to Reno that night to join him in a weekend of fun. The blonde, quick to do so, was still agog over what a wonderful time Santo had given her and how much money he had spent. What sort of money? Why, hundreds of dollars — in 20-dollar bills. He must have had several thousand on him. No, Beverly didn't know where Jack had got the money. She hadn't asked.

Shortly after this tip came in from Grass Valley, Sheriff Schooler received a letter from a Sacramento man, suggesting that he look into the activities of Gene Faris, a Chester painting contractor and sportsman. The letter writer said that an ex-convict, whom he did not name, had stayed at the Faris home on the night before the murders. And this man and the Farises had gone on a big spree in Reno immediately after the robbery-massacre. Investigation in Sacramento revealed that the informant was none other than the jealous ex-husband of Beverly Winter.

Big Jack Santo was already known to the Plumas County sheriff. In fact, he had already been questioned routinely, only a few days after the mass murders.

Santo, a known ex-convict of violent temperament, had visited a Chester tavern on October 10th. A pick-up order had been put out for him, along with other potential suspects. Big Jack, who did a lot of travelling, was soon being questioned by deputies in San Mateo County, on the San Francisco peninsula. Santo indignantly protested that he had spent all Friday afternoon at the home of Gene Faris, a reputable Chester citizen, who could vouch for him. He was released when a check with Faris confirmed his story.

On the strength of the new information about the Reno weekend, the spotlight swung back to Santo and his alibi. Sheriff Schooler questioned Gene Faris more closely. The contractor, a nervous little man, said that Santo had telephoned him and invited himself and Harriet, his common-law wife, up for deer-hunting. The couple had spent the night of October 9th at the Faris home. On Friday, Jack and Harriet did some drinking, got into a quarrel — and the brunette left in a huff. Faris understood she had caught a ride back to Auburn with some people she had met at a bar. Santo then invited Faris and his wife to go to Reno with him to watch a golf tournament. And he also phoned Beverly Winter, who joined them there.

The contractor assured the officers that he hadn't known Santo was an ex-con. He claimed that the Nevada weekend wasn't a "spree" by any means — and that Big Jack had not been particularly loaded with money. He thought that someone had to be exaggerating.

Faris ridiculed the idea that Santo could have killed Guard Young and the children. "Why, it just wouldn't be possible, sheriff. Jack was in and out of my house that day, but he was just around town here. I don't think he was gone for more than half an hour at any one time." Faris said it was about 4.30 p.m. when Jack called Beverly — and telephone company records substantiated this.

The contractor's wife confirmed his story, though she said she hadn't paid much attention to Santo's comings and goings. Faris enjoyed a good reputation and had never been in trouble. Still the lawmen were not satisfied. They noted that Jack Santo was a tall man with dark curly hair, just as little Sondra had described one of the killers. They also established that Harriet Henson had been wearing red jeans, which brought to mind the brunette reportedly seen near the logging road. Proceeding on a strong hunch, Sheriff Schooler and his colleagues took a long, close look at Big Jack's criminal record.

John Albert Santo, alias Jack Santos and Jack Mahoney, a powerful, hard-faced man of 48 who stood 6 feet 1 and weighed 14 stone, was well known to the police up and down the coast. His record dated back to 1924 in Portland, Oregon, when he was convicted of transporting a stolen car across a state line and drew two and a half years on McNeil Island. In 1932, he knifed a man in a fight over a poker game and did six months in the San Francisco County jail for assault with a deadly weapon. He had also been arrested for

kidnapping, suspicion of robbery, burglary and other offences.

Santo had spent most of his life around the Mother Lode
country, and for some years he had lived in a big old house
just outside Auburn. Of Spanish ancestry, he was ruggedly
good-looking. He had arrogant ice-blue eyes behind shell-
rimmed glasses, a pencil-line moustache and a debonair,
masterful manner. He kept his greying hair carefully dyed.
He was a notorious ladies' man, and had been married
several times and was reported to have three children.
Estranged from his latest wife, he had been living off and on
for four years with dark-haired Harriet Henson, a tough,
lynx-eyed woman of 30. Big Jack often strayed, but he
always seemed to come back to Harriet. He was currently
facing a $100,000 lawsuit for savagely beating a man who
made an offensive remark about the brunette.

Big Jack's source of income had long been a puzzle. He
had once owned an impoverished ranch and had a share in
an unproductive gold-mine. Vaguely understood to be a
"mining man," he was always hinting about mysterious big
deals. He passed himself off on occasion as a mining
engineer, a contractor, a gold-buyer and a real-estate
developer. No one saw him do any work other than hunting
or fishing, however, yet he always seemed to have plenty of
money.

For years, investigators had suspected Santo of "high-
grading" — dealing in illicit gold from the mines and selling
it on the international black market above the legal rate —
but nothing could be proved.

On July 2nd, 1950, two masked men hijacked $12,000 in
freshly mined gold from a truck on a lonely road near
Hammonton. On November 29th, 1951, Andrew Colner,
a gold-buyer, and his wife were cruelly tortured with lighted
matches, pistol-whipped and robbed of $4,500 in gold dust
by two men wearing rubber masks who invaded their home
near Folsom.

Then, on the snowy Christmas night of December 25th,
1951, two vicious marauders, one of them masked, forced

their way into the home of Edmund Hansen, owner of the famous Last Chance Mine at Nevada City. They demanded $20,000 in gold. When Hansen resisted them, protesting that he had no gold in the house, they shot him to death, riddling him with seven bullets before the horrified eyes of his wife.

Jack Santo was among several strongly suspected of these crimes. He was questioned and investigated, but nothing could be proved against him.

Early in 1952, Santo was able to produce enough cash to buy one of his favourite hangouts, a roadside tavern at Higgins Corner, between Grass Valley and Auburn.

For months, the Nevada and Placer County sheriffs had been checking intermittently on Santo and his associates. Then, in October, came the Chester mass murders and Big Jack's name cropped up yet again.

After studying the suspect's history, Sheriff Schooler had Santo picked up for further interrogation. Certainly, the arrogant ex-con snapped, he'd had a row with Harriet at Gene's house. She had gone back to Auburn, while he went to Reno to meet blonde Beverly. That was his personal business. Sure, he'd had a little money from a mining equipment deal, but he was far from wealthy. The blonde must have been trying to impress her girl friends, he leered.

Sullen-faced, waspish Harriet Hansen was likewise picked up. Obviously in love with Santo, she backed up his story. But there were some discrepancies in her account. She couldn't name the people who had driven her from Chester to Auburn, or tell which route they had taken.

After lengthy questioning the pair were released. And the investigators adopted the strategy of keeping away from Santo to lull him into a feeling of security.

The lawmen played it cautiously, keeping tabs on Santo, Harriet and Beverly without alerting them — while hoping for a break. They kept in contact with Gene Faris, who seemed increasingly nervous, as though he had something on his mind. They showed Santo's picture to little Sondra

Young, but she couldn't recognise him.

Meanwhile, as other avenues of investigation were pursued, the weeks turned into months. Early in 1953, Sheriff Wayne Brown of Nevada County — still working doggedly on the Edmund Hansen murder — became interested in a man named George Boles — a 28-year-old sanitorium attendant, a former barman and part-time newspaperman — with a minor police record. Boles, known as "The Professor," from his habit of quoting poetry, was a habitué of the Higgins Corner bar. When in his cups he sometimes dropped dark hints that he could tell plenty about the Mother Lode crimes if he wanted to. Boles was a pal of Santo — and phone records revealed that he had called Big Jack no less than 22 times from his hotel just before the Hansen murder. The investigators kept Boles under discreet surveillance.

That was the situation in March, 1953, when Jack Santo — who was still keeping both Harriet and Beverly on a string — borrowed the blonde divorcee's 1952 Oldsmobile for a trip to Los Angeles on one of his mysterious "business" errands.

It was at this point that the murder focus swung dramatically to southern California, 500 miles from the Mother Lode mountains — and Barbara Graham came into the picture for the first time.

On March 11th, 1953, a gardener found the body of Mrs. Monahan, a well-to-do crippled widow and former vaudeville star, crumpled in a hall cupboard in her big white home on West Parkside Avenue in the élite Mountain View district of suburban Burbank, Los Angeles. The fragile, grey-haired 62-year-old woman had been savagely tortured, beaten and choked to death, her hands trussed behind her. She had been dead for two days. The interior of the house was literally torn apart, as though the killer — or killers — had been frantically searching for something. Yet valuable jewellery in a handbag was untouched.

Mabel Monahan, who lived alone and feared burglars, had formerly been the mother-in-law of Luther B. "Tutor"

Scherer, the multi-millionaire Las Vegas gambling boss, a colourful figure known as the "Poet Laureate of Nevada." Burbank Police Chief Rex Andrews and his detective chief, Lieutenant Robert Coveney, sensed a connection between the murder and the gambling rackets.

The break came late in March with a tip passed to Detective Sergeant Ed Lovald of the Los Angeles burglary division by a reformed — and frightened — burglar and gambler, who said it was rumoured that Tutor Scherer kept a cache of $100,000 or more in undeclared gambling profits in a secret safe at the home of his former mother-in-law, in order to dodge income-taxes.

Two former aides of Tutor's principal rival, according to this informer, had had their eyes on the rumoured hoard kept in Mabel Monahan's home. One of the aides was Baxter Shorter, a husky, scar-faced 43-year-old ex-convict. The other was Bill Upshaw, a dapper, pudgy, silver-haired 34-year-old gambler and promoter.

"For the past year or so," the ex-gambler confided, "Shorter and Upshaw have been trying to get me to go along with them to help crack this safe and grab the loot. We cased the place a couple to times, but Upshaw got scared and kept putting off the job. Then I had a row with Bax and I pulled out. When I read that Mrs. Monahan had been bumped off, I decided I'd better get clean."

Baxter McCoy Shorter, who now called himself an "income property manager," and William Alvin Upshaw, who sold aircraft parts, were swiftly picked up, together with two other mobsters named by the informant.

Under persistent questioning, Bill Upshaw was the first to crack. Nervously assuring the officers that he hadn't been in on the actual murder, and given a promise of immunity and secrecy, he told what he knew. He named Jack Santo as leader of the murder mob. Upshaw said he had met the big fellow from the mountains when Santo visited Los Angeles to try to promote an illicit deal for high-grade Mexican gold. Upshaw had introduced him to Baxter Shorter, and Santo immediately became interested in the hoodlum pair's long-discussed plan to crack Tutor Scherer's reported cache in Mrs. Monahan's home.

Big Jack Santo man took charge of the operation. His chief lieutenant was a little buddy of his, a gambler whom Upshaw knew only as "Perk." There was another man named John, a northern Californian hunting pal of Santo's. And there was a shapely young, reddish-golden blonde called Barbara, who worked with Perk as a gambling tout. She was brought into the job in order to induce the timid widow to open her door.

The job was set for the night of March 9th. Upshaw was originally scheduled to go along, but the pudgy gambler was allergic to violence, and he didn't like the look in Big Jack's eyes. He backed out at the last minute. The next day, Shorter told him what had happened. Shorter had been posted outside as lookout.

When he went into the house, he found Santo, Perk and Barbara beating and torturing Mabel Monahan to make her reveal the hidden safe. They didn't find the safe. The frustrated mob finally fled, leaving the trussed-up widow at the point of death.

With Upshaw's information in hand, the jittery Shorter was soon persuaded to talk, on a similar promise of immunity. "I was there all right," the scar-faced cracksman acknowledged glumly, "but I don't go for murder. I'll tell you all about it."

Like Upshaw, he knew Santo's aides only as Perk, John and Barbara. Shorter said he had worried about having a woman on the job, but Big Jack had assured him that Babs was O.K. — that "she knows what happens to squealers."

As Shorter told it, Barbara went to the door and got the cautious Mrs. Monahan to open it by asking to use her telephone. The others piled in while Shorter kept watch outside.

When they called him inside to help look for the safe, Shorter said, he was horrified to see Barbara beating the moaning widow over the head with her gun. Perk was also hitting her. Shorter, who hadn't bargained for violence, got out fast. On his way home, he put in a call for an ambulance, but in his anxiety he gave the wrong address.

That was the shocking story of the Monahan murder. To cap the tragedy the crippled widow had died for nothing. The rumoured cache didn't exist. The cold-blooded killers had left without a penny.

Shorter promised to testify against the others, so he and the other informant were released. Jack Santo's record, of course, was known — and the wires hummed between Burbank and the Mother Lode country. Shorter's story was kept secret while he helped detectives to identify and trace the other three.

Big Jack's aides were soon identified. His jug-eared crony was Emmett "The Weasel" Perkins, alias Jack Bradley, a wizened, doleful little Los Angeles man who had spent more than half his 44 years in prison on multiple convictions, including bank robbery, burglary and car theft.

The blonde was Perkins's girl friend, Barbara Elaine Graham, a 29-year-old sometime prostitute and dope-user with a sordid police record up and down the coast dating back to 1937. The other man was John Lawson True, 38, a deep-sea diver from Sausalito, who had met and become chummy with Santo while working in the Mother Lode country, diving into flooded mines to salvage equipment.

All three had dropped from sight, along with Jack Santo. Baxter Shorter disdained police protection, declaring that he wasn't afraid of punks who would kill an old woman. But when the police moved to close a trap on the four fugitives, the plan misfired and there was a leak to the press. John True was arrested at Grass Valley, but the others got away. A few nights later, Baxter Shorter was kidnapped from his Bunker Hill apartment at gunpoint by a snarling little man whom Shorter's wife identified positively as Emmett Perkins. Shorter was whisked away in a car with another man at the wheel.

"The canary," as the newspapers nicknamed the luckless Baxter Shorter, was never seen again. His pal Bill Upshaw had fled to Mexico before the story broke. John

True blandly denied any part in the Monahan murder. With no one to testify against him, he was released.

The callous, vicious *modus operandi* of the Burbank murder made the northern lawmen feel strongly that Santo was also the killer of Guard Young and the three children — and of Edmund Hansen.

The missing trio were finally traced through some dud cheques issued by Barbara Graham. And on May 4th, a small army of Los Angeles police led by Deputy Chief Thad Brown closed in on their hideout in a boarded-up building in suburban Lynwood. The raiders found Big Jack Santo lying nearly naked, half asleep on a bed. Jug-eared Perk lay fully clothed in another room. Blonde Babs was wandering around the place in semi-undress. All three startled fugitives gave up without resistance.

Booked on suspicion of murder, the hardened, con-wise trio wouldn't give the police the time of day. They denied even knowing Baxter Shorter or Bill Upshaw, much less Mabel Monahan. Barbara Graham scornfully rejected offers of leniency if she would confess and implicate her companions.

If Barbara had known then what she would later have to face, she'd surely have squealed. But how could she have imagined that this was the last chance to save her life? Or that by co-operating with the police against the barbarous Santo crew, she would live to bring up her beloved child Tommy?

Events would show that others were more than ready to double-cross her and place her in the gas chamber. . .

Judge Fricke gathered the folds of his robe over his knee as he leaned forward and studied the lawyers at the counsel tables. They were divided into two camps. On their faces ran a gamut of expressions ranging from inscrutable calm to tense expectancy.

"Ready to proceed, gentlemen?" he asked quietly.

Prosecutor Adolph Alexander answered for the state. "The people are ready, Your Honour."

Jack Hardy, attorney for Mrs. Graham, ran his fingertips over the copy of the indictment on the table before him. "The defendant Barbara Graham is ready," he said.

"Ready for defendants Perkins and Santo," Defence Attorney S. Ward Sullivan called.

"Ask the jurors to take their places," Fricke instructed the bailiff. Nine men and three women filed into the courtroom and settled themselves self-consciously into the jury-box. Then two deputy sheriffs escorted the three prisoners into the courtroom proper. Barbara Graham came first, her red-gold hair braided in a double halo at the back of her head. She wore no make-up, other than a little powder and carmine lipstick. Her eyes were both defiant and demure. A flowered print dress hugged the smoothness of her hips and accentuated the fullness of her breasts. She took the seat next to Attorney Hardy and clasped her hands in front of her.

Emmett Perkins followed John Santo to chairs alongside Sullivan. Santo walked with brazen self-confidence. Perkins shambled in. In following Santo, he was doing what came most naturally to him. He had been following Jack Santo for a long, long time.

Prosecutor Alexander delivered his opening address to the jury. "Mabel Monahan was a widow, aged and crippled. She lived alone in her house at 1718 Parkside Avenue in Burbank, California. On the night of March 9th, 1953, she was brutally murdered. The gardener found her savagely beaten body at noon next day. A blood-soaked pillowcase was pulled over her head and face, her wrists were bound with a strip of torn bed sheet — and another strip was knotted around her throat.

"Here before you are three persons whom the state accuses of taking part in this crime. Murderers of this type are not hatched in the churches, or in the home of our community. They are spawned in the foul caves they infest. By night, they crawl out to perform their evil deeds. There are a lot of Mrs. Monahans in this world, in the sunset and twilight of their lives. They are entitled to live in the peace and sanctity of their homes. But there are a lot of Perkins and Santos and Mrs. Grahams who persist in crawling out from under slimy rocks. The dead voice of Mrs. Monahan cries out for justice from her grave. The entire state cries for justice. These crimes must not go unheeded.

"We will prove that the defendants Santo, Perkins and Mrs. Graham did wilfully and in concert with each other force their way into the home of Mrs. Monahan, under the impression that a considerable fortune in cash was hidden there. We will prove that they beat and tortured the old lady, hoping to extort from her the hiding place of the secret cache. We will show that, failing to locate this hidden hoard, they killed Mrs. Monahan in cold blood, rather than leave behind a witness who could point an accusing finger at them."

The jurors followed the prosecutor's eyes and looked carefully at the prisoners while defence counsel Sullivan looked over his notes as the state prepared to call its first witness. There was the body to be proved, then medical testimony by the coroner, the preliminary stuff. It would run through fast. No one was going to deny that Mabel Monahan was dead. The fireworks would come later when the DA tried to pin the crime on the defendants.

Big Jack Santo thought of Baxter Shorter. And he smiled. Baxter Shorter. All through California, in Nevada, Arizona and the Utah badlands, the cops were looking for Baxter Shorter, the canary, one-time henchman of Micky Cohen. Whatever had happened to Baxter Shorter?

Shorter was the wedge that cracked the Mabel Monahan case. When the old lady lay dying under a pillow-slip hood with fatal cranial injuries and a strangler's cord around her throat, somebody had phoned for an ambulance from a kiosk at Vermont Avenue and Sunset Boulevard. A man's voice told the operator that there was an injured woman at 1718 Parkside Avenue. He neglected to add that the address was in Burbank. The ambulance went looking for that house number in Los Angeles — and it was while those precious moments ticked by that Mabel Monahan died.

It was Shorter who made that call. He admitted it to the cops when they picked him up for questioning. It wasn't the only thing he admitted. They sweated him and he sang. He told the police who was in on the job — Jack Santo, Emmett Perkins, Barbara Graham and John True. He told about the underworld rumour that over a hundred grand in cash was stashed away in the Monahan house. Santo had gone to a lot of trouble to set up the caper. He brought Shorter along as boxman, to take care of a safe, should they find one. Barbara was to help them gain entry to the house. True and the Weasel were there to do the muscle work, while Santo rode herd on the crew as the brain.

The caper went sour. They went too heavy on the old woman. And they left without finding a dime when it became too hot to hang around any longer.

Baxter Shorter's information to the police resulted in a lightning raid on a mountain cabin in Nevada County. Cops from LA kicked in the door and grabbed John True, who was in the act of taking a bath. It was a hush-hush raid, made without the knowledge of the Nevada County authorities. True was hustled to the jail in Stockton and held there under an assumed name. He did not break under a continuous session of police questioning, and was finally released when a custody dispute arose between the officials of Nevada and Los Angeles Counties. The press got wind of the arrest and asked True for a statement, which appeared in the evening papers of April 14th. The first headlines hit the street at 6 o'clock. In effect, those evening editions set the seal on the canary's doom.

"They asked me did I know a party named Baxter Shorter," True told the reporters. "I told them I did not know any Baxter Shorter."

This was the gang's first intimation that the canary had sung. They acted fast. At 9 o'clock, Jack Santo and Emmett Perkins came to Shorter's hotel suite. Shorter met them at the door. Warning his wife to make no outcry, they forced Shorter at gunpoint to accompany them downstairs. No one ever saw the canary again.

When the gang was finally rounded up, their car was examined for some traces of the informer's one-way ride. Foliage specimens clinging to the undercarriage were studied by Bonnie Templeton, Curator of Botany at the Los Angeles County Museum.

"I found specimens of ribbonwood and *Metzelia affinis*," she told the cops. "The wood comes from a small shrub native to southern California, particularly the San Jacinto Mountains at elevations of 2,500 feet and above. The plant exists in two varieties. The smaller is found in the San Gabriel and San Bernardino Mountains, again at about 2,500 feet. The second variety is native to the desert."

To the cops, this meant that unless the buzzards led them to the corpse of Baxter Shorter, rotting somewhere up on the heights of the Sierras, or deep in the trackless desert, the remains of the canary would never be found.

Santo knew that the only evidence against his gang was the uncorroborated testimony of an accomplice — not sufficient to convict in a California court. With Shorter out of the way, there was an even wider margin of safety.

Then the cops upset his applecart by picking up William Upshaw, a natty, cherub-faced man who looked like a movie producer.

When he was first planning the Monahan caper, Santo had tried to interest Bill Upshaw in going along. Upshaw, therefore, knew the members of the gang. And because he wasn't in on the job, his testimony might well provide the independent corroboration which would pave Santo's last mile to the gas chamber.

Santo sweated in jail over ways and means to liquidate this prosecution witness. Then abruptly, he changed his tack and went to work on framing an alibi which would save his own skin. His common-law wife, Harriet Henson, could fix him up with a woman who would swear black and blue that on the night of the murder Jack was shacked up in a hotel somewhere in Fresno. A lot, of course, depended on how much True would blab.

Prosecutor Alexander brought deep-sea diver John True

to the witness stand on August 25th. He then proceeded to put him through his paces.

"What do you do for a living, John?" he asked.

"I'm a deep-sea diver," True answered.

"When did you meet Jack Santo?"

The diver, a big man in a well-cut jacket, contracted his eyebrows in thought. "Last January," he said. "I was living up in Grass Valley. Jack came up to do a little hunting."

Piece by piece, Alexander put together the background of the murder plot. At no time had True realised that Santo was anything other than a reputable business contractor with a wad of money. Santo promised to set him up in business, diving for submerged logs.

Early in March, the two drove down to Los Angeles and took a room in an El Monte motel. It was there that True met Emmett Perkins and Barbara Graham for the first time. He also met Baxter Shorter and Bill Upshaw.

"Describe that meeting," Alexander directed him.

"It was on the afternoon of March 9th," True said. "Perkins and Mrs. Graham showed up at the motel. We got in Santo's car and met Shorter and Upshaw at a drive-in. Santo told me that Shorter was a boxman. He asked me if *I* was a boxman. I asked him what kind of a box he meant, an apple-box or what. He said, 'That is a man who opens safes.' I told him that was something I never did."

"How did Santo get the idea that you did?"

"As a diver, I handle explosives. Dynamite, jelly."

At the drive-in, Santo talked privately with Shorter and Upshaw in their car. A few minutes later, Santo came back looking glum. He told True and the others: "Upshaw doesn't want any part of it."

The group then took off in the two cars, passing the Monahan home on Parkside Avenue in Burbank. Santo and Shorter pointed to the house as they drove by. Then Perkins said: "That must be the place."

"Weren't you curious about all this?" Alexander asked the witness.

"Sure I was," True answered. "When we got back to the

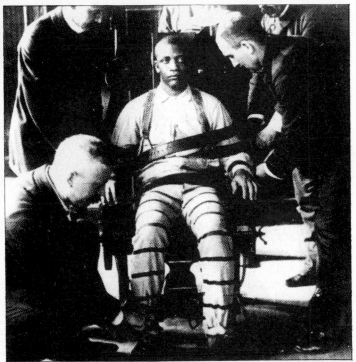

An unidentified man is strapped into an electric chair during the early part of this century

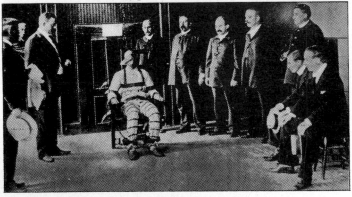

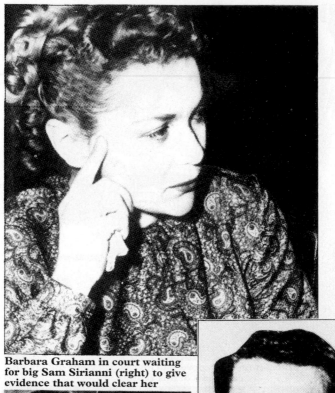

Barbara Graham in court waiting for big Sam Sirianni (right) to give evidence that would clear her

Jack Santo (above left) and Emmett Perkins died together in the gas chamber, sneering and defiant

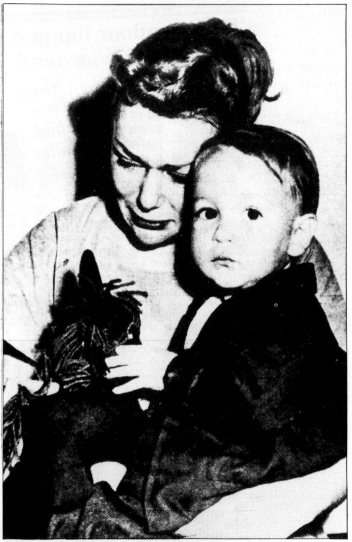

Barbara Graham with her son Tommy. "I wish I could see him grow up. But I know I won't"

Bloody Babs: page 36

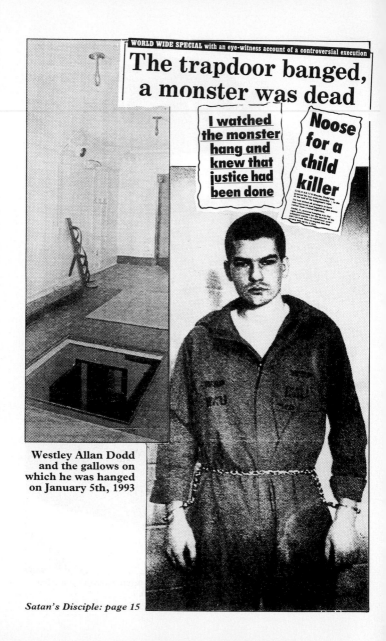

The trapdoor banged, a monster was dead

I watched the monster hang and knew that justice had been done

Noose for a child killer

Westley Allan Dodd
and the gallows on
which he was hanged
on January 5th, 1993

Satan's Disciple: page 15

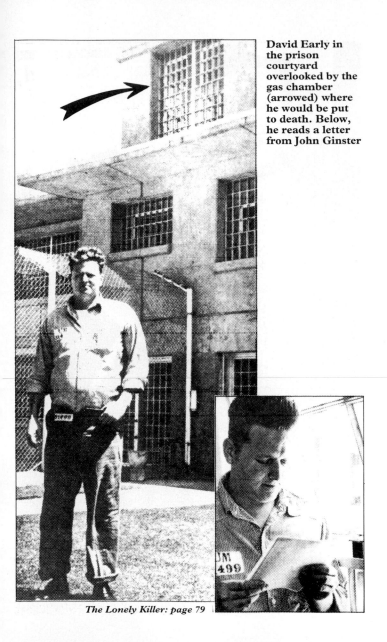

David Early in the prison courtyard overlooked by the gas chamber (arrowed) where he would be put to death. Below, he reads a letter from John Ginster

The Lonely Killer: page 79

Glenn Dague and Irene Schroeder.
"If I do go to the hot seat, Glenn will want to go too. We will love
each other always to the end"

The Trigger Woman: page 150

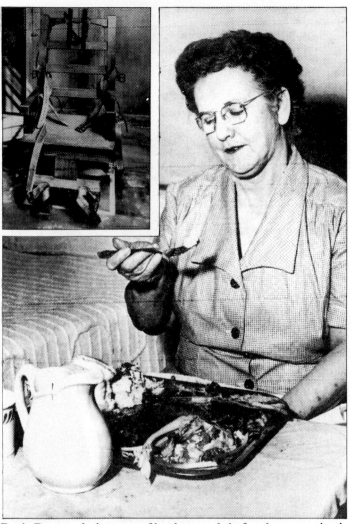

Dovie Dean tucks into one of her last meals before her execution in Ohio's electric chair. "She was one of the calmest persons I've ever seen taken into the death chamber. She looked like Whistler's Mother as she sat there with her arms folded"

Whistler's Mother: page 96

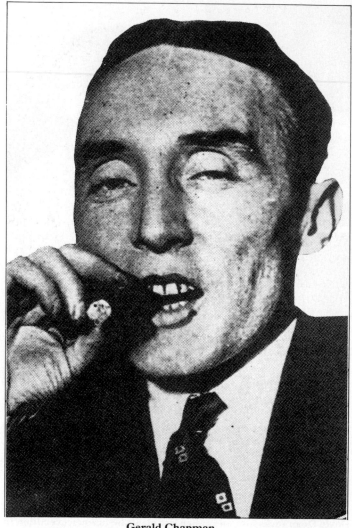

Gerald Chapman.
The black cowl was slipped over his head, the signal given,
and the rope hissed over it's pulleys. It took him nine
minutes to die!
The Count of Gramercy Park: page 164

motel, I asked Santo what the score was. He gave me a real cock-and-bull story. He said people were hiding black market money in a safe in that house and that all of us were going to get it. Later, he told me that some guy from Las Vegas had been bringing money there, 100,000 dollars at a time."

"Did you agree to go along on the job?"

"Only after Jack swore to me that nobody lived in the house and that nobody would get hurt."

Alexander was like an artist painting every detail of what had happened on that tragic night through the halting, troubled words of his witness. At 6 o'clock, Perkins, Santo, True and Mrs. Graham had supper at the Smokehouse, where they found Shorter waiting for them. Santo outlined the job.

Shortly before 9 p.m. they set out. Everyone wore gloves. Perkins, True and Barbara Graham were armed with revolvers. The two cars drew up across the street from the Monahan home. Barbara got out and ran up the steps. Her instructions were to ring the bell and ask to use the phone. A moment later, John True followed. He found the girl struggling with the widow in the doorway.

"Mrs. Graham was lambasting the old lady in the face with her gun. She had her by the hair with her left hand and was striking her with the right. I told Barbara to cut it out and put up my hand to stop her. The old lady collapsed. Pretty soon, Barbara put a pillowcase over the lady's head. Then Perkins came in and said, 'Let's get her away from the door.' He tied her hands behind her and dragged her by the feet up the hall till he got in front of a closet. Santo took a strip of cloth and tied it around Mrs. Monahan's face over the pillow-case. She was moaning, like she was hurt bad.

"We started going through the house, opening drawers and looking all over. There was a trapdoor in the den. I opened it with a knife, but it was only a floor furnace. There wasn't any safe there at all."

"Did you go back to where Mrs. Monahan was lying?" Alexander asked.

"Yes, sir. She was moaning. I'm a deep-sea diver, so I know how it's like to be down there with too little air. I cut a piece out of the pillowcase, so she could breathe just a bit more easily."

True identified a bloody patch of cloth as the piece he referred to. Alexander wound up fast, bringing out the details of the unsuccessful search of the house and of the flight afterwards.

"We went back to the motel and cleaned up. I felt pretty cheap and lowdown about what had happened. I hoped this Baxter guy called for an ambulance, like I had told him to on the quiet."

That night, True said, Santo drove him back to Grass Valley. The two men talked little, except for a few words about the possibility of the crime being laid at their door. "Sniffing gas in that chamber is an awful way to go," True told Santo.

Santo nodded. His voice was as cold as ice as he said: "Don't forget that there's two ways to go. If they catch you, you die. If you squeal, you die, too."

The defence failed to shake True in any essential part of his story. Then Bill Upshaw took the stand and added his clincher to True's damning evidence. The jury watched the defendants to see how they were taking it. Santo seemed a little worried. Perkins was, figuratively speaking, playing poker. He looked like a man who might still have an ace in the hole. Barbara Graham, alone of the trio, seemed completely serene. She gave the appearance of knowing for certain that she was betting on a sure thing.

Barbara listened more as an interested spectator than a defendant to the parade of prosecution witnesses. She had an alibi, custom-made and ready for delivery. She had made up to Elsa Prantile when she first caught Elsa's eyes watching her during recess in the prison yard. The minute she knew Elsa well enough, she laid her cards on the table. Elsa had a friend by the name of Vince who had connections. Vince sent big Sam Sirianni to the jail during the next visiting session. Sam identified himself with the password

that she had thought of, that line from Omar Khayyam —
"I came like water and like wind I go ..."

After that, it was easy to set up the deal. For 25 grand,
Big Sam would swear that, on the night of March 9th, he
and Barbara were engaged in a cosy session in a motel on
Ventura Boulevard. What was more, Sirianni would produce a receipted bill for that night, plus an obliging clerk
who would take the stand and testify that, on the night in
question, Sam and Barbara (registered as Mr. and Mrs.
John Clark) had disappeared into motel room No. 20 and
had not emerged until 7 o'clock the next morning.

On the morning of August 27th, the court clerk called
the first witness for the day: "Sam Sirianni!" he intoned.
"Sam Sirianni?" In the rear of the courtroom a tall man in
a dark blue suit rose from his seat.

"Come forward and be sworn," the court clerk instructed. The witness, carrying a neat black briefcase,
pushed through the gate and left his case on the prosecutor's table, then walked over to the clerk.

After being sworn in, Sirianni seated himself and let his
eyes flick over the counsel tables. The blood began to drain
out of Barbara's face. She stared uncomprehendingly at the
black briefcase on the prosecutor's table. If big Sam was her
alibi witness, why had he been called forward by the DA's
staff?

Deputy DA J. Miller Leavy picked up the briefcase and
walked around the end of the table. Instead of advancing
towards the witness stand, he stood with his back to the
railing, so that his questions, when he asked them, would be
delivered in a loud voice. And the answers, likewise, would
be easily heard.

"What is your occupation and title, Mr. Sirianni?"

"I am a police officer attached to the Intelligence Squad
of the Los Angeles Police Department," was his reply.

Barbara Graham's mouth sagged open.

Under Leavy's skilful questioning, Officer Sirianni disclosed the bizarre story of how he had posed as an underworld fixer who had connived with Barbara Graham to

frame the phony alibi calculated to leave her in the clear, while the maelstrom of justice sucked the other defendants under. Assigned to his undercover role on August 6th, Sirianni had been working under the direction of Detective Lieutenant Bob Coveney, the Burbank cop who had been in charge of the Monahan murder probe from the beginning. Coveney was actually the "Vince" whom Barbara thought was the intermediary between her jail acquaintance Elsa Prantile and big Sam.

Coveney and Elsa were old acquaintances. They had known each other when she was a waitress in Burbank. When Elsa was sentenced to one year in the county jail on a reckless driving charge, Bob Coveney visited her and learned about her new friendship with Barbara Graham. Elsa had agreed to lead Barbara on. She was to tell the redhead that her friend Vince (Coveney himself) would fix the details. He was to send someone to jail to speak to Barbara and arrange the details of an elaborate alibi. Barbara herself suggested the watchword by which the two would know each other. "Baby," she had written to Elsa, "I thought of a password. It is from Omar Khayyam. Hope your friend doesn't think I'm too weird, but then we can be sure. *I came like water and like wind I go*. Do you think he can remember that? If not, you can use something else and let me know."

Sam visited Barbara in jail on three separate occasions — August 7th, 10th and 12th. Each time he was equipped with a miniature wire-recording device bandaged to his back under his trouser belt and provided with a button microphone concealed under his shirt. The wire on which the dialogue was recorded was finer than human hair. The last such conversation was replayed in court for the edification of the jury. The miniature machine was amplified through another record-player.

There was a hushed silence in court as the first words of the transcription were played back. They were fuzzy, but just distinct enough to be followed.

"Hi, Barbara. How are you?"

"Pretty good."

"Has your attorney been up here to see you?"

"No. He's waiting to hear from *you*."

"Oh, well, that's all right. I want to go over everything today that we went over the last two meetings. Do you understand? I got a hell of a lot to say, so let's get things straight."

"OK by me. What do you want to know?"

The voice of Sirianni seemed tense. "Now first of all — for my own protection, in case there was someone else there that night — I want you to tell me where you were that night, who you were with. In other words, if you weren't there that night, maybe you were someplace where somebody saw you."

"No. I can assure you that no one saw me."

"In other words, if someone else *did* see you that night, they might show up in courts as witnesses. Do you think that will happen?"

"Not a chance."

"Take it from 10 o'clock Monday morning till 7 o'clock Tuesday morning. If anyone *did* see you, you know what that would mean to us," the officer pressed.

"I was home most of the time, Sam."

"Now listen, Barbara, I got a hell of a lot at stake. I want to get all that straight, because I don't want to make a chump out of myself when I go to court. I want everything pat. I don't know those other guys. I've heard their names. You say it's Perkins, True and Santo? You were with those three fellows that night? OK, you were with them. How about Upshaw?"

"Oh, no. I don't know him."

"OK — how about Bax?"

"You mean Baxter Shorter?"

"Yeah. That's one thing you'll have to assure me about. Where is Bax? I have no assurance that he won't be there in court."

"I can assure you that he'll not be there."

"You know for a fact that he won't be there?"

"Uh-huh."

"Do you personally know what happened to him?"

"Listen, Sam. If I wasn't sure that he wouldn't show up, I wouldn't say it. So you can use your imagination."

"OK. Now, on the motel. I've got one of those. You know, baby, 500 dollars is only chicken-feed for what I'm doing for you."

"I was always under the impression that I was going to pay more. I figured you for about 25 grand before you got done. What can I do? Without you, I'm a cinch for cyanide."

"You figured pretty good. Just remember this, Barbara. I'm only doing this as a favour, because that money means nothing to me. I can go out and make that much in one night. You're willing to pay me 25,000 dollars. Is that right?"

"It'll be on the line."

"About that motel, now. Now I can't do this without the clerk. Do you understand that he has to be paid off?"

"Uh-huh."

"How much are you willing to pay *him*?"

"Well, now, we don't have too much time — and he's also going to have to take abuse. Promise him whatever you think."

"He gave me this registration card. We have to fill it out. What names should we put? Our own names, Barbara? How about using your name and I'll pose as Mr. Graham?"

"No, Sam. It will be better if we use a fictitious name."

"Should I use Sirianni? No, I guess we better use a phony. How about Clark? Mr. and Mrs. Clark?"

"Sure. That's fine. Whatever you say, Sam. Only one thing — I don't want my attorney to know anything about this, Sam. This is between you and me and that motel clerk. Nobody else should know a thing."

"Sure. I understand. Now let's just get this last one thing straight. I want to know where you *were* that day. Because if anyone — I don't care who it is — if anyone saw any of you, they'll be in court and I don't mean maybe! Now,

Perkins, True, Santo — how about Bax? Was he there that night? If he *was* there that night, that would make four of them."

"Uh-huh."

"Perkins, True, Santo and Shorter. That's what I want straight. Don't worry about it. I want to protect myself too. You were with those four guys on the night of March 9th when everything took place? Now then — were you?"

"I was with them."

The jury listened to these words, to the recorded voices which detailed the plot to place Barbara Graham and Sam Sirianni in the motel. It was the connivance of a desperate woman clutching frantically at anything, no matter how foul, no matter how low, no matter how devious, if only it could serve to keep her from treading the last mile to the San Quentin gas chamber.

Barbara Graham looked at the jurors and abruptly lowered her eyes. In that one brief exchange she realised that she had looked at her fate.

When Officer Sirianni had completed his testimony, it was implemented by Elsa Prantile, who followed him to the witness stand. Placed into evidence were letters which Barbara had slipped to her fellow-risoner on the occasions they managed to meet in the county jail.

Policewoman Shirley Parker was another bombshell with which the prosecution demolished Graham's defence. Parker had also posed as a prisoner, being planted in the same cell as Barbara under the name of Shirley Olson. Parker claimed Barbara had admitted to her that she was in the company of the killers at the time of Mrs. Monahan's murder — and that she was frantically casting about for someone with whom to frame an alibi.

The trial of Barbara Graham, Jack Santo and Emmett Perkins moved swiftly and inexorably to its end. Only Barbara of the three defendants went on the witness stand. She was unable to explain away her disastrous efforts in prison to set up an alibi. Nor were character witnesses for Santo able to whitewash his obvious guilt. His common-law wife Harriet Henson — in attempting to provide him with an alibi — herself came to grief. For cross-examination proved that she had offered 1,500 dollars to a truck salesman to help her establish a false story.

Upon leaving the courtroom, Harriet Henson was taken into custody in connection with the murder of Edmund Hansen, the gold prospector shot dead in Nevada City, California, on December 29th, 1951. Hansen had been shot seven times — and there was good reason to believe that Jack Santo and his gang had been responsible. Just moments before the assassination, Jack and Perkins had attempted to buy 20,000 dollars in gold from the victim.

Meanwhile, in court Perkins's attempts to provide himself with an alibi in the Monahan case were no more successful than those of his colleagues. The prosecution soon poked holes in the story that he was visiting relatives on March 9th and 10th.

In his closing address to the jury, Prosecutor Alexander said: "We have been criticised for what the defence has chosen to call an entrapment. It is claimed that we have been too relentless in the prosecution of this case. We admit that the state went to great lengths in performing its sworn duty to the people. We fought fire with fire.

"The defence has hurled around the word 'deal' to explain our treatment of John True. Put yourself in the position of the prosecution. You have four vicious rats, or rattlesnakes — whatever you want to call them. They are infesting your home and are a menace to your neighbours. You have the opportunity of exterminating three and letting one go — or losing four.

"Any criminal case is tried on the facts. In this case, the facts are hideous, almost beyond belief. You are asked to decide the guilt — or innocence — of the prisoners before the bar on these facts alone. There is no place for sentiment. You are told that the children of Perkins and Graham will be orphaned. I tell you that they were orphaned long before this murder trial came before this court.

"If you want tears, there are tears aplenty in this case. But the tears should be shed for Mrs. Mabel Monahan and her fate, not for Perkins, Graham and Santo.

"We do not ask for revenge — only for the proper administration of justice. You swore that you would perform your duty. Under the evidence of this case, there is but one duty which you can perform. The lives of Barbara Graham, Emmett Perkins and John Santo must be forfeited for what they have done . . ."

On September 22nd, nine men and three women entrusted with the fates of the three defendants retired to the jury-room to deliberate upon a verdict. After five hours and 20 minutes they notified the clerk that they had reached an agreement. Judge Clement D. Nye, designated to receive the verdict on behalf of Judge Fricke, mounted the bench and instructed the bailiff to bring the jurors into the courtroom.

"Ladies and gentlemen of the jury, are you unanimously agreed on a verdict?" Judge Nye asked.

Foreman Robert Dodson rose. "We are, Your Honour," he said. He handed the written slips to the bailiff, who passed them to the judge to read. He in turn conveyed them to chief clerk Cecil J. Luskin, who read the fateful words.

"In the case of the People versus Barbara Graham, we the jury find the defendant guilty of murder, a felony, as charged in the indictment — and find it to be murder in the first degree." He read two more identical pronouncements in respect of John Santo and Emmett Perkins.

Pronouncement of sentence was deferred until Friday, September 25th, although this amounted to a formality. Under the law, there could be only one penalty — and that was death.

The three prisoners were ushered out of the courtroom. Each was stoical. Each had heard other guilty verdicts before. Even Barbara Graham remembered how she had been found guilty of prostitution, guilty of perjury, guilty of possessing narcotics. But this time it was different. "Why did this have to happen to me?" she murmured. "Life is so short. Why does mine have to be even shorter?"

Still to be resolved were the investigations into the murders of Edmund Hansen and of Guard Young and the three children.

Harriet Henson was questioned daily. And though she finally confessed to driving the getaway car in the massacre of Guard Young, his daughters and their young playmate, she flatly refused to implicate Big Jack, with whom she was still apparently very much in love.

Detectives continued to question Harriet, dropping frequent mentions of Santo's association with Babs Graham and his blonde girl friend Beverly. They stressed that big Jack had cast her off and had used her only as an alibi dupe. He wouldn't even reply to the daily love-letters Harriet was still writing to him. Finally, after three weeks, the brunette broke down and told the full story of the Hansen murder — and also of the Chester massacre.

On the afternoon of October 10th, Harriet said, Santo and Perkins had left her in a Chester tavern and picked her up again an hour later. They were excited and shaky. Though Harriet insisted that the pair never told her in so many words what they had done, she quoted Perkins as remarking: "This has been a pretty gruesome day for us." And later: "If I'd known the kids were along, I wouldn't have gone through with the caper."

Big Jack and the Weasel were in a hurry to leave the vicinity. Jack told Harriet to drive Perkins back to Auburn, while he himself went on to Reno. On the way, Perkins changed his clothes, and gave Harriet a wallet — Guard Young's — and some papers to destroy. At her home, Harriet told the lawmen, Perkins counted out $2,000 from a fat envelope and handed it to her as her share of the day's profits.

While investigators wrapped up loose ends in the Guard Young massacre, Santo, Perkins, a suspected accomplice named George Boles and Harriet were indicted for the murder of gold prospector Edmund Hansen.

At the opening of the Hansen murder trial in December, Harriet Henson reluctantly agreed to testify against the others in return for the dropping of the charge against her. A statement made by George Boles was introduced.

A major witness was the Modesto garage man who had exploded Santo's alibi attempt in the Monahan case. An old hunting companion of Santo, he related how Big Jack had tried to enlist him for the Hansen job and other crimes. Asked if he weren't afraid to testify, the witness said contemptuously: "No! He seems to be better with children and old women!"

Santo, Perkins and Boles were found guilty of murdering the gold-mine proprietor. And on January 15th, 1954, Judge James Snell sentenced all three to life terms, which was of course superfluous in the case of Big Jack and the Weasel. A local mechanic drew three years for smuggling the hacksaw blades to them.

Meanwhile, the investigation of the Chester massacre was also completed. A grand jury indicted Santo, Perkins and Harriet for the massacre of Guard Young and the three children. This time, the murder monster's common-law wife wasn't able to get out of it by singing. The district attorney produced two surprise witnesses, a laundry truck driver and a rancher, who testified that while driving past the mouth of the logging road they had seen Harriet Henson in Young's car with the three children, while Santo and Perkins were standing beside their own car, talking to Guard Young.

Thus, the sullen brunette fell into a trap of her own making. The true story appeared to be that the lethal pair had taken Harriet along to lull their victim's suspicions when they flagged him down on the road, probably pretending that their car had broken down. Harriet's counsel bitterly assailed the new version, claiming that if the witnesses had actually seen a woman at the scene of the massacre, then it must have been Barbara Graham, not Harriet Henson.

Other evidence was damning. Beverly Winter testified that three days before the Chester murders, Santo had been broke and had borrowed 15 dollars from her. On the night of the 10th in Reno, he was flush. He told her that he had received the money for his part in a hold-up in Redding. Beverly had been afraid to divulge this originally. Gene Faris and his wife told their stories — and Harriet's statement to the sheriff was offered in evidence.

The district attorney introduced a transcript of a secretly recorded conversation between Harriet and Santo in his cell at Nevada City, in which Big Jack rasped at the woman: "If you hadn't opened your mouth, they'd never have found anything in the Chester deal!"

On May 7th, 1954, the jury found Santo, Perkins and Harriet Henson guilty of the Guard Young massacre. Judge Ben Curler sentenced the two men to die a second time — a grim legal technicality — and Harriet to life imprisonment at Corona.

Babs Graham continued to assert her innocence, claiming she had been framed by True and Upshaw.

Questioned about the fate of Baxter Shorter — with the implication that she might still win clemency if she told all she knew — Babs only shook her head and denied ever meeting Shorter, True or Upshaw until she saw the latter pair in court. She insisted that the vanished True and Upshaw had framed her to save their own skins. She couldn't explain why they should have ganged up on her, if they hadn't even known her.

"If I die in the gas chamber, those two are guilty of my murder," Barbara declared, referring to True and Upshaw. "They'll pay for it some day, one way or another. All the rats, all the liars, all the ones who want me dead, will pay!"

Only two women had been executed previously in Californian history, but Barbara Graham was destined to be number three . . .

Perkins and Santo chatted and chuckled as they sat strapped side by side in the chamber of death. They reminded your author, who was one of the reporters who witnessed the executions, of scared kids whistling their way past a grave-yard.

But Barbara died hard. For on that fateful June morning, the state of California played a grim game of cat and mouse with her. Twice she mustered her courage for the 15-foot walk to the gas chamber, only to be told there was still a slim chance that she would live. One delay was granted after she had walked more than half the distance from her cell to the sombre tomb where death patiently waited.

She fought down the rising hysteria within her and clung momentarily to each straw of hope held out to her, only to have it snatched away, leaving her more desolate than before. Finally, when she could stand the strain no longer, she cried out in agony:

"Why do they torture me so? I was ready to die at ten o'clock!"

That was at 11.10 a.m. on June 3rd, 1955, just 32 minutes before she would be finally pronounced dead.

Father Dan McAlister, former chaplain at San Quentin, who consoled Babs in her last hours, declared that she had undergone a "complete transformation" during her two years in prison. And after her death, he declared with conviction: "She was a deeply religious woman."

Perhaps it was from her newly found faith that the attractive 32-year-old mother of three drew the courage and strength that kept her from cracking up under the most appalling circumstances.

She arrived at San Quentin at 4 p.m. on the day before she was to die. She hadn't taken solid nourishment since she left the women's prison at Corona early that morning. For her last meal, she requested only a dish of ice-cream.

She was suffering from a severe toothache. And when she was taken to her special cell, she had to walk past the chamber in which she was to die some 19 hours later. Given a sedative for her throbbing jaw, she changed into a pair of scarlet lounging pyjamas, then began preparing herself for her fast-approaching death.

She was about to become the third woman to be executed in the history of California. And since there was no accommodation for female prisoners in the sprawling prison on San Francisco Bay, she was placed in a special apartment just a few feet from the ghastly chamber.

There she told Warden Harley O. Teets that she would talk to no one but her attorney and Father McAlister.

Barbara refused to eat a chicken dinner that had been brought to her cell and commented wryly to Warden Teets:

"Why waste good food on me? Give it to someone who can enjoy it."

Through the long night, the light burned in her cell as she prayed with Father McAlister. Telephone lines were kept open all night to the executive mansion in Sacramento, where Governor Goodwin Knight remained ready to consider any legal manoeuvre that might warrant a stay of execution.

The final battle for Barbara Graham's life really began at 2 a.m., when the governor received a call from Attorney William Strong, one of the condemned woman's attorneys. Strong raised a legal point that Knight deemed worthy of consideration.

The governor promised him an opportunity to present it to the state supreme court in Los Angeles later that morning. He also told the attorney that he would alert Chief Justice Phil Gibson immediately and notify Warden Teets of an impending stay of execution.

At 9.5 a.m., two petitions for writs of *habeas corpus* and *mandamus* on behalf of Barbara Graham were hurriedly filed with the supreme court. By that time, Barbara was making her final preparations in her apartment-cell, unaware of the legal tussle going on 500 miles away in Los Angeles.

She laid out the stylish beige suit she'd worn at her trial, showered, dressed, applied her make-up and meticulously groomed her hair. The only jewellery she wore was a gold wedding band and a pair of shimmering rhinestone earrings.

At 9.20 she was told that Governor Knight had granted her a delay to give the supreme court time to consider the petitions now before it. For the next hour, Barbara wavered between hope and despair.

At 10.27, the governor phoned the warden, told him the petitions had been denied, then added: "There is nothing further in my office, or before me, to prevent the carrying out of the sentence."

The warden went to Barbara's cell and told her that she would enter the gas chamber at 10.45. But then, at 10.40, a new writ was filed in the state supreme court.

At 10.44, Barbara left her cell with Father McAlister and had just come into the view of the newspapermen and police officers in the witness-room, when she was notified that another delay had been granted.

Her eyes were brimming with tears as she turned to Father McAlister and clutched the black sleeve of his cassock, sobbing hysterically:

"Maybe they've found out that I'm innocent?"

She was led back to her cell, where she remained until 11.10. Then the warden informed her that her petition had been denied and that there was now no further barrier to her execution. She would enter the gas chamber at 11.30.

It was then that the beautiful murderess broke down and wept disconsolately: "Why do they torture me so? I was ready to die at 10 o'clock!"

But she had regained her composure by the time she again walked past the newsmen in the witness-room, stepped daintily into the chamber and requested that a blindfold be placed over her eyes.

"I don't want to look into people's eyes," she murmured to the guard, referring to the shocked faces of the newsmen not five feet from the gas chamber's window.

Taped to her chest and looking incongruous against her neatly-pressed suit was the black stethoscope that was to be connected to the gauge outside the chamber. Her lips moved in prayer as she was strapped in the chair and instructed to count to 10 and then take a deep breath. Finally, she was alone in the locked death cell.

At 11.34, the cyanide fumes began filling the chamber and Barbara's head dropped to her chest. Most of the witnesses were certain she was dead and I was relieved that she had died quickly and easily after the long, nerve-shattering delay . . . But I was wrong.

For, in a moment of horror that sent shivers down my spine, Barbara slowly lifted her head. From the strained, piteous look on her face, it was clear that she was holding her breath in a frantic attempt to cling to life just as long as she could.

I watched with growing terror, until she could hold her breath no longer. Then with what seemed to be a sigh of despair, the breath burst from her lungs and, a second later, she gulped in the lethal fumes that snuffed out her life.

The prison physician reported that on June 3rd, 1955: "She died *easily* at 11.42."

Not one of us newspapermen would have described her death as "easy", but then that had to be the official verdict.

By 2.30 p.m., with the lethal green chamber aired out, Jack Santo and Emmett Perkins were strapped side by side in the twin chairs. Sneering and defiant, they kept their grim secrets intact to the end.

"Don't do anything I wouldn't do," Santo quipped to the warden. The Weasel succumbed quickly. Big Jack died fighting for breath.

Barbara Graham's body, claimed by a woman friend, was interred at San Rafael. No one claimed the bodies of the two men, so they were sent to a state hospital for cremation.

The bloody curtain had run down on at least seven savage murders. Justice was satisfied — and one of the blackest chapters in Californian crime was officially closed. But the aftermath to the Santo-Graham story continued for a long time.

Bloody Barbara had cursed and prophesied early death for those who wanted her dead.

She'd threatened: "All the rats, all the liars, all the ones who want me dead will pay." Weirdly enough, soon after her execution, a parade of deaths began. No one thought much of it when Barbara's original court-appointed defence counsel, Jack Hardy, aged 51 — who had quit the case in disgust when her lying alibi attempt was exposed — died of a heart attack just a month after Babs was executed. A year later, in October, 1956, Barbara's nemesis, District Attorney Roll, died of cancer at 52. In August, 1957, death by apoplexy struck down aged Tutor Scherer, the innocent bystander whose mythical $100,000 cache had sparked the murder of his former mother-in-law Mabel Monahan.

Next to go was the man who, in a strictly literal sense, was directly responsible for Barbara's death, even though he often said he had no relish for the grim task his duty imposed on him. He was San Quentin's Warden Teets, who died suddenly of a heart attack on September 2nd, 1957, aged 50.

The passing of these four principals in the final tragedy of Barbara Graham's life and death was still in the natural order of things. But in January, 1958, the pace of death stepped up. And it now struck at those whom Bloody Babs had specifically singled out for ultimate retribution.

On January 22nd, the Dutch freighter *Bonita*, steaming up the Mississippi channel in a fog south of New Orleans, rammed a converted shrimp boat and cut it in two. One man was saved as the smaller craft swiftly sank, but the other four aboard were drowned. All the dead were professional divers on their way to a salvage operation in the Gulf of Mexico. One of them was John True, then aged 42, the man who had wriggled out of a murder rap by testifying against his accomplices.

Just a few days later, on January 28th, Judge Fricke, the Los Angeles judge who had pronounced the death sentence on the unholy three, succumbed to cancer at 75. Barbara's attorney had called Judge Fricke "the 13th juror."

On the rainy night of February 19th, 1958, less than a month after the diver took his last dive, pudgy Bill Upshaw's borrowed time ran out with equal abruptness. Driving his Cadillac convertible at high speed along US Highway 99 in the desert near Indio, Upshaw pulled out to avoid an oncoming bus. He failed to note that the road had narrowed for a bridge over a wash. Before he could swing back, the car crashed into the bus. Upshaw and a companion were killed instantly in the splintering crash.

That wound up the death roster and chillingly closed the books on the infamous murder mob, of which not one member was left alive. Bloody Babs could at last rest easy in her hillside grave overlooking the prison.

But she wasn't destined to rest for long. Within a few months, her grim story was resurrected and blazoned all over the world with the release of the screen sensation *I Want To Live.* Susan Hayward won an Oscar for her performance in the role of the convicted and executed murderess. The trouble was that the screenplay, while claiming to be "based on the actual facts," took artistic liberties with them. It left the strong implication that the state of California had railroaded an innocent woman to the gas chamber, apparently because she had a dubious past — and because she had refused to co-operate with the police.

The film, seen by thousands of people who had never heard of the Mabel Monahan case before, stirred world-wide controversy over capital punishment. Foes of the death penalty hailed it as a classic documentary exposing the tragic futility of "legalised murder." California and Los Angeles lawmen, on the other hand, condemned the picture bitterly, branding it as distorted.

Deputy District Attorney Miller Leavy, who had prosecuted the Monahan case, called the movie "a black mark on the administration of justice in California." Leavy blasted the film's contention that Babs Graham was left-handed, while Mrs. Monahan had been pistol-whipped by a right-handed person. He produced jail records to prove that Barbara was definitely right-handed.

It was also pointed out that the picture was confined entirely to the question of Barbara's involvement in the Monahan case — that it lightly skipped over the Santo mob's gory background of mass murder.

The furore over the Barbara Graham film had barely died down when her case was revived on the emotional impetus of the worldwide clamour generated over the pending execution of another condemned Californian criminal, the late Caryl Chessman. The haggard ghost of Bloody Babs walked once again in March, 1960, when Deputy DA Leavy was called to testify before a state senate judiciary committee which was weighing Governor Edmund Brown's bill to abolish capital punishment. The governor had just given the latest stay of execution to Chessman.

The Los Angeles prosecutor came up with the startling revelation that Barbara had reportedly confessed her guilt to the late San Quentin Warden Teets after her transfer from Corona. Leavy said he had received this information in June, 1959, from San Rafael District Attorney William Weissich, to whom Teets had confided it only two days before his sudden death in 1957. Teets had reportedly told Weissich that he could see no reason to make the confession public, since Bloody Babs had already been convicted. Weissich had considered the information confidential.

Besieged by reporters, Weissich confirmed that Teets had told him of Barbara's confession. Associate Warden Louis Nelson then revealed that Teets had told him the same thing in 1956. When Nelson had told Teets that he was haunted by a gruesome Death Row confession made to him by another prisoner, he explained, Teets had said: "I know how you feel about it. It's part of the job. I had to listen to Barbara Graham tell me how she pistol-whipped Mrs. Monahan and split her head open. It's a load I've been carrying a long time." Nelson and Weissich, some time after the warden's death, had discussed the matter and decided to keep it confidential, since revelation would serve no purpose. Weissich had later passed the information to Leavy.

Asked why he had not revealed the confession before, Leavy said he had been waiting for an opportune occasion. He said that by the time he had received the information the film had already "done its damage" to the cause of law enforcement.

A final footnote to the bloody chronicle was written on June 2nd, 1960, when Mrs. Olivia Shorter, after the necessary seven years, filed a superior court petition to have her long-missing husband Baxter declared legally dead, so that she could get clear title to money received from the sale of their house.

On June 21st, Judge Frank Balthis granted her petition. Thus, the grim total of the Santo mob's killings stands officially at seven.

4

THE LONELY KILLER

Richard Banks

"Sure would like to take a little holiday about now, but they like me so well they won't let me go." Extract from a letter written by David Early from Death Row.

When you read this, I may be dead. I have been sentenced to be executed in the Colorado gas chamber. My stay of execution, originally to August 10th, has been extended indefinitely while the appeal on my conviction awaits action in the state Supreme Court.

On Death Row, without hope, I wait.

I'm 29, with 10 years behind bars. I killed a relative by marriage, his wife and their daughter. I pleaded insanity. I hope that telling my story will help somebody, because somewhere there is a person like me, and he must be helped before it is too late.

What happened along the line? Will others with my beginning end in the gas chamber for needless killing?

Let's go back and try to determine what went wrong with me.

I was born in Salt Lake City, Utah, on November 14th, 1929. No brothers or sisters. My father left my mother before I was a year old and my mother remarried in practically no time at all; she and my stepfather were together about 10 years.

They had little or no interest in me. I never knew what to expect from them — a beating or affection.

From the age of six, I spent much of my time running away from home. The police would bring me back and there would be more beatings. I played truant from school so often that they finally gave up and threw me out.

Trouble became my middle name. Starting out as a small-time thief, I moved down the road that led to armed robbery.

I saw the inside of jails all the way from Albuquerque to Sante Fe, El Reno, Amarillo, Lewisberg, Canon City to Levenworth. And it was at Levenworth that the big trouble really began.

I started day-dreaming. At night, I had dreams of killing those who had hurt me or given me a bad time in the past.

I was sent to the psycho ward. After 30 days the doctors said I had a split personality.

I was discharged on April 22nd, 1958. If I was dangerous, why didn't they treat me? Why did they release me on parole?

As Warden Harry Tinsley of the Colorado State Penitentiary said, "There are three hundred and fifty people now on parole in Colorado, and one in every ten paroled from Colorado penal institutions is listed as a dangerous paranoid psychopath.

"We are the biggest gamblers in the world. We have to bet on human behaviour — not sure things like dog or horse races. Under the law we can't keep such people any longer than their sentences. And if we could, our facilities wouldn't hold them all."

With $30 in my pocket I travelled from Leavenworth back to Denver on a bus. I arrived at the bus station with $20 left and scouted for two days for a job. I was desperate, but no one would help. Finally I registered at the YMCA under a false name.

I found out later that my cousin whom I called "Uncle Merrill" was leaving for a holiday in Las Vegas.

I think one of the main things I needed was understanding. I don't think anyone can understand how it feels to walk in the world and not be a part of it; to have words, but nobody to listen to them.

I was back to the old point. I wanted a pistol and I was definitely going to rob, and if anybody got in my way it would be too bad. But Denver had changed its laws and I needed identification to buy a gun. I decided on a burglary to get the money.

No. There was another way. I decided that I was angry at my Uncle Merrill Knight, who lived just outside Denver. Maybe that hatred had grown through the years since childhood. I remember I'd always wanted a bicycle. One of my first offences was theft of a bicycle. In my childhood, I would visit the Knights. His first son had a bicycle and I didn't.

On one visit they borrowed a bike for me to ride. I wasn't used to riding and accidentally smashed into the side of a car backing out of a driveway. I was afraid to tell my stepfather for fear of a beating, but I told Uncle Merrill about it.

Merrill paid to have the bike fixed. That was well and good, but he never let me forget it. He reminded me of that incident for the rest of his life. He said he didn't have to do things for me. He did them out of the goodness of his heart.

Back in 1954, I recall, I was broke and he gave me $5. It was the same old routine. He kept saying how good he was to me, he'd even paid for that bike when I was a kid. Once he told me not to go to his house, but to see him at his office. He inferred I wasn't good enough to go to his home. In anger and frustration, I decided to rob him and show him who was best. I couldn't bring myself to grovel before him and beg for help.

I looked up his address in the telephone directory and found he lived near Littleton on the outskirts of Denver. With the last of my money I took a bus to Littleton and a cab from the bus station to the Knight home.

It was a big tri-level place on a four-acre tract with a circular driveway leading to the front. His first wife had died of polio in 1949, and his daughter had a slight case of it, so they'd moved to the suburbs for her health.

It was about noon that Friday, April 25th, when I reached

the Knight house. No one was at home and the back door was unlocked. The nearest neighbour was almost a quarter of a mile away.

I went in. There were some notes in the kitchen, instructions on watering plants and bringing in the milk. Later I learned that the Knights had written the notes because they were planning to leave the next day for a week's holiday in Las Vegas, celebrating their sixth wedding anniversary.

I roamed through the house, ransacking it, searching for money to finance a trip to Mexico, or somewhere. There was a basement bedroom and it was strewn with baseball mitts, rack shoes and car magazines. It was the bedroom of their 16-year-old son, Kenny. Up a stairway from the kitchen was the master bedroom, and beyond that on the top level was their 15-year-old daughter Karen's room.

I found a .22-calibre pistol in one of the bedside cabinets and shells in another drawer. I decided to wait until the Knight family came home. I would rob them and head for Mexico. I always wanted to go to Mexico.

I found a little money in the house, but not enough. I found another gun, a .22 rifle, and ammunition. I also found a .410 shotgun, but no shells. I was afraid they might know where the ammunition for the .410 was and use it against me, so I hid it under the mattress in the basement bedroom. I went through the house collecting knives, meat cleavers, anything they might use as a weapon against me when they got home. I hid these things under Mrs. Knight's bed in the master bedroom.

I sat down on a settee in the living-room, smoked one of their cigarettes and looked around. No wonder Knight was self-righteous, with a layout like this. How could he know how it is for an ex-convict like me to be alone in the world?

I waited at the house almost two hours before anyone came home. They arrived one at a time. Mrs. Knight, whom I had not met, was first. I met her at the door, the gun in my hand. She was tall and slim. She had a fancy hairdo and a light coloured coat thrown over her shoulders.

I ordered her into the bedroom and made her lie on the floor. She was scared, but she didn't say a word. I assured her all I wanted was money. I pulled some nylon stockings out of the drawer and tied her hands and feet, then took about $60 from her purse. As she lay on the floor of the bedroom she looked uncomfortable, so I moved her onto the bed and put a pillow under her head. Her hands were tied behind her back. She still looked uncomfortable, so I retied them in the front.

I removed my shoes so I could walk quietly and watched from the windows. I had no desire to hurt them, to cause physical revenge. I wanted to take something from Knight that I did not have.

About an hour later, at 3, Karen came home from high school. I showed her my gun and ordered her into the bedroom where I had tied her mother.

Mrs. Knight told the girl to do what I wanted. I had assured Mrs. Knight six or seven times that I did not want to hurt anyone.

I tied the girl's wrists and feet with nylons and put her in her own bedroom. First, I made sure she was comfortable, that the knots were not too tight.

The son — I didn't know him, either, because Knight had remarried — arrived at about 5.15. I met him at the back door, showed him the gun and took him to his mother. Mrs. Knight told him to obey me. The boy lay on the bedroom floor, not far from his mother. I tied his wrists and ankles and put a pillow under his head. Now I was waiting for Knight.

It took less than an hour. He arrived at 5.55 p.m. I ran upstairs to the bedroom and told Mrs. Knight to tell her husband to come up there. She did. Knight saw me as soon as he entered the bedroom.

"So this is gratitude, Dave?" he asked stiffly. I said, "Take it easy. All I want is your money. Nobody will get hurt."

I took him to the basement bedroom and tied his ankles and wrists. He kept telling me not to hurt his family and I said I wouldn't. He said he wouldn't call the cops if I'd just take the money and leave. I took some money from him — making a total of $260 from the whole family — and told him I would leave the house when it got dark.

I watched the windows for visitors. One man knocked on the door with a letter for Knight. I kept running back and forth, checking the four persons and looking out the windows.

Once I caught Knight trying to hobble to his desk and I told him to get back on the bed. That happened several more times. I don't know why. Once he reached the desk. He kept telling me if I'd leave his family alone and go he would help me. But I didn't believe him. He kept struggling.

When I decided it was dark enough to leave I got ready to place gags on them. I got some gauze and gagged Mrs. Knight, then went downstairs to take care of her husband.

Knight was on the bed and I put the pistol on the bedcover behind his head. I was bending over him to put the gag in place. He kept insisting that I was going to shoot him, but I said I wasn't. The gag was now in place and I reached for the pistol and started to get off the bed.

As I was pulling back my hand with the pistol in it, Knight started to get up off the bed. I stepped back quickly. Knight was sitting on the bed, facing me. Suddenly he made a dive and I saw him coming.

I shot him three times with the .32 revolver. Twice in the chest and once in the back of the head.

"There's no use leaving any witnesses behind," I thought, so I went upstairs and walked to the side of the bed where Mrs. Knight was. She had heard the three shots.

Mrs. Knight stared at me and tried to scream through the gag. I shot her through the temple.

The pistol was then out of bullets. I grabbed the .22 rifle and raced upstairs to the girl's room. She just looked at me and moaned. I shot her twice in the stomach and twice in the head. She died with a tiger doll beside her.

As I went downstairs to get the boy, I heard him running. He wasn't in the bedroom. He had got himself loose and was opening the front door. I ran after him. When I reached the door he had got to the front gate. I fired one shot, but missed. Then the rifle's shell ejector wouldn't work.

I knew I had to move fast. I grabbed my shoes and a jacket and got in Mrs. Knight's Plymouth convertible parked outside.

The boy ran to the nearest house about a quarter of a mile away. I saw people with a rifle and shotgun getting into a car. I was speeding down the driveway when they rammed the car I was in. I had only the empty .32 in my hip pocket, so I jumped out and started to run.

I ran about a quarter of a mile before I gave up. The Knight boy caught up with me and tried to grab me. I turned and hit him in the face, but as I whirled to run again, the others reached us and I was caught. They threatened to shoot me if I took another step.

One of them was Varian Ashbaugh, the man who had brought the letter to Knight's door. He and his wife were guests of my captor, Glen Wilson.

I was mixed up. I wasn't normal. I must have been insane. The killing didn't seem to bother me. Even the day after I had no remorse.

I told officers, "I had to do it. Knight forced me to kill. Naturally, I was forced to kill the rest of them so there wouldn't be any witnesses. I had to keep them straight. See, they came into the house in a certain order, and that's how I had to kill them. Knight was out of order, but that was because he jumped me. I wanted to keep them in order.

"I stepped over the boy and went upstairs. I shot the girl then because she came into the house second.

"I admit that was a mistake. I should have shot the boy right away, instead of keeping them in order. Somehow he got free. That was my mistake. I knew I had to kill them all so there wouldn't be any witnesses. That's just sense — if I had it all to do over, I wouldn't do any different. To get away after that I would have killed anyone, only I didn't have ammunition for the gun. I would have killed them all . . . I didn't go out there with the intention of killing anybody. I just wanted some money, but they forced me into killing them.

"Sure, I realise I'll probably go to the gas chamber, but I'd do it all over again if I had to. There's some things you have to do. Knight always had more than me and he always let me know it. Now he has nothing."

I guess it was building up in me all my life. I hated society and its mistreatment. All I wanted was money. No one cared about me, and I didn't care about anyone.

Until a couple of months ago I considered myself as dangerous as they come. I had no compunction over killing. If somebody got in my way, killing didn't bother me. But in prison I got to thinking about everything. I had let religion slide, but only recently I was baptised a Catholic. I believe there is a God and that I must straighten myself out before the end. Now I feel remorse. It was a terrible shame they had to die.

I'm 29 now and I may die before I'm 30. The gas chamber is on the third floor of the building where Death Row is located. I am resigned to the future and have no fear of dying.

I never had close friends until I got in this jam. There is one now who is interested in me. He is John Ginster, 53, a former professional golfer from Pueblo, Colorado. I believe he understands me. He volunteered to correspond and visit me in prison. I have asked John and his wife, who are childless, to be my foster parents until the end. They have agreed. John will claim my body and I have consented to be buried in a plot they have in Whiteboro, New York. That's better than being buried in a prison graveyard.

I call John Ginster Dad now. He is the only one who ever stood by my side, to be my friend. When I walk the last mile I'll know that someone cares. But when I sit in the gas chamber, I will be alone.

What could have prevented all this? Looking back, I see a lot of signposts pointing the wrong way. Was it a broken home, alcohol, lack of understanding? Come to think of it, I haven't heard from my mother since 1955. Undoubtedly she has good reasons.

Or was it within my power all along to straighten my life and change fate? The way I was it would have taken a miracle.

I hope parents and mixed-up kids will read this, the mess I've made of my life. Maybe it will help someone — prevent a kid from ending up like me.

The way I see it now, it was inevitable for me to end here.

How does a man wait out the long days and months before society takes his life by legal execution? What does he do on Death Row? What does he think? How does he feel about the society that is punishing him? How does he live with his conscience?

So readers can better understand the short life of a condemned slayer, the following excerpts from David F. Early's letters are reprinted.

John L. Ginster from Pueblo, Colorado, wrote his first letter to Early in late 1958. Ginster, a former professional golfer, was 53 years old. Early answered the Ginster letter. Out of this strange death cell correspondence, friendship grew.

Early called Mr. and Mrs. Ginster Mom and Dad. Ginster offered, and Early accepted, burial beside John and Freda Ginster in their family plot in Whiteboro, New York.

The correspondence started in December, 1958, when the Ginsters read that Early, in the Arapaho County jail, Littleton, Colorado, had no family, no friends and no money.

"He had no one, nothing to remind him ever so temporarily that this was the time of the year when all Christians proclaim their love of all mankind," Ginster said. "He had passed the point of no return with nothing to look forward to except death in the gas chamber."

So John Ginster started his first letter to David Early, Death Row, Canon City, Colorado. He wrote:

Before asking you one question, I would like to tell you that if I had been so fortunate as to be your father I would have changed the colour of the 'sit'-uation with a size 12 boot the first (and quite possibly the last) time I caught you smoking. However, since apparently you have acquired the habit, what brand of cigarettes would you like to receive as a little Christmas present? . . .

Early answered in pencil, on plain white stationery:

Sunday Morning
December 6th, '58
John:
I was so glad to receive your letter last evening, since yours is the first one that I have received that wasn't written by a religious fanatic, or someone wanting to tell me off.

Even my so-called family hasn't written or contacted me since I got in this mess. I guess I don't care too much.

You and your size 12 boot might have done me some good in more ways than smoking, since from the tone of your letter you don't seem at all like my family or stepfather.

It has been at least 10 years since I have had any reason to look forward to Christmas, as I was usually in the penitentiary . . . when nobody else cares, a person tends to ignore Christmas because if I had thought about it I would have had to face up to how lonely I was at times like those and now.

If you feel that you would like to write me further, I would gladly answer as long as I can.

And Early mentioned his cigarette brand. He said his lawyer had been supplying cigarettes. But he had no money, and if Ginster were to send some chocolate it would mean a lot. He ended:

Many grateful thanks for the letter and the kindly thought.

"So it appeared," Ginster said, "that I had acquired a mail order son who might like to pour out his heart to an understanding old man whom he could trust."

Yes, Early was eager to correspond. He addressed his next letter "John!" with an exclamation mark:

Dec. 11th, 1958
John!
I received your letter this afternoon and I really appreciated it as today is visiting day and it is lonely for me here on visiting days. So I'm sure you see that I will be glad to see you any time you want to visit me, not only because I'm lonely (even Mother doesn't visit or write), but because you seem from your letters really understanding.

As to you being a funny-looking old man, remember that the body is not a true representation of the person, and there are a lot of funny looking people in the world . . .

I'm sure that if I had a father who had cared enough, I would not have turned out as bad as I did . . .

On January 5th, 1959, he wrote.

I had my hearing this morning and it was a farce. They denied me a retrial, and I was sentenced to die on April 13th this year. They will probably take me to Canon City today or tomorrow. I received your package and card just after I returned and was feeling downhearted. It helped an awful lot because I knew that somebody cared even at this moment.

They transferred him to the state penitentiary, and on January 7th, he wrote from Death Row. From then on, all his letters were written with pen, not pencil, according to prison regulations, and on lined prison stationery:

Solitary confinement in this case means that I am kept confined by myself on Death Row. But I am treated much better here than at the county jail. I have run into none of the animosity that characterised my stay in jail.

As far as parcels go, I think that you will have to get permission from the warden to send any at all. You can send money orders and I can buy anything at the canteen that I could get at a store (almost).

As to visiting here, I am sure that I can get permission for you to see me.

The food here is much better than at the county jail, and all things considered I'd much rather be here than there.

I have a cell about 10 feet by eight feet, with a good sized window (barred of course) in the east wall, and the west end of the cell, open barred, faces a long hall. I have a set of earphones that play from breakfast 'til 10.30 at night with a pretty good selection of programmes. I have been told that I can write and receive letters every day, so there will be no worry on this account. You know I am always looking forward to your letters. They are the bright spot of the day.

Towards the end of the letter he said:

I have been looking up the law in my case and have found where I have been deprived of my rights and due process of law. The DA and his assistant made some very libellous remarks about me personally, and the only reason they didn't spit at me and throw rocks is because of the so-called dignity of the court, not from lack of desire.

They used every means at hand to inflame the minds of the jury and the courtroom at large . . . There is going to be an appeal in my case, but I have no confidence that it will do me any good. I don't believe that my lawyer really wants to save my life, and maybe it is all for the best that I go and leave the world full of people who hate me.

This evening I have been listening to the New York Philharmonic Orchestra. I really like classical music. In fact, I can't seem to enjoy the so called popular music of modern day.

He commented on a current bill before the Colorado legislature:

I was hoping that the bill that passed the Senate would make it through the house before adjournment this year, but it doesn't look like it will, although it would mean a lot to me if it did as it gives a new definition of insanity in criminal cases. It says that anyone who commits a crime as a result of a mental condition is not guilty . . . not as it is now, that you must be deficient in the ability to know right from wrong, or not be able to resist, which is stupid because it does not cover all the different possibilities.

Aren't the papers a mess lately? It seems everybody in the government is in a wastebasket. If the world isn't careful somebody will pull the plug and we'll all go down the drain.

I see J. F. Dulles' cancer is about to finish him, and from what medical reasoning and reading I did in Leavenworth, it seems probable that not only is the cancer in his neck now, but also in his brain. So he won't last long.

(Secretary of State Dulles later died of cancer.)

January 7th, 1959
Other than you and your wife, the nicest people I know are convicts. At least they understand how I could get into this mess.
January 15th, 1959
Hi, old man!
How's things? You can rest assured I don't hate anyone. I don't hold a grudge against my stepfather. I remember all he did and all he didn't do when I was a child. So I have little or no affection for him, only a kind of pity.

I am reading some books given to me by Father Justin, and I think I'll become a Catholic before the end. I am reading a book by Bishop Sheen Preface to Religion and it is the most sensible book on religion I've ever read.

I am just about to eat a bowl of bread and milk, although it is near midnight. My ulcer is hurting a little, and the best thing I can do for it is to eat a bowl of bread and milk or drink a glass of milk straight, but since I don't like the taste of milk, I have the bread and milk.

On January 20th, 1959, he told his adopted 'Dad':

Beetle, my budgie, is getting ready to talk. I have the nicest bird you've ever seen and he is as friendly as a pup. I have lots of fun *with him, and he seemed to take to me right away, so we get along fine. He makes the time go easy.*

The days are very quiet and peaceful here. Nobody but an officer or one of the priests ever comes in. The other fellow [unnamed] in the next cell is quiet. I have a lot of time to read and think and sleep.

The article you sent me about the bill to abolish capital punishment is OK! But even if it were passed it wouldn't do me any good, because the way I understand that bill, it will not be retroactive . . .

January 28th, 1959

. . . Beetle, my bird, sure got in a mess. At suppertime he got excited and jumped off my shoulder and landed in the beans. He looked like a plucked chicken. The bean juice made his feathers clot and left bare spots. I had to wash him with soap and water before he looked like a bird again.

February 9th, 1959

. . . In regard to those two boys, it is a shame that murder charges have been placed against them. It is obvious that boys that young could not visualise the consequence of their act in robbing and beating that old man.

It won't be long 'till I will be baptised and accepted in the church.

Ginster had written to Early telling him about a beautiful neighbourhood collie that had been poisoned by someone. Tears had come to Early's eyes, and he answered:

I'm sure that anybody who is a dog poisoner is to be pitied, for he or she is so unhappy with the world that he must strike back at animals who are defenceless. I love dogs and birds and animals, and I have no respect for people who mistreat them. My budgie Beetle is doing fine. He can say "pretty bird" as clear as anything and I would like to see someone try to hurt him. I'll safely bet be wouldn't want to hurt any more pets!

February 12th, 1959

Since I have made my peace with God and have peace of soul and freedom from fear, I can pass it on to helping others.

February 18th, 1959
I'm getting as fat as a hog in a turnip patch. I get six bowls of
milk a day for my ulcer. Milk always did fatten me up.

And he added, with obvious pleasure and excitement:

I don't get visits except from the press and officials, but in your
case we would visit in a special room in the deputy warden's office.
But that is better than a regular visiting room.

Early slipped a disc in his back while shovelling snow in
the Death Row yard. His letter ended with the prosaic,
every-day comment of information on health:

My back is feeling pretty good. I can stand up straight, but
cannot put the least strain on it; but I manage OK.

His letter of February 20th, 1959, told the Ginsters:

I think I have a terrific sense of humour as the cartoons and
funnies amuse me no end, and I dearly love a good joke.
Beetle had an accident. He broke both tail feathers and I had
to pluck them out so that he would grow some new ones. He looks
kind of bare from the rear. I suppose that it will take about a month
before he looks decent again.
Glad to say that my back is almost completely well now. If I
don't put any great strain on it.
I went out in the yard today, and it was cold and grey, so I
moved around to keep warm. When I came in I was pleasantly
tired, and it is catching up with me as I keep yawning.
March 12th, 1959
I am still taking religious instructions and am doing fine. But
it takes quite a while to read and learn and make up your mind
about all the things they expect you to know. The priest comes to
see me every week now.
April 24th, 1959
It was real nice and sunny here today. I spent most of my yard
time soaking up the sun and trying to get a nice suntan.

I'm going to be baptised this Sunday (April 26th) and I know you'll be as happy as I am over this.

But the toll of living on Death Row was being exacted:

As I told you at our visit, I've been falling down on my letter writing for I seem to be having trouble setting down my thoughts on paper . . .
April 30th, 1959
My bird is getting a little more venturesome and scampers all over the table at times. He likes to play and pull the chain around my neck when he sits on my shoulder.

His letter of April 30th, 1959, displayed one of Early's few forays into humour:

Sure would like to take a little holiday about now, but they like me so well they won't let me go . . .

Perhaps for David Early there was little humour, because as far as he knew, there was so little time . . .

His days on Death Row, his days in this world, were drawing to a close, and now — more important than a quip — was the meaning of time . . . the meaning of time for the condemned:

I sometimes think of how people outside pass hours or days and never really notice them. Time just slips away, almost unnoticed. But here for me it is a major problem, something to fight, either to fill or pass. Awareness of time, minutes, seconds, hours acquire a new meaning in jail. Days are not so bad. But the nights are terrible. I don't sleep much. Nights afford one's conscience unlimited opportunity and I have only philosophical rationalisation to retaliate with. It is a bitter and hard fought battle, never won, only fought again and again . . .

David Early continued to communicate with the Ginsters over the next two years. However, his long-fought struggle to stay out of the death chamber eventually came to nothing. For on August 11th, 1961, he was put to death in Colorado's gas chamber for his crimes.

5

WHISTLER'S MOTHER

Charles Morehead

"No! No! I didn't kill him. It was my son who killed him. It was Dan." Dovie Dean's response when accused of murdering her husband.

Confronted with a diagnostic problem, Dr. Joseph Batsche was extremely puzzled. His patient, 69-year-old Hawkins Dean, had been brought to the hospital two hours previously, suffering from agonising stomach cramp. Originally, the doctor believed that the man had eaten some contaminated food, but clinical examination had proved that this was not so.

Joe Batsche had administered several other tests to the patient, but had so far been unable correctly to diagnose Dean's ailment. Tentatively, the physician decided that Dean might be suffering from cirrhosis of the liver. So he prescribed a sedative to relieve the pain and ordered a further series of tests to be given to the sick man.

Two days later, Hawkins Dean was remarkably better. His pain had gone — and his pulse and temperature were normal. The doctor was mildly surprised, but medicine is not an exact science. The behaviour of the human organism often surprises. It was enough that Hawkins Dean was well again. The doctor released him from hospital, and Dean returned to his prospering farm near Owensville, Ohio. The date of Dean's discharge from the hospital was August 15th, 1952.

In the early hours of Friday, August 22nd, the telephone at Batsche's bedside rang insistently. The doctor propped himself on his elbow and answered drowsily. He heard the alarmed voice of Hawkins Dean's wife, Dovie, at the other end of the wire. Apparently, her husband had taken a swift and painful turn for the worse. Would the doctor come at once?

So he climbed out of his comfortable bed, jumped into his car and headed for the Dean farmhouse. Dovie Dean and Dan Reed, her grown son by a former marriage, awaited the doctor in the living-room. Mrs. Dean said that she had been suddenly awakened by her husband's groaning. He had told her that he was in unbearable pain. She had given him some aspirin and surrounded him with hot-water bottles. Neither of these had helped much, so she had called the doctor.

The doctor went into the bedroom, where he examined Dean carefully. The symptoms appeared to be similar to those the patient had exhibited while in hospital. And diagnosis was just as baffling as it had been before.

The early summer dawn was grey in the east as Joe Batsche emerged from the bedroom, his face tired and drawn. Dovie Dean and her son looked up anxiously. The doctor regarded them solemnly. "I'm sorry," he said. "I did everything I could. Hawkins is dead."

Dovie Dean burst into uncontrollable weeping, while her son attempted to comfort her. The doctor put on his coat and walked to the door. "I'll be back later in the day," he said. "And I'll bring the death certificate."

Dovie Dean hardly heard him as he left the house. She seemed deranged by sorrow. She was no stranger to trouble, though. It had haunted her all her life. Her parents had died when she was but a small child. She was taken into the home of a distant cousin of her father, remaining there until she was 20 years old, when she married and moved to Charleston, West Virginia. The marriage had produced six children.

But the marriage broke up in 1937, when her husband was sentenced to imprisonment in the West Virginia state penitentiary, having pleaded guilty to rape. Later, a daughter had died in childbirth. In 1952, her son John was killed in an explosion at the factory where he was working. Now, in addition to Dan, who lived with her, Dovie had three other surviving children.

Dovie married Hawkins Dean in April, 1952. Hawkins was a widower whose married daughter Alice Way lived in Owensville. Both Dean and Dovie told their friends that they had been suffering from loneliness until they met and married each other. Their marital life had apparently been quite happy.

At noon on the day on which Hawkins died, his daughter and her husband called at the farmhouse to console the stepmother and make arrangements for the funeral. They asked Dovie what had caused Hawkins's death.

Mrs. Dean shook her head. "I don't know. I don't even remember if Dr. Batsche told me. I was so upset at the time. I do recall him saying that he'd call back with the death certificate. But he hasn't done so yet."

It was agreed that Hawkins Dean's funeral should be held on Monday, August 25th. The daughter and her husband remained at the farm until dusk. Then they got into their car and drove back to Owensville. Their route took them past the house of Dr. Batsche. Alice Way asked her husband to stop the car.

"I may as well ask him about the death certificate," she said. "Besides, I'd like to know just what it was that killed Dad. You can wait outside. I won't be long."

Joe Batsche told Alice candidly that he had not yet delivered the death certificate because he had not decided exactly what had been the cause of Hawkins Dean's death. "His symptoms were baffling," said the doctor. "Apparently, he died of the same thing which caused me to send him to the hospital earlier. But, quite honestly, I don't know what it was. There's only one way to find out — and that's to hold a post-mortem."

Alice, having thought that over, decided that she was in favour of a post-mortem. "I want to know what killed him," she said.

Batsche explained that, since no crime was involved, the Dean family would have to pay the cost of the post-mortem. Moreover, he believed it would be necessary to obtain Dovie Dean's permission. After Alice offered to defray the cost of the post-mortem, she asked Dr. Batsche to obtain the necessary permission from her stepmother.

At first, Dovie Dean protested. It seemed all wrong, she argued, to operate on a dead man. However, when the doctor said that he thought that it should be done, son Dan supported the physician.

"Well, O.K.," said Dovie. "If everyone thinks it should be done, go ahead. But I can't see that it'll serve any good purpose. Hawkins is dead. Nothing will bring him back to me."

On Saturday, August 23rd, Dr. Batsche made the arrangements for Dean's body to be taken to Cincinnati, where Dr. Frank Cleveland would conduct the post-mortem. Dr. Cleveland, who completed his task on Sunday, found a severe congestion in the digestive tract and other organs. He sent these organs to the laboratory for further examination. Meanwhile, he released the body for burial.

On Monday, Hawkins Dean was buried in the Owensville cemetery. While the solemn service was being held, Sheriff Clyde Dericks read the laboratory report rushed to him from Cincinnati. It was a startling report, for it stated that Hawkins Dean's vital organs contained enough arsenic to kill half a dozen men!

Dericks called in two of his deputies, Sam Skinner and Charlie McNutt. He showed them the report, then said: "I'm going to talk to Joe Batsche. Sam, you go out to the Dean farm. See whether it was possible for Dean to have swallowed all that arsenic accidentally. If it wasn't, ask a few questions. See what you can find out." Dericks also sent Charlie McNutt to the office of District Attorney Ray Bradford with a copy of the Cincinnati report. Then he called on Dr. Batsche.

The doctor listened to the sheriff and frowned. "No wonder *I* couldn't diagnose Dean's illness!" he said. "I never suspected arsenic."

"Would it be possible for him to have taken the poison accidentally?" asked Dericks.

"According to the lab. report, his organs were full of it. Naturally, there could be a certain amount of arsenic around a farm. It's used in sprays, for fertiliser and as a rat-poison. But it seems incredible that Dean could have swallowed such a large amount of it accidentally."

"Could Dean have been deliberately poisoned?" Dericks persisted.

The doctor shrugged, then said: "That's a natural conclusion, perhaps. But where's the motive? Who'd want to kill him?"

"You didn't notice any suspicious actions among members of the family when you were attending Dean?" the sheriff inquired.

The doctor shook his head. He had noticed nothing like that, he said. It had seemed to him that the Deans were a pleasant, close-knit family. "They all appear to be on good terms with one another."

Meanwhile, Deputy Skinner was at the Dean farm-house. Dovie Dean was stunned to learn that her husband had died of arsenic poisoning. "It's impossible," she said. "We don't keep any kind of poison in the house at all. Hawkins couldn't have swallowed any arsenic here."

In spite of this assertion, Skinner asked for — and received — Mrs. Dean's permission to search the house. He did so thoroughly. Nevertheless, he was unable to find any trace of arsenic in the house, or the outbuildings. When Skinner returned to the sheriff's office, he found Dericks in conference with McNutt and DA Bradford. They were grave, as befitted a group of officials who had a probable murder on their hands. Dericks asked Skinner if, during his visit to the Dean house, he had learned whether anyone else stayed there, other than Dovie Dean and her son Dan.

"There's a son-in-law," said Skinner. "A son-in-law of Mrs. Dean's. His name's Cliff Norrell. From time to time, he stays at the Dean farmhouse. He was there on several occasions recently, Mrs. Dean told me."

During the next few days, the son, the son-in-law and Dovie Dean were exhaustively questioned. To all of them, it appeared incredible that Hawkins Dean had died an unnatural death. All denied knowing how the elderly man could have swallowed arsenic. All assured the investigators that there was no conceivable reason for anyone to do away with the popular farmer.

DA Bradford, after consulting with Hugh Nicols, Hawkins Dean's lawyer and executor of the dead man's estate, informed the sheriff of the contents of the will. It had been signed on April 12th, 1952 — the day before Dean's marriage to Dovie. The estate was worth some $20,000. It included 65 acres of farmland, the house, plus two savings accounts. In his will, Dean stated his intention of marrying Dovie. He directed that all his property, real and personal, go to her in the event of his death. The will stipulated that, upon the death of Dovie, the property was to go to his daughter Alice Way.

On the Wednesday following the death of Hawkins Dean, the phone rang in Dericks's office. Deputy McNutt picked up the receiver. A strained, hoarse voice, which sounded as if the speaker were trying to disguise it, said: "I have some information about the Dean murder."

"Why don't you come in and talk to the sheriff?" asked McNutt.

"I can't afford to get mixed up in this. But I understand you are looking for the stuff that poisoned that man. Well, I suggest you look in the glove compartment of Cliff Norrell's car." There was a sharp click as the caller hung up.

McNutt flashed the operator and asked to have the call traced. It appeared that it had been made from a phone booth at the railway station. McNutt immediately informed the sheriff of the mysterious call.

Dericks instructed the deputy to visit the booth from which the call had been made and try to trace the anonymous caller. Then Dericks picked up Deputy Skinner and they set out in search of Cliff Norrell's car.

They found it in the car park belonging to the motor company in nearby Batavia, where Norrell worked. The glove compartment was unlocked. Dericks opened it. He found, among other things, a cellophane-wrapped parcel. Inside the parcel was a small bottle, about which several paper cups had been telescoped. There was a skull and crossbones poison label on the bottle.

Dericks handed the bottle to Skinner. "Rush that to the crime lab. in Cincinnati," he said.

"Have the contents analysed. I'll pick up Norrell right away."

Dericks entered the works and informed Norrell that he wished to question him further because of the cup-encased bottle found in his car. Norrell became immediately indignant. "I'm being framed!" he cried. "I haven't seen that bottle for months! I swear it wasn't there the last time I looked in that glove compartment!"

He insisted that he had bought the medicine as a remedy for barber's itch, from which he had suffered several months ago. "I haven't used it for a long time," he said. "I never carried it in my car. I didn't put those paper cups around it. I don't know how it got in my glove compartment."

Norrell recalled that he had purchased the medication in a Batavia chemist's shop in the spring. He had last used the lotion in June. Then he remembered that a pile of paper cups, similar to those which the sheriff had told him were telescoped about the bottle, were kept in a cupboard in the dining-room of Hawkins Dean's home.

Deputy Frank Hutchinson was sent to the Dean farm. There, both Mrs. Dean and her son freely admitted that the cups had been in the cupboard for some time. Both denied any knowledge of the bottle found in Norrell's car.

Cliff Norrell was still under interrogation in the sheriff's office when word came from Cincinnati that the laboratory had found the medication in the bottle to be laced with arsenate of lead. Dericks promptly telephoned Dr. Cleveland in Cincinnati. The doctor gave it as his opinion that the death of Hawkins Dean could have been caused by drinking some of the contents of the bottle. Told of this, Norrell emphatically insisted that he was in no way involved with the death of the elderly farmer.

"All right," said the sheriff. "If you are innocent, you should have no objection to undergoing a lie-detector test."

Norrell did not hesitate. "Why not?" he said. "I'm quite willing. But I think that, if I take the test, so should everyone else concerned."

"That's exactly what *I* was thinking," said the sheriff. "I intend to pick up Dovie and Dan as material witnesses. I'll ask them to volunteer for the polygraph test."

Mrs. Dean and her son were taken into custody by the sheriff. Dericks explained why they, along with the son-in-law, were being held. He explained that Norrell had agreed to the test — and he hoped that Dovie and her son would be equally cooperative.

Both were, at first, more hesitant than Norrell had been. But they finally agreed to take the test. When it took place on September 4th, the technician who operated the machine reported that the graph indicated that Norrell was telling nothing but the truth. The tests on Dovie Dean and her son indicated that they were not entirely frank in certain areas, but produced nothing really conclusive.

After a week of questioning brought no further results, the sheriff suggested a second lie-detector for each of the three. Norrell, however, was indignant. "How many times must I go through this?" he demanded. "I've taken one test. I want to go back to work. I have a family to support."

The sheriff assured him that, if he again passed his test, he would certainly be released. Reluctantly, Norrell agreed to go along. So did Dovie and Dan.

On September 11th, Norrell was once more the first to take the test. Again, the experts, after thoroughly examining the results, announced that they were convinced Norrell was telling the truth. However, it was decided to hold him a little longer.

Dan also appeared to be speaking the truth during most

of the examination. However, when he was asked if he had any suspicions concerning the murderer of his stepfather, the needle wavered.

When Dovie Dean was questioned, the graph indicated strongly that she was not telling the truth. When the tests were over, the sheriff and the DA resumed their questioning of mother and son. Again, both stoutly denied any knowledge of Dean's poisoning, but Dovie and Dan were returned to the Clermont County jail.

Throughout the day of September 12th, the interrogation continued. At 5 p.m., Mrs. Dean was returned to her cell, where Mrs. Dericks, the sheriff's wife, served their dinner. After she had eaten, Dovie Dean told Mrs. Dericks that she would like to make a new statement to DA Bradford.

She was escorted into the sheriff's office, where Bradford and Dericks awaited her. She sat down, wiped tearful eyes with a handkerchief, then said: "I haven't told you the real truth. But I'm going to now."

"All right," said Bradford. "You are now willing to admit that you murdered your husband?"

"No! No! I didn't kill him! I've been trying to protect someone, but I can't do it any longer. It was my son who killed him. It was Dan!"

Dericks and Bradford exchanged glances. This was not quite what they'd expected. "You're quite sure of this, Mrs. Dean?" asked Dericks.

"Positive. He did it with rat poison. It's called 'Zip.' He put it in Hawkins's milk. I saw him do it."

"But why?" asked Bradford. "Why should Dan kill his stepfather?"

"He never liked him."

That seemed a rather inadequate motive for murder. Dovie Dean was returned to her cell and Dan Reed was brought from his. He seemed stunned when he was informed of his mother's accusation.

"Of course I didn't poison my stepfather!" he stormed.

"Why should I? I had nothing against him. I knew the terms of his will. I knew I would never inherit anything. After my mother died, his entire estate was to go to Alice Way."

He was returned to his cell and Dovie Dean was brought back into the sheriff's office. By this time, both Dericks and Bradford had a good idea as to which of the two suspects was lying.

"Your son denies your accusation," said Bradford. "He insists that he had no reason to kill his stepfather. The sheriff and I can't think of any motive for him, either. But *you* had a motive, Mrs. Dean. You are Dean's sole heir."

"Isn't it quite possible," Dericks put in, "that a mother who would accuse her own son of murder could be guilty of the crime herself?"

There was a long silence. Dovie Dean moaned softly. "Yes," she said, finally. "Dan had nothing to do with it. Neither did Cliff. *I* killed my husband. But I had to do it. I had to do it, before he killed me." She went on to explain that her marital life had been most unhappy. Dean always refused to give her any cash, refused to take her out anywhere. "And," she said, "he was unable to consummate our marriage. Because of that, he threatened to kill me and then kill himself. I decided to act first."

She first put the rat poison into his milk on the day before he was taken to the hospital, she said. She repeated the dose on the two days prior to his death, each time putting the poison into Dean's milk.

The trial began in December, 1952. On the 13th of that month, Dovie Dean was found guilty and sentenced to be executed at the Ohio state penitentiary in Columbus. Her lawyers filed notice of an appeal. The matter was considered by the courts for almost a year before Ohio's supreme court upheld the original verdict. The new date of execution was set for January 15th, 1954.

Dovie Dean's behaviour in the Marysville reformatory was impeccable. She remained very calm. During the final week of her life, she sat in her cell, together with her parakeet, which the authorities had permitted her to bring with her. She read the Bible constantly. On January 11th, she sent for the Rev. George Wilcher, pastor of the Methodist church in Marysville. She requested that the minister baptise her.

Using one side of her bed as an altar, the clergyman knelt at the side of the convicted murderess and asked the solemn question: "Do you truly repent of your sins and accept and confess Jesus Christ as your Lord and Saviour?"

Later that day, Superintendent Marguerite Reilly provided Dovie Dean with a new dress, new shoes and new underwear. Throughout the week, a special telephone connection was held open between the reformatory and the governor's mansion in Columbus, where Governor Frank Lausche, the only man who could spare Dovie Dean's life, heard a final appeal made by the condemned woman's lawyers.

Early on the afternoon of the last day of her life, Dovie was escorted to the reformatory beauty salon, where she obtained a hair-do of her own choosing. When she returned to her cell, she presented Velma Wet, a Cleveland murderess, with her parakeet. "Take good care of him," she said. "I loved him very much."

Then she made arrangements for the little crocheted items she had made in her cell to be sent to each of her grandchildren. It was arranged that she should eat her last meal in the reformatory before being taken to Columbus. She ordered it, calmly remarking, "Of course, it doesn't matter. It will probably be just as good as I've been having."

The meal she requested consisted of roast chicken, mashed potatoes, asparagus, green salad with French dressing, coconut-cream pie, angel-food cake and "lots of coffee" with cream. She ate the meal with a hearty appetite. Never once did she ask her guards whether or not the governor had called the superintendent.

At 4 o'clock in the afternoon, a limousine pulled out of the gates of the Columbus penitentiary. In it were the driver, a guard captain and two matrons. At 5.30, the car stood before the gates of the Marysville reformatory, where the Rev. Wilcher escorted Dovie Dean from her cell. He accompanied her on this, her last ride.

Dovie Dean entered the Columbus prison at 7 p.m. A Catholic and a Protestant chaplain joined the Rev. Wilcher as Dovie was taken to a cell from which a radio had been removed a few minutes before. This had been done on the specific orders of Warden Ralph Alvis.

For Governor Lausche had announced, after hours of conferences, that he would not prevent the execution. The news was at this moment being broadcast by radio. The warden did not wish the prisoner to hear it.

Dovie Dean had promised Superintendent Reilly at Marysville that she would die bravely, without hysteria and without tears. A few minutes before 8 o'clock, she was brought from her cell. She marched to the death house, preceded by Rev. Wilcher. It was apparent to the 24 official spectators and reporters that Dovie Dean was keeping her promise.

Her head was held high, her chin thrust out. Her face was pale, but her eyes were dry. She appeared more self-possessed than the majority of the witnesses.

She entered the death chamber and sat quietly in the chair under the sightless gaze of the 261 killers whose pictures adorned the walls — the 261 murderers who had died in this same room before her. It took the guards exactly three minutes to adjust the straps and the helmet. Dovie Dean seemed utterly unafraid.

"Fear thou not, for I am with thee," intoned Rev. Wilcher. "Let not your heart be troubled, for where I am ye may be also."

At 8.03 p.m., 1,950 volts of electricity coursed through the body of the second woman ever to be electrocuted in the state of Ohio. Four minutes later, the prison physician pronounced Dovie Dean dead, just as a sudden driving rain pelted down upon the roof of the squat, rectangular death house in the south-east corner of the penitentiary yard.

Dietician Frank Cheel, who had taken cakes to Dovie Dean's cell immediately prior to the execution, said: "She was so calm. She was one of the calmest persons I've ever seen taken into the death chamber. She looked like Whistler's Mother as she sat there with her arms folded."

There is no doubt that Dovie Dean died with courage. Equally, there is no doubt that she did not look like Whistler's Mother to Hawkins Dean, as he lay dying in agony. Nor did she appear like the artist's mother to the sheriff and DA Bradford when she accused her son of a crime she had committed herself.

6

THE RED LIGHT BANDIT

Harrison Bentley

"All I can say is that this is a hell of a way to start a week." Caryl Chessman's remark upon waking on a Monday morning, the day of his execution.

The case that was to become a 12-year nightmare, involving the highest courts of the United States, started out like a routine holdup — and the scene was a long way from the San Quentin gas chamber, where the grim saga came to its belated end . . .

It all began on January 18th, 1948. On that warm Sunday evening, a young man, visiting California from his native Kansas, parked with a girl friend on a winding road in the San Rafael Hills, on the outskirts of Pasadena. The time was 7.30 p.m.

They had spent the day at Santa Monica beach and dined early at a drive-in. Now, heading for home, the youth braked the car at a lookout point on the drive above the Chevy Chase Golf Course to enjoy the view over Los Angeles and the twinkling lights of the San Gabriel Valley.

As the couple sat chatting, a car came up the road from the opposite direction and a red spotlight suddenly bathed them in its glare. "It's only a cop, honey," the youth said. "Just checking up, I guess."

The coupé approached slowly, its lone occupant craning to peer at them. Then it ground to a stop just in front of the youth's sedan and the red light was switched off. A tall man got out and walked towards them. The boy drew his wallet from his hip pocket and opened it to his driving licence as the man approached the car from the passenger side, snapping the beam of a pencil torch in their faces.

"Here you are, officer." The youth leaned over and showed the open wallet. "Everything's all right. We were just—" Then his voice died in his throat, and the girl beside him stifled a scream of terror.

For the ugly snout of a .45 automatic came into view beside the torch. And now the youth saw that the man did not look at all like a cop. He was hatless, dressed in sports clothes, while there was a vicious leer on the elongated face distinguished by a large hooked nose and protruding chin.

"Give me your dough! This is a stick-up!" he snarled. As the young couple hesitated, he nudged the girl's arm with the .45 barrel. "Let's have the dough, or I'll give you both the works! I'm not fooling!"

"Here, take my wallet," the youth said quickly, leaning over the girl and extending the leather wallet. "I think there's about 15 dollars in it —"

The gunman snatched and pocketed the wallet, then turned to the petrified girl. "Where's your purse, sister?"

"I—I haven't any. I didn't bring it with me—" Her voice wasn't convincing, though. And the robber flashed his torch, saw the purse lying on the back seat, jerked the rear door open and grabbed it. As he straightened up, he noticed that the girl was staring at his unmasked face, plainly revealed in the light of a nearby street lamp. "Turn your face, sister!" he barked, slapping her on the cheek with the back of his hand. He stood beside the car, automatic levelled, eyeing the girl speculatively.

"You've got our money, why don't you leave us alone?" the boy protested.

"Shut up!" the gunman snapped. Then he moved to open the right front door. But at that moment, the lights of another car flashed around a curve some distance away. With a snarled curse, the gunman loped back to his car, gunned the motor and zoomed off.

"He's not going to get away with this!" the youth declared, starting up his car. He swung the vehicle around and took off down the road.

In a few minutes, the irate youth and the frightened girl were telling their story to deputy sheriffs at the Montrose substation. "I'd recognise him anywhere," the girl said positively. "That long crooked nose and that jutting jaw—" She shuddered. "No one could forget that face!"

Then came a report made belatedly to the Malibu substation. At 4.35 a.m. that same Sunday — 15 hours before the Pasadena ambush and 25 miles away — a lanky gunman using a red spotlight had stopped the car driven by John Wako on the Coast Highway near Malibu Beach and robbed his woman companion of $15. Wako described the same young man with a crooked nose — as though it had been broken and improperly set — well dressed, carrying a worn-looking Colt .45 automatic and pencil torch. It had been too dark to see his car.

Next night — Monday, January 19th — police cars patrolling the San Rafael Hills were on special alert, though it was thought unlikely that the Red Light Bandit would strike in the same area on successive nights. But when the alarm came on Monday evening, it was again in Montrose territory, little more than a mile from the scene of the Sunday night robbery.

A couple — we will call them William Kaner, 34, and Mary Ryanal — were out for a drive together.

At about 8.30 p.m., they stopped for a moment on St. Katherine Drive to look down at the Devil's Gate Reservoir, shimmering in the almost-full moon.

A car came up the road, flashed a red spotlight and stopped some yards away. After the red light went off, a tall man got out and approached them on foot. Like the youth the previous night, William Kaner reached for his wallet, assuring his companion that it was only a policeman checking up.

Suddenly yanking open the car door, the tall stranger pressed the .45 automatic into the startled man's side. "This is a stick-up," he told them. "Turn your faces the other way."

Thinking the gunman didn't want them to get too good a look at him in the bright moonlight, they obeyed. Concerned for Mrs. Ryanal's safety, Kaner froze as he heard the automatic's hammer go back to full cock. "Go ahead — take our money. Just don't harm us. The lady here isn't well," he said tensely.

The gunman pocketed Kaner's wallet, then walked around the back of the car and opened the right-hand door. Now he had put a white handkerchief over the lower part of his face. "Come on, get out!" he ordered Mary Ryanal.

"I can't walk!" she protested truthfully. "I've been sick — I'm just out of the hospital. Here, take my handbag. There are a few dollars in it — and some jewellery —"

"Get out!" the masked man repeated, ignoring the handbag and prodding her with his gun. "Get out, or I'll kill both of you! I've killed before!"

"She's sick, don't you understand?" Kaner pleaded desperately. "For God's sake, take our money and leave her alone!"

"Either she gets out, or you both go out in a casket!"

Sobbing in terror, Mrs. Ryanal clambered out of the car and leaned on the door for support. The gunman seized her roughly by the arm. "Don't make a move, or I'll let you both have it!" he told Kaner.

Helplessly, wanting to put up a fight, but vividly aware of the cocked automatic and the fiend's ice-cold eyes and voice — and bent on saving his companion's life at any cost — Kaner sat frozen, his hands on the wheel, watching mutely while the masked man half carried and half propelled the weeping blonde, still clutching her handbag, to the light coupé. He forced her inside, climbed in after her and slammed the door.

There was a scream, cut off by the gunman's hoarse commands telling the terrified woman to perform oral copulation on him. Kaner gripped the wheel, wanting frantically to go to his companion's aid but convinced that any move would endanger Mary's life.

Finally, Mary Ryanal, sobbing hysterically, stumbled to

the open door of Kaner's car. Then the coupé's motor sprang into life. Kaner lifted her inside. Her clothing was disarrayed, her face scratched. She was trembling and near collapse.

Kaner hastily started his motor and jammed the car into gear. As he got rolling, the light coupé sped past him, tearing off down the hill. Kaner stopped at the first house and phoned the sheriff. Soon, the wooded hills were swarming with deputies and roads were blocked off, but the sexual attacker had escaped again.

"I'd have given both my arms to save her," William Kaner told cops unhappily. "But I was helpless. He'd have killed her. He was a killer —" The officers agreed that Kaner had followed the wisest course and probably saved both their lives.

Shortly after 2 a.m. on January 22nd, Hollywood police received an excited call from a youth. He said he was phoning from a house on Mulholland Drive, where it winds down over what was then a sparsely inhabited part of the Hollywood Hills. "This fellow — we thought he was a cop — he took Helen with him —" he stammered.

Patrol cars were in the area within in a few minutes and radio car officers were interviewing the scared 20-year-old student. His story was a grim one. He and a girl we will name Helen Tarpley, a high-school girl he had just met, were on their way home from a party in the San Fernando Valley. They had parked in the moonlight on Mulholland Drive, in the forested heights above Laurel Canyon, overlooking the panorama of Hollywood's lights.

A light-coloured coupé, a 1946 or 1947 Ford or Plymouth, the youth thought, cruised up with its red spotlight, stopped in front of them and a tall man got out. The young man started to produce his identification. Then he saw that the approaching man wore a handkerchief mask.

"Sit still, this is a stick-up," the Red Light Bandit told him, as the blunt-nosed .45 came into view. But this time, the bandit ignored the wallet as his eyes studied the girl in the glow of the pencil torch.

He stepped around to the right side of the car, opened the door and pulled the terrified girl out by the arm. "You're coming with me," he told Helen. "And you -" he glowered at the boy — "you drive on ahead. I'll follow you. Just keep going. Do what I say and don't try any smart stuff, or I'll plug you both!"

Frozen with fear, they had no choice but to obey. The gunman marched the girl to his car and got inside with her, ordering the youth to start up and drive slowly ahead. As the boy's car moved ahead, the bandit's car turned around and hung on his bumper, trying to force him into the ditch. No other traffic was in sight as the frantic youth turned down Woodrow Wilson Drive. Suddenly, the bandit's car swooped ahead, cut in and forced him off the road. The youth heard a grating laugh over the horrified cries of the girl as the gunman whipped his coupé around and shot off again, disappearing up Mulholland Drive. The youth, unhurt, but shaken, wandered afoot in the darkness for almost an hour before he could find a house and phone the police.

An urgent alarm sent police cars scurrying throughout the hills. Meanwhile, the youth — who did not even know the girl's address, since he had just met her at the party — was brought down to the Hollywood police station, where he tried to remember details under questioning by Detective Sergeants Colin Forbes and Arnold Hubka.

"I didn't get a good look at him," the boy said. "He had a handkerchief over his face and I was worried about the girl. He talked tough. God knows what he's done with Helen!"

Detectives searched the youth's car and, jammed down behind the front passenger seat, they found the girl's black handbag. A card had her address on it, and the officers sped there, arriving at about 4 a.m. The lights were on. And the girl's mother, peering through a crack with the door on the chain, was crying.

"Yes, Helen's here," she sobbed. "That fiend brought her home an hour ago. But he said he'd come back and kill us both if we told the police!"

"Don't worry," Detective Sergeant Forbes assured her grimly. "He won't be killing anybody. Just let us talk to your daughter briefly and find out what happened."

Suffering from hysteria and shock, the girl could barely speak. She lay rigid in bed, moaning, her eyes tightly closed, as though to shut out the nightmare she had been through. Bit by bit, they elicited her story. After ditching her escort's car, she said, the abductor drove down a lonely dead-end ravine, threatening to kill her if she didn't do as he said. Parking finally in thick shrubbery off the road, he ignored the girl's prayers and sobs and forced her at gunpoint to take off all her clothes. When she balked, he ripped them completely off.

Details of the sexual act he had forced upon Helen Tarpley were much the same as those Mary Ryanal had endured. At gunpoint, he had forced her to perform fellatio on him. More than an hour later, he ordered Helen to dress, asked her where she lived — and then, repeating his warnings that she and her mother would both be killed if she reported the attack to the police, he drove her to within 100 yards of her home. Before putting her out of the car, he took down her name, address and phone number. As she got out, he levelled the gun at her and warned her not to look back at the car's licence number.

A bulletin on the Red Light Bandit was broadcast by radio and teletype throughout Los Angeles County. It was read in all squad rooms at the evening roll call:

"White male American, about 26 years old, 6 feet, 180 pounds, dark brown wavy hair, brown eyes; prominent long hooked nose, possibly broken; protruding jaw. Grey 1946 Ford business coupé with spotlight, either attached or carried in car, red lens cover possibly concealed in glove compartment, possibly equipped with police radio. Use extreme caution, this man is armed and dangerous."

Every half an hour, the urgent bulletin crackled out to all police units.

At 5 p.m. Forbes received a near-hysterical phone call from Helen Tarpley's mother. She reported that the Red

Light Bandit had just phoned Helen! "Just a personal friend," he had affably assured the mother, who answered the phone. But Helen had recognised his voice at once and hung up with a scream. Forbes reassured her and sent police to guard the house.

At 7.50 p.m., Patrolmen John Reardon and Robert May, who had already stopped and checked four grey Ford coupés, were cruising south on Vermont Avenue, just off Hollywood Boulevard, when they spotted another Ford, going north at a fast clip. "Here we go!" exclaimed Reardon, the driver, as he swung the police car in a U-turn. "It's a '46 — and it has a spotlight!" He trampled on the gas pedal to overtake the coupé, which appeared to have two men in it.

The grey car slowed abruptly, then pulled into a closed petrol station. As the police car went by the Ford circled through the grease rack and emerged on Vermont again, heading south.

"That's our boy!" cried May. "He did that to see if we were on his tail!" So Reardon swung the patrol car around again and took off after the speeding Ford. May got busy on the radio and, in a matter of seconds, half a dozen other police cars were converging on the area. By the time the chase hit busy Melrose Avenue, the Ford was doing 80 miles an hour.

"He's really asked for it," May declared grimly, taking out his .38 and leaning out of the window. The crack of shots came over the radio as May, gun in one hand and microphone in the other, fired at the zig-zagging coupé. At Vermont and Beverly, two police cars with red lights oscillating tried to block the intersection, but the Ford, without slackening, headed straight at one of them, forcing it to stop to avoid a crash.

One of May's shots shattered the fleeing car's rear window. With a shriek of tortured rubber, the fugitive car turned east on Sixth Street, veering crazily up the wrong side of the road, then twisted north on Shatton Place.

Reardon's car was only a few yards behind as the driver suddenly braked and started to swing around in a teetering

U-turn. The Ford spun out of control on the slick surface. Without hesitating, Reardon crashed the police car head-on into the coupé's left front wheel and bumper, bringing both cars to a shuddering halt.

Two men clambered dazedly from the Ford as Reardon and May leapt out, guns ready. One man, short and stocky, had his hands in the air. Reardon seized and handcuffed him — without a struggle. The other man, the driver, tall and stooped, took off up the street, ignoring May's shouted commands to halt.

May gave chase, firing over the fugitive's head, as other police cars raced up and more officers poured out with revolvers and riot guns. The tall man ducked between two houses into a back garden and ran for a low wire fence. May fired twice more, directly at the blurred figure in the darkness. At the second shot, the runner staggered, recovered himself, then collapsed against the fence. In a moment, he was surrounded by officers and handcuffed. The bullet had only grazed his temple, leaving a bloody but superficial furrow. He cursed as he gasped for breath.

On the front seat of the Ford, the officers found a fully loaded Colt .45 automatic, plus a plastic toy pistol that looked like the real thing. The back of the coupé was jam-packed with brand-new suits, sports jackets, slacks and shirts, all on hangers. The captured men had more than $300 in their pockets.

Taken to Hollywood police station, the manacled pair turned out to be well known to the police. The tall man — with elongated head, curly hair, prominent beaked nose and protruding lower jaw — was Caryl Whittier Chessman, a 26-year-old Highland Park resident. As an adolescent, he had been a constant headache to police till he was sent to San Quentin in 1941 for a series of armed robberies. He now admitted that he had been paroled only the previous December 28th, 1947, some four weeks before.

His shorter, hard-faced pal was David Hugh Knowles, 32, who also had a lengthy record of burglary and robbery. Just as they were brought in, a teletype bulletin came in from neighbouring Redondo Beach that explained the stack of new clothes. At 6.45 p.m. that evening, two gunmen had held up the Town Clothing Shop there, forcing proprietor Melvin Waisler and his assistant Joe Lescher into a back room and slugging Waisler viciously over the head with the butt of a gun. They got away with $320, besides the clothes.

An extra pair of licence plates, apparently the original ones, were found in the back of the Ford. And the police "hot sheet" showed that the car had been stolen on January 13th from a Pasadena woman.

The pair denied everything. Knowles claimed that Chessman had picked him up at Hollywood and Vine a few minutes before they were caught, while Chessman declared that he had just borrowed the Ford from a friend he wasn't at liberty to name. He hadn't known it was stolen, he knew nothing about the clothes or guns — and he had fled from the police because a paroled convict isn't supposed to drive a car without special permission.

"You only got me because that car was a lemon," he said, grinning crookedly. "It's the first time I've ever been caught in a car."

"Where's the red spotlight lens, Chessman?" Forbes demanded.

The lanky prisoner looked at him incredulously, then threw back his head and laughed. "Are you trying to pin that on me, too?"

Chessman's record showed that they were dealing with a criminal who knew all the ropes — and a few more. He had been in trouble since the age of 16.

Two terms in the Preston State School of Industry, punctuated by escapes, had netted him the broken nose and other scars in fights. He had also acquired an education through reading everything from Nietzsche to criminal psychology in the reform school library. Interviewed in 1940 by a psychologist who found him of unusually high IQ, but a confirmed criminal dedicated to outwitting the law, Chessman blamed his criminal quirk on childhood asthma and encephalitis, adding that he had stolen to raise money to help his mother, who was paralysed and bedridden from a traffic accident.

Married in 1940 to a girl who tried to help him, Chessman went to school for a time and planned to join the Royal Canadian Air Force. But he soon turned up as the brains of a youthful gang which staged a wild series of robberies, climaxed by holding up two deputy sheriffs and stealing their cars and guns, beating up a highway patrolman and shooting and wounding a citizen.

Police eventually rounded up the gang. And on February 2nd, 1941, Chessman and his chief lieutenant were sentenced to prison terms totalling 16 years to life. Articulate and intelligent, the self-made crime genius took up literary work and impressed San Quentin authorities so favourably that in May, 1943, he was transferred to the minimum-security institution at Chino, from which he promptly escaped.

Recaptured in Glendale, California, Chessman told a wild story of having broken out in order to masquerade as a Nazi agent and kill Adolf Hitler. Taken to the maximum-security prison at Folsom, he made articulate applications for parole and finally won his release to join his parents for Christmas, 1947. His young wife had meanwhile divorced him.

No red spotlight equipment was found in the stolen Ford, but the rim of the ordinary white spotlight was loose. And in Chessman's pocket, Detective-Sergeant Forbes found a small nut that fitted the rim tension bolt. He believed the lens had been covered with disposable red Cellophane. There was no police radio, but there was a pencil torch in the glove compartment.

Another incriminating item found on Chessman was a sketch-map of part of the wealthy movie colony at Malibu Beach, drawn on Folsom prison stationery, with the homes of a number of film notables marked, along with the floor plans of some. Asked about this, Chessman said that a fellow-inmate — a former butler for one of the stars, serving time for forgery — had drawn it for him in connection with a book Chessman was writing.

Forbes and Hubka took Chessman to the home of his last victim, Helen Tarpley, where the 17-year-old girl, cringing in terror, identified him instantly and positively as her attacker. Next morning, other victims, including Mary Ryanal and William Kaner, unhesitatingly picked him out of a lineup at the county jail, positively identifying both his face and his voice.

Meanwhile, investigation linked Chessman with at least three other crimes: the robbery of a Pasadena clothing store on January 3rd, in which $800 was taken; the attempted burglary on January 17th of a home two blocks from the gunman's own home; and the sexual abuse of another Hollywood girl who did not want to risk publicity by filing a formal complaint.

Faced with all this, Chessman made partial admissions concerning some of the robberies, including the Redondo Beach job — in which he implicated Knowles — but refused to admit to the Red Light sex atrocities. "Those are tough raps," he was reported as saying. "I'm allergic to that little green room!"

Pressed, he finally came out with a new story. He now said that he knew the Red Light Bandit. It was a fellow named Pete Azevedo, who looked very much like Chessman himself. Pete had stolen the Ford — and was actually in it with Chessman on Friday night when police spotted it. Pete had jumped out as they swung through the darkened garage, Chessman claimed.

Chessman supplied the names of several of Pete's hangouts on Hollywood Boulevard. The detectives traced and questioned several men with similar names, but checked them out. They were convinced that Chessman's story was a fabrication, especially since Officers Reardon and May were certain that no mysterious third man had jumped out of the car as they pursued it.

The district attorney prepared a complaint charging

Caryl Chessman with 18 felony counts, including three of kidnapping with bodily injury for the purpose of robbery — which carried a death sentence under California's "Little Lindbergh Law" — armed robbery, burglary, grand theft, attempted robbery, attempted rape, plus two morals offences. Only one of the victims involved in these several crimes failed to pick out Chessman in a lineup. All the others positively identified him as their assistant.

David Knowles was charged with two counts of kidnapping with bodily injury, two of armed robbery and one of car theft. Witnesses also identified Knowles at the brief preliminary hearing. On February 4th, both Chessman and Knowles were remanded in custody.

In a separate trial, David Knowles, still protesting his innocence, was found guilty on four counts. On April 27th, Judge Harold Landreth sentenced him to serve two consecutive life terms, one without possibility of parole, plus two terms of five years to life.

Chessman went on trial before a jury of 11 women and one man in the court of Judge Charles Fricke. Deputy District Attorney J. Miller Leavy demanded the death penalty. Branding the Red Light crimes as "worse than murder," he cited Chessman's partial admissions, then introduced a damning parade of witnesses, including Helen Tarpley and Mary Ryanal, both of whom positively identified Chessman and related their nightmare experiences at his hands.

On May 21st, after 30 hours of deliberation, the jury found Chessman guilty of 17 of the felony charges, acquitting him only of the Highland Park burglary attempt, in which identification was not positive. For the kidnapping and assaults on the two girls, the jury returned the mandatory death verdicts.

On June 25th, 1948, Judge Fricke sentenced Chessman to die twice — a grim legal irony — in the gas chamber at San Quentin. He added a sentence of life imprisonment without parole, eight consecutive terms of five years to life and four lesser terms. It was the first time a man had been sentenced to death in California for a crime other than murder, under the "Little Lindbergh" kidnapping statute in 1933.

"Your Honour," Chessman said to the judge, with a slight smile, "I still owe the state another 260 years for violating parole on former sentences."

"Those may be served concurrently," Judge Fricke replied, with a straight face.

Chessman was taken to Death Row at San Quentin to await the outcome of his automatic appeal to the State Supreme Court, mandatory in all death penalty cases. But it developed that the death sentence, instead of marking *finis* to his career, was merely the signal for him to begin to fight and wriggle in earnest. He obtained law books from the prison library and the state law library at Sacramento, wangled a typewriter in his death cell and spent all his time poring over books and preparing legal documents.

He got an unexpected break when the elderly court reporter who covered his trial died before he had a chance to transcribe his old-fashioned shorthand notes. Thus, there was no record ready to submit for the appeal. The district attorney's office collaborated with the judge in preparation of as complete a record as possible from the deceased reporter's notes.

Chessman cried that this was unfair. He fought certification of the pieced-together record and demanded a new trial. He carried his appeals and petitions as far as the U.S. Supreme Court — and the proceedings dragged on.

Another technicality arose in Chessman's favour when the state appellate court ruled in the appeal of David Knowles — in which Chessman had collaborated — that kidnapping or detention for robbery was the same as robbery, and hence reversed Knowles's lesser robbery convictions, while letting the kidnap counts stand.

This moved the California legislature in 1951 to amend the "Little Lindbergh Law" to require specifically a kidnapping or carrying away for the purpose of robbery itself. The legislature at the time granted eligibility to anyone who had been sentenced under the old statute to life without parole.

Thus, Knowles was made eligible for parole, but Chessman, sentenced to death, was not. Chessman claimed that this action was discriminatory, that he was being punished illegally for the atrocious nature of the alleged sex crimes, not legitimately for the offence of kidnapping. But, finally, Chessman's court appeals on these points were exhausted. And he was re-sentenced to die on March 28th, 1952.

But he was far from finished. Two events aided his campaign for a new trial: William Kaner was killed by a runaway car, while Helen Tarpley was committed to a state hospital with a mental breakdown brought on by her hideous experience at the assailant's hands. These witnesses would not be available for a new trial — and Chessman redoubled his efforts with even greater zeal.

He kept right on, consulting more than 1,000 law books, typing thousands of pages and firing petitions and appeals broadside to every state and federal court within range. But, one by one, Chessman's petitions were denied — and Judge Fricke pronounced sentence again and again.

Early in 1954, with his execution date now set for May 14th, the convict prodigy popped again into the limelight with an announcement that he had become a successful author as well as a lawyer. He had sold a book, *Cell 2455, Death Row*, the story of his life of crime and his current fight to stay alive. The book appeared in May, shortly before its author, his latest plea denied by the U.S. Supreme Court, was scheduled to die in the gas chamber. His will provided that the proceeds, expected to be some $100,000, should go into a fund for three children in whom he was interested.

A number of leading authors, psychologists and penologists appealed to California's Governor Goodwin J. Knight for clemency, on the grounds that the book was an invaluable contribution to the literature of criminal psychology — and that Chessman should be spared for the further work he could do in this field. Chessman himself asked time to complete still another work.

But Judge Fricke pungently remarked: "If we are going

to grant leniency solely because a man who richly deserves the penalty he got from a jury is able to write English and get a book published, we might as well throw the criminal law into the trash can!"

Governor Knight rejected the appeals, declaring that there was nothing in the case file to give grounds for reprieve or commutation.

A last-minute plea for a new psychiatric examination was granted, but Chessman was again pronounced legally sane. Then Judge Thomas J. Keating, of San Rafael, in whose jurisdiction San Quentin lies, granted his petition for hearing on a writ of habeas corpus and thereby stayed his execution.

At his habeas corpus hearing in San Rafael, Chessman's newly retained attorney renewed the attack on the validity of the trial transcript, pointing out that one of the stenographers who had prepared it from the dead reporter's notes was a relative of Prosecutor Leavy. But Judge Keating found no merit in the arguments, denied the writ and rescinded the stay. Judge Fricke immediately sentenced Chessman — for the fifth time — to be executed on July 30th, 1954, the first Friday after the necessary 60-day minimum.

Grinning triumphantly, justified anew in feeling that he bore a charmed life, Chessman relaxed in his death cell and set to work on his new book, while his attorney prepared further appeals.

A film studio announced that it had bought the screen rights to Chessman's book for $15,000 and was planning a film to be based on it. The producer, stressing that the studio had no intention of glamorising the convicted Red Light Bandit, said: "The story will be handled as a horrible example, perhaps a lesson to boys who might be starting out as Chessman did."

That was in 1954. But the sands were still a long way from running out in the case of Caryl Chessman. In his autobiography, he wrote: "If I had a potential bag of tricks, why should I hesitate to use them?"

Elsewhere in his autobiography, we read:

It was Monday morning, October 25th, 1954. I was waiting — locked in a tiny, maximum- security death cell in San Quentin Prison's Death Row. Again my life hung precariously in the balance, with the odds overwhelmingly against me.

The chips were down. Minutes from now the wire services would flash word from Washington that the Supreme Court had rendered a decision. Then the long wait would be over. Then I'd know.

I lit a cigarette, grinned wryly, and shook my head in wonder. It was a hellish spot to be in.

For the fifth time — the seventh, counting petitions for rehearings — the much-publicised case of *Chessman versus California* was back before the nation's highest court, awaiting decision.

For me, a summary denial of relief would mean death in the prison's squat "little green room" before the end of the year. And here was real irony. For now I had everything to live for, I'd found myself; I had a meaningful future — and two death sentences.

I sat and smoked and thought. I hardly dared hope. The stakes were high — my life against a little more time.

Behind me were more than six years, six eternities, of living in the shadow of the gas chamber, of fighting a dogged and seemingly endless battle for survival, of watching nearly five dozen men take that last grim walk past my cell. It had been an incredible, nightmarish experience, and during the first four years of it I hadn't given a damn whether I lived or died. I'd been interested only in cheating the executioner and in seeing that Death Row didn't break me, didn't whip me. It hadn't.

Out of the experience had come an ultimate awakening and an overriding determination to give some affirmative meaning to an existence shaped, controlled and directed by psychopathic bondage and crime.

Out of it, too, had come a book, one written against the clock and the mounting pressures and tensions of Death

Row, while I held off the executioner.

I wrote it because its author is both haunted and angered by the knowledge that his society needlessly persists in confounding itself in dealing with the monstrous problems of what to do with criminals. Tied, consequently, is the cause of the criminally damned and doomed. It's time their voice was heard. And understood.

Cell 2455, Death Row, the unprettified story of my life in crime and my years as a doomed man, was published in the spring of 1954 — just 13 days before I was scheduled to die. The book became an immediate bestseller, attracted international attention. It would be translated into more than a dozen foreign languages.

A film studio had bought the screen rights for $15,000. All this gave meaning to my life. And my rugged fight for survival would go on just like it had for six years. Just like back in May this year when I was only 16 hours from death and Judge Keating finally held that my appointment with the executioner on the following day was definitely off. The stay created a storm of controversy. It was terminated two weeks later when, after a careful study of the case, Judge Keating ruled I should seek relief in the California Supreme Court, rather than in a superior court.

I was resentenced to die at 10 a.m. on Friday, July 30th, 1954. The California Supreme Court denied my petition for a writ of habeas corpus. Again time was running out on me. The papers reported my life "hung by a thin legal thread." It did, for a fact. My only hope was to win yet another stay of execution while the case was taken, for the fifth time, to the United States Supreme Court. The odds against me, I knew, were a conservative hundred to one.

The days passed. The tension mounted.

Thursday, July 29th, 1954. I was packed up to go. I had my last visits, executed a new will, made arrangements with a mortician to claim my body. This time it definitely looked like the end. Then San Quentin's Warden Harley Teets brought me some news. My hours away date with death was off! Justice Jesse Carter of the state Supreme Court had granted a stay to give the Federal Supreme Court, then in summer recess, a chance to act on my petition for review.

In an opinion filed with the order, Justice Carter had said, "To my mind it is a clear and obvious violation of the (constitutional) due process provisions . . . for the California Supreme Court to decide a death penalty case on an incomplete or inaccurate record, where such record is procured by fraud and connivance of public officials," as I had consistently maintained.

The stay had some explosive repercussions. The California attorney general urged the governor to appoint a committee to study the whole question of capital punishment in the state. Newspaper editorials blasted Justice Carter's action, other commended him on it. Public opinion was sharply divided.

In August, the attorney general's office challenged the legality of the stay order and, in an unprecedented move, made a motion asking the California Supreme Court to set it aside. This motion was argued in September before the full seven- man court in a packed courtroom, then taken under advisement.

Speculation was rife on what the court would do. Its answer was handed down on Thursday, October 7th, 1954. While not "approving" the stay order, the full court, following a lengthy written discussion of the legal history of the case, refused to set it aside. Justice Carter wrote a separate, strongly worded opinion in which he again voiced the conviction that my claims should and must be heard.

Thus ultimate disposition of California's most controversial and sensational case was left squarely up to the United States Supreme Court — and today, Monday, October 25th, 1954, was decision day.

I lit another cigarette, put on my earphones to listen to the news. Seconds later the newscaster's somewhat breathless words told me the long wait was over.

It was, inevitably, a headline-producing decision: CHESSMAN LOSES IN U.S. SUPREME COURT. *High Court Rejects Chessman Plea But Offers New Loophole.*

"The United States Supreme Court said 'no' to Caryl Chessman for the seventh time today. But it did it in a way opening a whole new vista of lower court actions. There was virtual assurance to the doomed convict-author he will still be around in 1955, and maybe in 1956."

Maybe even, with any kind of a break, for the duration of a long life.

The Supreme Court's tersely phrased order contained exactly 26 words — "The petition for writ of certiorari (review) is denied without prejudice to an application for a writ of habeas corpus in an appropriate United States District Court."

And those 26 words spelled the difference between certain death in San Quentin's gas chamber and a fighting chance at life, a future, freedom. They meant I would get what I had vainly sought for years on end — a full dress judicial hearing on my claims.

What, in substance, were those claims? That, while admittedly I had been hijacking bookies and "knocking over" collectors for a huge bookmaking syndicate in the area, I was not southern California's notorious Red Light Bandit. That, forced to stand trial unprepared and denied an adequate opportunity to defend myself against the Red Light charges, I had been wrongly and illegally convicted. That I hadn't had a fair trial because of the prosecutor's persistent misconduct throughout the trial, because of his introduction in evidence, by a subterfuge, of my criminal record and false and coerced "confessions," and because of the trial judge's erroneous instructions to the jury.

That, on appeal, I had been foreclosed from establishing these facts because the court reporter had died at the conclusion of the trial, with the result that the trial record, uniquely fashioned from the dead reporter's old-style Pitman shorthand notes, was grossly incomplete and inaccurate. That the substitute reporter was addicted to the excessive use of alcohol, was incompetent and in fact unable to read the notes, and that he was a relative of the prosecutor and had been under the latter's domination during the period the record was being prepared.

I had never asked any court to take my word these contentions were true. Rather, all I had asked was the opportunity to prove they were by competent evidence. Finally the chance had been given to me and I was elated. My fantastic ordeal hadn't been in vain.

If, after this judicial hearing before the United States District Court, the hearing judge found my charges to be proved, the convictions would be thrown out. I would stand then in the same position as though I had never been convicted in the first place. The state would, of course, be free to retry me. But I welcomed a retrial. I was confident of an acquittal, vindication.

But what would Chessman do — how did he hope to use his life — if miraculously he got it back?

The question had been asked by Ed Fitzgerald, the editorial director of the American magazine *Saga*.

Two days before the Supreme Court's decision, Fitzgerald wrote to Chessman:

"It's my thought that you have nowhere, other than briefly in your book, set down the sum of your thoughts concerning the kind of life you would like to lead in the years ahead."

That was true. I had been too furiously busy fighting for a future, working from 12 to 18 hours a day to complete my second book, that I might leave it behind, whatever happened to me. Yet, pacing the floor of my cell in the small hours of the night, I had given considerable hard-headed thought to exactly what I would do with my life if the state relinquished its demand that I forfeit it in the gas chamber.

It was an intriguing question. As I turned it over in my mind. I stood off and surveyed myself. There stood a battered-faced, 190-pound, 33-year-old six footer, a guy who had been through one of the damnedest experiences in modern times. He'd spent more years, months and days on Death Row than any doomed man in California's history, waging an obstinate, seemingly impossible battle for survival. Surprisingly, his sense of humour and irony hadn't deserted him. He was a ruthlessly self-disciplined work-horse, a voracious reader, reasonably intelligent, something of an enigma. A complex guy, probably both dreamer and realist, with a violent past. But not really the thoroughly bad guy legend makes him out to be.

His problem wasn't dying; he'd lived with death too long to react emotionally or subjectively to the prospect of being gassed out of existence. If necessary, he could die tomorrow with a shrug, without dramatics or bravado. But he didn't want to die; he wanted to live, literally to write some meaning into his existence. .

Here, then, are the results of a cross-country interview. The questions are Ed Fitzgerald's. The answers are mine. They're written here in my death cell, between legal rounds, while preparations are being made for court action that will finally decide my fate.

"Would you get married? Is the girl you were thinking of marrying still seeing you regularly and still interested in your future?"

"A girl in the life of a doomed man whose name, to many, is a dark criminal legend? Yes. A pretty, blue-eyed, brown-haired young woman with two small children by a former marriage. Her name is Frances, and she still sees me regularly, is still vitally interested in my future. So far as we are concerned, the unusual thing is my situation, not the way we feel towards one another.

"Frances entered my life in almost story-book fashion. She was born and raised in Maine. When she was 20, against her parents' wishes, she married an enlisted man in the Navy, a youngster her age. A year later, after travelling about the country and after her husband had received his discharge, they moved to Glendale, a city adjoining Los Angeles, where Frances hoped to establish a home. Her husband, however, wasn't ready for marital responsibility. He didn't want children; Frances did. One day he walked out. Later they were divorced.

"At one time things looked bleak for her. Fundless, she had David, now six, and was expecting Cheryl, now three. She got a job as a waitress in a restaurant in Glendale. My father regularly ate his meals there. He was an elderly, lonely, heartbroken man. My mother had died a few months before and his only son was on Death Row. He and Frances became friendly. She would drop in to see him on her days off to cheer him.

"My father, knowing her predicament, suggested she move into our house and be his housekeeper. She did, and little Cheryl was born the following April, 1951. My father's health was failing him; Frances coaxed him to eat, watched over him. The children were also a wonderful medicine for him. He was the only grandpa they had ever known, and a marvellously kind one. Frances came to feel closer to him than she had to her own father.

"I was writing to my father regularly, but he wasn't much of a letter writer and he had a crippled hand. Frances began to answer for him. Facing death day after day as I was, she felt I would want to hear from my family. Then, in March of 1953, she drove my father north to visit me. That was when I first met her. She later confided she was frightened at the prospect of meeting face to face a man whom the press, with characteristic extravagance, had labelled everything from "fiend" to "criminal genius." She discovered I was a human being.

"A heart attack killed my father a year later. Good soldier that she was, it was Frances who made all the funeral arrangements. It was she who came to see me, who sensed how helpless I felt, who acted for me, who shyly offered a love that was selfless and sacrificing and warm. She believed in me and had become convinced I was innocent of the Red Light crimes. If I had a future, she wanted to share it with me. David and Cheryl wanted me to come home and be their daddy.

"It was a beautiful dream and, it appeared, a hopeless one. Twice thereafter I came within hours of execution.

Twice we had what we thought were last visits. The last time Frances brought an engagement ring. I slipped it on her finger, moved by her love and loyalty. Death Row had given me far more than it could ever take away.

"Then my execution was stayed. Now I have a fighting chance to see the dream translated into fact. I'm glad, and so is Frances, whose faith has never wavered throughout an experience that has been hell for her. She writes and visits me regularly. Not long ago she brought the children with her. David is my pal and Cheryl is my tiny sweetheart. They asked me to promise to come home as soon as I could. I promised.

"I hope I find it possible to keep that promise. There is nothing I would like better. Believe me, Caryl Chessman's days of rebellion are over. And whatever finally happens to me, the proceeds from my book are giving these two tiny friends an even chance at life. This gives me a good feeling.

"When I thought my string had run out, I explained to Frances the arrangements I had made in my will for her and the children.

"I won't forget her answer. 'But we don't want the money, Caryl. We want you.'

"And the state won't let me forget that it also wants me — dead."

"What kind of work would you want to do? Obviously, writing would play a part in your life. Would you strive to make that your primary means of making a living? What kind of writing would you want to do?"

"Writing would play a full-time part in my productive life. If freed, I would go to New York and learn that writing and publishing business from the ground up at Critics Associated, under the tutelage of Joseph E. Longstreth, the agency's managing editor. Joe Longstreth is my literary agent; he is also one of the finest and most understanding friends I have ever had, a warm, human and gifted man. I know I would be in good hands, and that if it even remotely appeared I was on the verge of backsliding Joe wouldn't hesitate, if less drastic therapy failed, to bend an encyclopedia over my head.

"Seriously, his agency isn't one of those high-pressure, strictly commercial outfits. It's composed of people genuinely interested in helping develop creative talent and getting the sincere writer a start. I saw that demonstrated in my own case. It was Joe Longstreth who arranged for publication of my first book by Prentice-Hall. He, his staff and the trade book editor of the publisher freely sacrificed their time to work out with me the million and one details surrounding publication, and to rush the book into print. They knew how much the book meant to me; I can't and won't forget that.

"Joe has offered me a place in his agency. I jumped at his offer. Besides presenting the opportunity of a lifetime for me, it will give me a chance to help other beginning writers as I was and am being helped. I'd like that; I'd like to prove that this guy Chessman is grateful.

"Meanwhile, I'm not sitting on my hands. I like to think that my future began the day I started my first book here in Death Row. That way, if the future gets cut short, I still will have something to show for it. *Cell 2455, Death Row* was the first of a planned trilogy.

"The second, *Trial by Ordeal,* will be completed pretty soon. I've been giving my Underwood a fierce workout in hammering together, within a tight, dramatic framework, the story of capital punishment, life in Death Row, and, without self-pity, my own stranger-than-fiction trial by ordeal.

"If I get a chance to write it, the third book in the trilogy, *These Places Called Prison,* will take a sharp and critically objective but unstuffy look at today's prisons in terms of theory, practice and social goal. It already is outlined and extensively researched.

"As well, in the planning stage, is a serious novel of our times, and a determination to do a major overhaul of a gentle satire of Hollywood (also a novel) I wrote some years back, titled *Nov Smoz Kapop?* This is not to mention the whimsical, Runyonesque shorts I turned out when the face

of Death Row gets to looking especially dour and formida-
ble and I needed a breather. The latest of these is *The
Gladiator, the Disrobing Danseuse and L'Amour*. Nor is it to
mention the off-beat, allegorical boxing yarn I just completed, or the novelette I'm presently working on in my
"spare time."

"Five days from death last July, when queried, I told
George Flowers of the Long Beach *Press-Telegram* of my
writing plans. He shook his head and marvelled. Later, in
a feature story, he called me "the world's most optimistic
writer."

"He's doubtless right. I never have thought much of that
line of Shakespeare's, "My ending is despair."

Ed Fitzgerald then asked:

*"What means would you want to seize to prove your usefulness
to society and thus demonstrate your gratitude for the second
chance of life?"*

"Up until a couple of years ago my answer to such a
question would have been brusque and barbed. 'Gratitude!' I'd have exploded. "Gratitude for what? After what
I've been through, I'm supposed to be grateful if the courts
finally decided I never should have been convicted in the
first place?

"Now I feel differently. I've radically revised my thinking. Guilt or innocence aside, Death Row is doubtless the
best thing that ever could have happened to me. Since I was
sixteen, it was a race between Death Row and the morgue
as to which would claim me first. Luckily for me, Death
Row won. Then followed a lot of gruelling years. I shudder
when I look back on them. But at the same time I recognise
they forced on me the sustained, rugged psychological
shock therapy I needed, needed desperately. They jolted
me into wakefulness. They made me my own man.

"And when this happened a concerned penologist, San
Quentin's Warden Harley Teets, challenged me to make
some sense out of my life if I could, to tell why I'd
rebelliously done my damndest to throw my life away. No
whining plea for mercy, *Cell 2455, Death Row* was my

earnest effort at an answer.

"I think my greatest usefulness lies in that I've had and will continue to have the opportunity to demonstrate that the most 'hopeless' criminal in existence can be salvaged; that, moreover, he's worth salvaging, on both humanitarian and hardheaded social grounds.

"Retributive justice and execution chamber, in my opinion, aren't the answer. In seeking a solution to the crime problem, I firmly believe that vision can and should be substituted for vengeance. I'm convinced that there is much that is narrow and negative and wrong in society's attitude towards and treatment of the man who is said to be at "war" with it, and who often is at war with himself. Unhappily, tradition has a way of handcuffing progress.

"By putting my views and experiences in the market place, by giving people an opportunity to see all sides and facets of the crime problem, I believe I can make a material contribution towards its ultimate solution. And that, above all else, I'd like to do, without know-it-all pretensions.

"I don't kid myself. I know it's nothing less than a miracle I'm still alive, and that I find myself out of the brutal psychological jungle in which I was trapped for so many years. It took the kill-or-cure medicine of Death Row to give me a future. I would regard myself as a phony, ungrateful bastard if I took the attitude: 'From here on I'm strictly looking out for No. 1. I saved myself; now I'm out, free, and through with crime. Let the other guy starting out as I did look out for himself. He's society's problem, not mine. Sure, maybe by working like hell I could arouse public opinion and help him and society. But I've got my own life to live, my own future to think about.'

"To adopt that attitude would make me a real fine guy, wouldn't it?

"I agree. It would like hell."

Do you think it would be hard to remain away from your old associates and surroundings? What, in short, would be your attitude towards the life you used to lead?

"The questions are mutually exclusive, and the first one

is a loaded non sequitur.

"To answer them in order. No, it literally wouldn't be hard to remain away from my old associates and surroundings but the fact has no real relevance. Criminal careers are a result of a complex of conditions, not geography. The popular notion that the "criminal element" are habitués of pool halls, smoke-filled back rooms and other such unsavoury places is largely a fallacy. For example, I don't think I've been in a pool hall twice in my life, and the only time I've visited smoke-filled back rooms has been to relieve some poker-playing pimps of their cash, or bookies of their operating capital.

"Some of my old associates are dead; some are doing long stretches in one prison or another; some are still living outside the law; some have straightened out and are hardworking, well thought of members of their communities. None of them ever tried to talk me into a life of crime. I wasn't an innocent led astray by "bad companions." Rather, I was a youngster who got lost, who rebelled, and whose compulsive psychopathic rebellion very nearly destroyed me.

"Do I regret the life I've lived? Of course I do, keenly. Yet at the same time my attitude towards my past life is and will continue to be more clinical than emotional, more objective than subjective. For me to indulge uncritically in loud confessions I would be futile, meaningless. That much is obvious.

"But what triggers rebellion? How much is really known of the anatomy and dynamics of criminal psychopathy? Actually very little. And there are thousands of youngsters following in my footsteps. Denunciations and righteous demands for a public display of abject penitence aren't solutions; they're evasions. That's why I feel a heavy obligation to dissect, evaluate and help the public understand what happened to me, what I let happen. In short, I believe my past makes me valuable as a social guinea pig to be studied and understood rather than as a symbol of what is to be hated, damned and destroyed."

"*What makes you feel sure you can free yourself from whatever mental chains kept you enmeshed in criminal activities in the old days? How would your prison experiences, and particularly your death cell experiences, be likely to affect your future thinking and living?*"

"Just as cancer is a ravaging disease of the body, so is criminal psychopathy a like affliction of the mind or soul. When intelligently regarded as such, it's both treatable and curable. For years I've been regarded as a "dangerous psychopath," seemingly a violently hopeless case. And four defiant, rebellious years in Death Row only confirmed this view.

"But then the impossible occurred. Virtually overnight I 'straightened out.' I changed, radically — and there was nothing phony about the change. What had happened? I got a stay that I didn't expect. And with it came a blunt-spoken challenge from the warden, whose stinging words made me think, made me see myself for what I really was. In the public mind, places like Death Row made sense, I bitterly realised, only because guys like myself didn't. Well, I could do something about that. I could tell the story of my life, without pulling punches. I could and I did. Ironically long after I should have been dead, I wrote myself back to sanity.

"And writing changed the world for me. It was a catharsis and more. It meant, live or die, I could salvage something from my destructive past — and write some positive, creative meaning into my life. I'd been through the mill, through reform schools and jails and prisons, through guns, battles and hell. I wasn't a damned bit proud of that record; but there it was. Make some sense out of it! I told myself. Either examine your condemnation and all that preceded it in terms larger than your own predicament or admit you're a glib fraud!

"I set to work. Reaching the concluding chapter of *Cell 2455, Death Row,* I wrote with perfect honesty: 'The long years lived in this crucible called Death Row have carried me beyond bitterness, beyond hate, beyond savage animal violence. Death Row has compelled me to study as I have never studied before, to accept disciplines I never would have accepted otherwise, and to gain a penetrating insight into all phases of this problem of crime that I am determined to translate into worthwhile contributions towards ultimate solution of that problem. This book is a beginning contribution; I would like to believe that it also signals the beginning for me of a journey back from outer darkness.'

"Miraculously, it did signal such a beginning. The reception of the book had an incalculable impact upon me. People, I found, were genuinely concerned with the problem. They were, moreover, interested in me. I won friends the world over. I was grateful beyond words and humbled. As my fight for life went on, I threw myself into my second book, *Trial by Ordeal*. Now the manuscript is nearly completed. And now I know what I want. Now I have a future. There isn't a chance I would or will throw it away."

Finally Fitzgerald asked:

"Specifically how do you feel your release can be accomplished? What steps do you expect to take, what outside assistance would you like to attract, and what do you personally think your chances are?

"Statistically, the odds against my leaving Death Row by any door but the solid steel one leading to the execution chamber are at least one hundred to one. But, then, the odds against my remaining in Death Row longer than any doomed man before me ever had were more than 500 to one. On the merits of the case itself, statistical comparisons aside, I believe my chances for survival and eventual release are better than fifty-fifty, partly because I'm not under sentence for murder, but for a highly technical kind of kidnapping for the purpose of robbery. The "kidnapping" in one instance involved a movement of eighteen feet.

"My release can be accomplished in one of two ways:

"By establishing on the habeas corpus proceedings in the Federal District Court that my conviction as southern California's notorious Red Light bandit was illegally obtained, and, if retried, by proving my innocence of the charges. That would result in my being returned to prison to serve out my time on prior, unexpired commitments.

"By a commutation of my death sentence to life imprisonment by the Governor of California, in which case it would be up to me to win parole eligibility and to convince the parole board that I am a good parole risk.

"For five years and ten months following conviction, I represented myself, doing all my own legal work here in my cell in Death Row. Now I'm assisted by three attorneys — Berwyn A. Rice, Jerome Duffy, and Rosalie S. Asher — who believe in the case, in me, and in my innocence. They've been doing a remarkable job. Recently San Francisco's J. W. Erlich, a legendary lawyer in this part of the country, stepped into the case on my side to resist the state's motion to throw out my latest stay of execution, and has offered us the benefit of his tremendous experience. If there is a legal win in the deck for me I know these four dedicated attorneys will see that I get it.

"Literally thousands of people in all walks of life — throughout the state, the country and the world — have written to the governor, urging clemency. These include doctors, church leaders, psychiatrists, writers, criminologists, lawyers, and columnists — old friends and new. As well, many reputable groups and organisations have gone on record as favouring clemency. One, a committee of well-known writers headed by Wenzell Brown, was formed to do everything it can to save my life. These people and all who may join them may be assured that I shall never do anything to let them down or cause them to regret their vote of confidence.

"Hence I'm most grateful to *Saga* for this opportunity to tell what I would do with my life . . .

"Downstairs are two doors. One leads to the gas chamber; the other through the prison proper, to a future.

"Which door will open for me?

"After six and half years in Death Row, I'll soon know."
Caryl Chessman, 1954

He was not, however, soon to know which door he would take . . .

Nearly six years after the correspondence with Ed Fitzgerald, Caryl Chessman was still on Death Row.

We take up the case with Father Byron Eshelman who knew Chessman for 10 long years in San Quentin.

In his remarkable book, *"Death Row Chaplain,"* Byron Eshelman recalls:

In February, 1960, Caryl Chessman was again waiting to die. He had survived the judge who sentenced him and quite definitely was no longer alone.

From juke boxes across America, the mournful "Ballad of Caryl Chessman" was dirging: "Let him live, let him live . . ." An auto caravan from the University of California brought to Sacramento a petition signed by 384 distinguished members of the faculty urging Governor Edmund Brown to spare Chessman's life. There were hunger strikes, pickets, demonstrations all over the world. Petitions were circulating by car, foot, plane, and horseback. Governor Brown's office received more than one thousand letters a day, averaging three to two in favour of Chessman.

A motion picture, *Justice and Caryl Chessman,* was playing in movie houses from New York to Hong Kong. Belgium's Queen Mother phoned Governor Brown asking him to spare Chessman's life. So did the Social Democratic membership of Italy's Chamber of Deputies.

The Vatican newspaper, *L'Osservatore Romano,* urged clemency. In Brazil, a petition to save Chessman got 2,500,000 signatures. Ten hours before Chessman was to die, Governor Brown received word from the State Department. President Eisenhower was soon to visit Uruguay, and the government of Uruguay was seriously concerned about hostile demonstrations in the event that Chessman was executed. The governor granted Chessman a 60-day reprieve, and called a special session of the state legislature to consider his proposal to end capital punishment. The proposal failed, by one or two votes, to get out of committee.

What had happened in twelve years, in a death cell four and a half feet wide by ten and a half feet deep? Many things had happened. A noted legal expert said Chessman had become "one of the sharpest and best-trained lawyers I've ever met." Chessman himself told me he had read hundreds of legal books after coming to the Row. He became a student of philosophy, a linguist, a mathematician. But I know that all of these accomplishments were secondary, even to him. The real key to understanding Chessman, and his impact on the world, is the almost incredible clarity with which he came to understand himself, and others who were troubled.

No matter how you feel about Chessman, Eshelman tells us, you will find it difficult not to believe that the man society finally executed was a far cry from the petty hoodlum who first came to Death Row.

But, as the chaplain wrote, in spite of all the reports, letters, petitions and pleas, Caryl Chessman moved inexorably towards his final date with the gas chamber. The execution was set for Monday morning, May 2nd, 1960, at ten o'clock. He was to go down to the holding cell on Sunday afternoon. That day Chessman began writing to Mary Crawford, reporter for the San Francisco *News-Call Bulletin*:

"Dear Mary," Chessman began, "they say the child is father of the man. Tomorrow morning, barring last minute court action, I shall be executed. The physical man will die. What of the child?

"What sort of person was this lad who, figuratively, sired Caryl Chessman?

"Initially, in these last hours of life, I must tell you frankly that memories of my boyhood are often blurred. The images of the present and immediate future are sharper in my mind than are those of the dim past when I and the world each were younger ...

"Now, so far as I know, the man that boy became — after twelve years on Death Row — has no more birthdays to look forward to. With death so close, you have asked: 'What could have been done to reach the troubled, rebellious youngster that boy became, in the period between childhood and adulthood?'

"How could he have been changed from an angry, undisciplined young man, filled with mistrust of the world and even of himself, into a useful citizen?

"In larger context, where and how are we failing those we call juvenile delinquents?

"Almost certainly there is no easy answer, and it would be presumptuous if not ridiculous for me to suggest there is. Nevertheless, I feel a few reflections are in order.

"Since the death watch will be here in a very few more minutes, I'm obliged to postpone writing further until I am transferred downstairs."

(At this point, the letter changed from typing to longhand.)

"It is now past six a.m., less than four hours remain to me, and, after a busy night consulting with attorneys Rosalie, Asher and George Davis, and writing personal letters to my friends, I'll return to your questions.

"Let's start with what I'm convinced the answer is and is not. It is not, ethically, morally, legally or philos-ophically, a problem in seeking to coerce or compel passive obedience to authority on the part of young persons whose deeds we label criminal.

"Thus, I believe that so long as we seek a negative answer with punishment and the threat of punishment, deluding ourselves with the witless fiction that punishment *per se* is either a correction or a cure, we will continue to see the problem get worse.

"For the youthful offender can be likened to a kettle filled with water under which a fire has been lit.

"Steam begins to generate — and when we seek to solve by punishment in reality we do no more than attempt to hold back the potentially explosive pressure of the steam by plugging the spout and holding down the lid, meanwhile scolding the kettle and holding it responsible for this phenomenon.

"We leave the fire burning, and the pressure grows greater, until inevitably there is an explosion.

"These physical explosions we call crime, and when the explosions express themselves homicidally, we have our gas chambers ready.

"We say we 'punish' to protect ourselves, by example to deter others from repeating the proscribed act.

"We haven't learned yet that, while young human beings are not kettles, there are pressures inside them (conflicts, needs, anxieties, wants, hopes, dreams) which must and will find or force outlet.

"Repression externally applied only can result in these internal pressures increasing. Accordingly, it is more than futile and, in final analysis, more than absurd.

"It does not explain how or why the flame is ignited in the young person's mind and emotions and soul. It does not recognise — because of the logical fallacies we cling to about the efficacy of punishment and retribution — that, even once generated, these pressures can be given legitimate social outlet and, when this is done, that the results can be positive and socially useful.

"I think this letter is evidence of the social validity of my thesis.

"My background as a violent young psychopath (putting to one side my guilt or innocence of the Red Light Bandit crimes for which I wait to die) is well known.

"Punishment didn't control me; it didn't relieve the pressures.

"I might have spent this, my last night on earth, cursing my plight and society. I didn't.

"Instead, even though I realised no matter what I wrote or didn't write my fate would remain unchanged, I put these pressures, these tensions to work. They are producing this letter.

"They will permit me to walk into the gas chamber and, paradoxically, die calmly. For I have learned the hard, the lethal way to put them to work.

"I earnestly submit my society can learn to reach those

thousands of youngsters following in my footsteps to do the same in a much easier way, provided only if it is willing to call upon its reason and its humanity rather than its executioners and its desire to punish, punish, punish.

"I die with the hope that someday this will come to pass. I want to believe no man ever again will have to know the twelve-year hell I have now, since, especially, there is such a reasonable, rational and human alternative.

"Yet, as Voltaire said, 'the more ancient the abuse, the more sacred it is.'

"Sincerely, Caryl Chessman."

Eshelman recalls how Chessman's last days were hectic. There were almost constant interviews with reporters and attorneys. His publisher, Stuart Daniels, editor-in-chief of Prentice-Hall, came to see him.

The pressures on Chessman were enormous. He had to maintain his poise and his purpose under the glare of increasing public scrutiny. And he had to direct the delicate manoeuvrings in his fight to live.

On the final days before execution, Eshelman was with Chessman. He relates:

When I came to Death Row on that last Saturday afternoon, the TV set was already moved to the front of his cell, a grim reminder that his time was short. Chess-man was just being brought back from the associate warden's office, where he had participated in a group interview with a pool of reporters representing most of the world's major wire services, papers and magazines. He hadn't had time to eat, and now was carrying a tray of food to his cell. One of the officers on guard put the television set earphones on his tray. I had started talking with Louis Moya in the cell next to Chessman's, and continued doing so in order to give Chessman a chance to eat.

I didn't step over to Chessman's cell until he was sipping his coffee. He looked tired.

"How was the interview?" I asked.

"Rough," he sighed. "Those news conferences are always rough."

"What happened?"

"Everything went okay, I guess . . . but I've got to be so careful — for my own interests and for this whole cause of abolishing capital punishment . . ."

"Are you afraid of saying the wrong thing?"

"I wouldn't say anything I didn't believe, but it's more subtle than that. They're all looking for some little sign of weakness — and they're ready to pounce like a bunch of hounds."

"What's next?"

"My attorneys are putting an action into the courts this afternoon. They've got another for tomorrow, and one for Monday morning."

He took another sip of coffee and smiled faintly.

"Of course, the state also has an action for Monday morning — about 10.01 a.m."

Eshelman went on: He showed me the paperback edition of his latest novel, *The Kid Was a Killer*. He also had an attractive, multi-coloured dust jacket of a hard-back edition to be published in Italy.

"This has been a long time getting into print," he said. "I feel good to see it finally out."

For a few minutes he talked about the thin, tangled legal threads from which his existence hung. The State Supreme Court had been voting four to three against him. One member of the court had been expected to change the balance, but had not yet done so.

"I've still got a chance," he said thoughtfully, "but if the break does come, I'll have to sweat for it . . . It's a dead certainty I'll go downstairs again tomorrow."

As I left, he invited me to come down to see him.

The pressure was still on Sunday evening in the ready room. Chessman's attorneys, Rosalie Asher and George Davis, were there much of the time. Warden Dickson came by. So did the associate warden and an officer who had known Chessman years before on Death Row. When Chaplain George Tolson and I walked in, Father Ding-berg was already there. Chessman was stripped down to his white T-shirt and new blue denims. The small table in his cell was covered with stationery and a yellow legal pad.

"I don't expect anything more from the governor," he was saying, "except maybe a short delay to get additional writs to the federal courts."

He glanced up at the clock on the wall, and reminded his attorneys:

"I've still got to sign my will . . . I couldn't die without signing it, could I?"

He also noted that he had some letters to write, and should start them about midnight.

I left just before midnight. Chessman looked up from conferring with his lawyers and asked:

"I'll see you in the morning, Reverend?"

"I'll be here," I told him.

Chessman stayed up all night, writing.

The following are the notes made by Byron Eshelman of the events of May 2nd, 1960. The vivid and chilling account reads:

"I walked back to the gas chamber and went in about eight twenty a.m. Father Dingberg was talking with Chessman, standing at the bars of his cell. The officers were there. I said, 'Good morning — I guess it is still a good morning.' Chessman said, 'No good news, no especially bad news.' Then he added: 'All I can say is that this is a hell of a way to start a week!'

Father Eshelman recorded: "Chessman said he had heard the flash that the Supreme Court had gone in session about eight a.m. The radio was up, and we all waited. It was playing music; one song was 'Keep Your Sunny Side Up.' We switched stations, and the announcer said he would bring us the bulletin as soon as it came. Chessman started a last letter to his attorney, Rosalie Asher. He wrote on yellow, legal-sized paper. He crouched on the mattress or stood and bent over the metal folding shelf to write, using a pencil."

Eshelman recalls the drama in that cell as they waited for the news:

"The newscaster broke in and we all sucked in our breaths. The bulletin was that the Supreme Court had denied Caryl Chessman's petition. Further details later. This was at nine fourteen a.m. Chessman looked a long time at the clock. It's unfair they took so long,' he said. 'It's practically killed any chance to go further.' He looked at the clock again, and said, 'We'll have to face it. This is it.'

"At nine forty-five there were still no further details. Chessman said, 'Let's get packed and ready to go here.' He straightened up all the papers on his table, and told the guards, 'Well, let's get started with this white shirt routine.'

"He called Father Dingberg 'Father,' and me, 'Reverend.'

"'I appreciate knowing both of you,' he said. 'I feel a little foolish about not having a religious faith, and seeing things like you see them. In fact, I feel like a damn fool. I thought I might have a feeling now, but it's just not there. It went out of me years ago and just never came back. I don't feel I should pretend about it when it isn't there.'

"Father Dingberg said, 'Speaking for myself, I have always appreciated your straightforward attitude.'

"I told Chessman, 'Your life has left a tremendous impact on the world. Your books will be classics.'

"Chessman shook his head. 'In spite of being accused of such great ego,' he said, 'I don't believe my books will be classics, but I do hope they will have some effect on the whole problem of capital punishment.'

"Nothing was happening. Chessman paced around his cell. 'Sure I'm uneasy,' he said, 'but don't worry. I'll be able to hold up and go through with it . . . There's no use denying fear; it's just what you do with it — how you handle it — that counts.'

"He paced some more, then checked over his own body. 'I don't think I've lost any controls,' he told us. 'My ass isn't twitching either . . . I remember one guy who came down to wait. When he came back up, the boys asked him if his ass twitched. Hell, he said, it jumped clean out of the socket.'

"Warden Dickson came in at ten to ten. Chessman asked him if he knew anything more. The warden said he'd been on the phone, but couldn't find out any more than came over the radio. Chessman gave him all the letters and documents he had written. The warden promised to take care of them.

"Chessman said he knew the warden would be asked if there were any confessions at the last minute. 'I just want to keep the record straight,' he said. 'I am not the Red Light Bandit. I am not the man. I won't belabour the point; just let it stand at that.

"Chessman took off his shirt when the doctors came in. 'How are the adrenalins working?' a doctor asked him. Chessman said, 'I can't tell you just how they're working, Doc, but I know they're working.'

"Father Dingberg gave him a cigarette and lit it for him. Then he shook hands with him. I shook hands with him and said, 'I'm in your corner.' He said, 'Thanks.' I wanted to say 'God bless you,' but I knew he didn't want me to.

"They waited until about one minute after ten, and then the warden gave the signal. Chessman said, 'So long, Father . . . so long, Reverend.' He walked straight past us to the gas chamber and sat down in the chair. He looked completely composed, hair combed, white shirt collar open at the neck. He smiled at the warden, and said, 'I'm all right.' Then he turned and said the same thing through the window, so that someone out there would be reassured.

"Warden Dickson nodded for the pellets to be dropped. They were. Chessman seemed to flinch each time he took a breath. There was a whispering and commotion over where the warden stood. Later I heard this was the business of the phone message from Federal Judge Goodman who was trying to stop the execution for thirty minutes to give Chessman's attorneys time to make their appeal.

"Chessman's head was back. His mouth open and his eyes closed now. When I looked in again, his head was down and saliva was dripping from his mouth.

"The witnesses filed out into the sunlight. Father Dingberg and I stood a moment by the chamber. 'I didn't think it would ever happen,' I said. He said, 'The horrible thing is what does it prove after all?'

"A minister outside stopped us and asked if either chaplain had got Chessman into the faith. I just told him no. One reporter asked me, 'Were you in there?' I said, 'I'm not authorised to talk to the press.'

"I could have cried. I came as close to breaking down and crying as I ever had at an execution. Walking home alone, I cried to myself. I'm crying now . . ."

FOOTNOTE: Just moments after the cyanide pellets had been dropped, the telephone call came through with news of a last-minute reprieve. But Warden Dickson decided that it was too late to stop the execution. He was heavily criticised afterwards for not doing everything in his power to save Chessman.

He could have switched on the powerful blowers in the death chamber, drawing off the gas that had generated and was still forming. He could also have told the executioner to don a gasmask, cut the straps fastening Chessman to the chair and lead him to safety.

Watchers said Chessman had been holding his breath at the start of the execution. Will Stevens, a reporter, had prearranged a signal that the condemned man was to give if in agony. That signal came five minutes later.

So there is reason to suppose that Chessman could have been saved; and if so might well be alive today.

7

THE TRIGGER WOMAN

D. L. Champion

*"I don't like deputy sheriffs. They shouldn't be
allowed at large. Get in the car." Irene
Schroeder's response (with gun in hand) when
asked to produce her driving licence.*

Irene Schroeder married rather hastily when she was 16
years old. She spent the next five years in leisurely repent-
ance.

This was not really the fault of her husband, Don
Schroeder. He was a man possessed of an unusually high
percentage of husbandly virtues. He was a serious youth,
hard-working and ambitious. He had rented and furnished
a modern apartment in Wheeling, West Virginia, at the time
of his marriage. He toiled diligently to maintain it, and to
provide for his wife and his son Donnie, who was born in
1924.

In her day Irene was a pretty girl. Her hair was blonde,
her complexion was fair and her skin as soft as her heart and
mind were hard. She was vain and domineering, and as
strong-willed as reinforced concrete.

She was a girl with a thirst for excitement and a hunger
for what she called good times. But these things required
more money than her harassed husband was able to
produce. This led to arguments. It also led to Irene's
protracted absences from home, during which she sys-
tematically did some serious damage to the Seventh
Commandment.

While engaging in these activities, she met Glenn Dague.
He possessed a wife, two children and an unblemished

reputation. He was an insurance man, a Sunday school teacher and an active worker in the Boy Scout organisation.

Shortly after meeting Irene, Dague voluntarily exchanged all these virtuous assets for the passionate embraces of the blonde who one day was to accompany him to the death chamber.

Dague had fallen desperately in love with Irene Schroeder. Apparently she felt the same way about him. She divorced her husband and took a job as a waitress in a restaurant.

Dague didn't bother about the formalities of divorce. He simply left his wife and children to fend for themselves, then moved into a cheap hotel near the restaurant where Irene worked.

Within a week after this move Glenn Dague was dismissed from his Sunday school job and asked to resign from the Boy Scout organisation. Within the month the insurance firm for which he worked also decided that his services were not indispensable. He was sacked.

At this point in her life Irene was still unhappy and disappointed. She was no longer married. She was independent. She had found a lover. Yet her life remained almost as dull as it had been before.

Her own earnings as a waitress were meagre, and now Glenn was out of work. What Irene wanted above all else was to live high and expensively. She certainly couldn't do that just now. She considered the problem and came up with an answer which horrified Glenn Dague.

Clad in her best gown and wearing her most alluring perfume, she visited Dague's hotel room late one evening. "Honey," she said, "we're living like hillbillies. We were made for better things."

Dague agreed and put his finger on the crux of the matter. "We need money," he said. "But I can't think of any way to get it."

"I can," Irene said. "I've got it all worked out. We'll get a car. We'll travel all over the country, stopping at the best hotels, eating in the best restaurants. We don't want to stay here all our lives."

Dague agreed that this was a good idea. But, he pointed out, the problem was money.

Irene shook her head. "No," she said. "That's part of the plan. As we drive around we pick up what cash we need."

"Where?" Dague asked. "How?"

"Oh, service stations, stores, places like that. We just hold them up. It'll be easy."

Glenn had deserted his family, lost his job and dedicated himself to illicit love. But some of his conscience remained.

"We can't do that," he said. "First, it's wrong. Second, we'll get caught." He shook his head. "No, Irene, the first man we try to hold up is bound to call the police."

"Not if he's looking into the business end of a revolver," Irene declared.

Dague blinked. "You mean we're going to carry guns?"

Irene looked at her lover with some contempt. "Did you ever hear of a hold-up artist who didn't carry a gun? Do you think a guy will hand over his money because he likes our sweet little faces? Of course we'll carry guns. What's more, we'll use them if we have to."

Glenn stated firmly that he wanted no part of it. However, before long Irene's iron will and her complaisant body had changed his mind. Dague agreed to join his mistress in this new career.

Later that day Irene picked up another recruit. This was her brother Tom Crawford, who already had a minor criminal record.

In August, 1929, the three were ready for action. Irene bought a Buick, which she registered in the name of her father. Somehow she acquired three guns, and at the last minute she decided sentimentally that she could not embark on the trip without her five-year-old son Donnie.

She picked up Donnie at her father's home, where he had been staying, loaded him in the rear seat of the Buick with Tom Crawford, got into the front (where Glenn Dague sat at the wheel) and they set out.

They travelled first into Ohio and pulled their first job on September 1st, holding up the Meadowlark Inn on the outskirts of Cadiz. The whole affair was unbelievably simple.

Tom Crawford remained in the car with young Donnie while Irene and Glenn advanced upon the inn's proprietor, W. A. Willett. Each carried a gun. It was Irene who took the cash from Willett's pocket and relieved the cash register of its burden. The getaway was clean and fast.

The trio celebrated for three days, then headed back to West Virginia. Late on the afternoon of September 5th the Buick rolled down the Waynesburg turnpike and through the town of Moundsville, stopping eventually at Jack Cotts's lunch-room and filling-station some four miles from town.

Here they all bought pop and ice cream cones while they cased the place. Then they drove off, to return at midnight when, under cover of darkness, their business was efficiently transacted.

Jack Cotts stared at the two menacing gun barrels and hastily co-operated. He handed them $30 from his own wallet and watched helplessly as they took $40 more from the cash register. The Buick was 30 miles away before the sheriff arrived in response to his call.

Glenn Dague was now prepared to admit that Irene Schroeder had been absolutely right. Their venture thus far had been easy, and no more risky than selling insurance.

A week later Irene looked up from the newspaper she was reading and laughed. Her brother and Dague looked at her. "What's so funny?"

"I told you this'd be a cinch," she said. "Not only are we clean, but the sheriff's picked up a guy and his wife for that Moundsville job we pulled. No one even suspects us. We should've been in this business a long time ago. We've been wasting our time."

They wasted no more time during that autumn of 1929. The black Buick, carrying three criminals and an innocent boy, raced through West Virginia, Ohio and Pennsylvania. In a score of places their drawn guns magically opened wallets and cash registers. Miraculously, they escaped each time, evading all road-blocks, all police nets.

On Friday, December 27th, Irene Schroeder's mob engaged in its most ambitious exploit. The black Buick pulled up before Kroger's grocery store in Butler, Pennsylvania. They left the engine running and little Donnie in the back seat as they entered and cowed the employees and customers with three revolvers.

Within five minutes the register was empty and the Buick was speeding down the road towards New Castle. By that time the store manager was talking to the state police on the phone.

Only a week before, Governor John Fisher and Major Lynn Adams, head of the state constabulary, had inaugurated a police teletype system which connected 95 cities and towns throughout the state of Pennsylvania. Now this system had its first real test. The results were notable.

Lawrence County officials, among others, were notified that a black car containing a woman and two men was heading for New Castle. Two highway patrolmen, Corporal Brady Paul and Private Ernest Moore, were despatched to Highway 422 to watch for the fugitive car.

A few minutes later a saloon which seemed to answer the teletyped description roared down the road. Moore turned the police car around, blocking the highway. The car, a Buick, halted. Corporal Paul stepped out of the police car and approached the other vehicle. As he did so he saw a woman and a child in the back seat.

"This can't be the bandits," he said over his shoulder to Moore. "There's a kid in the car."

Paul approached the man at the wheel and asked to see his licence.

"Sure," said Tom Crawford. He opened the door, got out on the road and fumbled in his hip pocket as if seeking his wallet. He did not produce it. He produced a revolver instead.

Paul had no chance to reach for his own weapon. He yelled to Moore: "Get your gun out! I'm covered! I—"

He never finished that sentence. For Irene Schroeder leaned out of the rear window of the Buick. She fired twice at Paul. As he fell to the road she calmly transferred her aim to Moore. She fired two shots in his direction.

"All right, Tom," she said. "Let's get out of here. And we'd better get another car. This one's hot."

"Where," Glenn asked, "can we get another car?"

"Don't be a fool," she retorted. "With a gun you can get anything."

As they raced down the road, Dague peered out of the rear window at the huddled figures in the road behind them. He closed his eyes and shuddered. Maybe this wasn't such an easy living after all.

But again Irene was to prove her point: "With a gun you can get anything." Speeding out of the town, they overtook a car driven by Ray Horton of New Castle. On orders from Irene, the Buick passed the Horton car. Then, with a sudden swerve to the right, it blocked the road completely. Horton stamped on his brake to avoid crashing into the Buick.

At the same time a young blonde alighted from the Buick. "Get out of that car, and make it quick!" she ordered the startled Horton. There was a gun in her hand — and Horton did as he was told.

"Come on, boys," the blonde ordered. "Let's go."

Dague, carrying Donnie, leaped into the Horton car followed by Irene, who still held her gun on Horton. Tom Crawford drove the Buick ahead for a short distance then ditched it in a patch of woods alongside the road. He rejoined the others and they headed west in Horton's car. Horton headed back towards town on foot.

Back on Highway 422, Private Ernest Moore, unconscious from a bullet that had grazed his skull, was conveyed to hospital. Corporal Paul was not so lucky. He had died instantly.

Police of Pennsylvania, Ohio and West Virginia were mobilised to search for the killers. Scores of road-blocks were set up, but somehow the murdering trio eluded the law.

Newspapers carried the story in large type. One reporter

christened the killer of Corporal Paul the "Trigger Woman." The name stuck.

The abandoned Buick was found by the Pennsylvania state police and the licence was traced to Henry Crawford from the town of Wheeling, West Virginia. In the car were a suit of child's clothing and a woman's red scarf. Private Moore, questioned at the hospital, said that the woman who shot Corporal Paul had worn such a scarf.

Captain Jacob Mauk, in charge of the investigation, journeyed to Wheeling. He was accompanied by Private Moore, who had recovered enough to make the trip and was eager to do his part in capturing Corporal Paul's murderer.

The officers drove to the isolated country home of Henry Crawford. Crawford admitted them with obvious apprehension when they displayed their credentials. Aware of the character and careers of his son and daughter, he must have anticipated eventual disaster.

In answer to the officers' questions Mr. Crawford said that Irene had been there the day before accompanied by her brother and Glenn Dague. She had left the child with him and had gone off with the two men. Her father had no idea as to their destination or their whereabouts.

Moore was staring at a small boy playing with his toys on the living-room floor. "Captain," he said to Mauk, "that's the kid who was in the car with the woman who shot Corporal Paul."

Mauk obtained from Mr. Crawford a photograph of Irene. This was copied and distributed to newspapers all over the country. Now that they knew the identities of the trio they sought they hoped to trace them quickly.

West Virginia officers kept a guard at the Crawford home, believing that the Trigger Woman would steal back to visit her son. She did not do so. Two weeks passed, and none of the officers searching for the fugitives came upon any clue to their whereabouts.

The first officer to lay eyes upon the Trigger Woman was Deputy Joseph Chapman of Pinal County, Arizona. A few hours later he was to wish that he hadn't done so.

On January 13th, 1930, Deputy Chapman stood on a street corner in the town of Florence. He observed a car pull up at a refreshment stand opposite him and noted a striking blonde at the wheel and two men seated beside her.

Chapman recalled the report on the Trigger Woman and her companions. Certainly one of the men in this car resembled Glenn Dague. The blonde at the wheel could be Irene Schroeder. However, the other man obviously did not answer to Tom Crawford's description.

Chapman decided to investigate anyway. He crossed the street and said to the blonde: "May I see your driving licence?"

The woman regarded him with open hostility.

"Who the hell are you?" she demanded.

"A deputy sheriff," Chapman told her.

"Oh, that's different. Just a minute." She opened her handbag and fumbled in it. She did not, however, produce a driving licence. She produced a .38-calibre revolver instead. She thrust its muzzle into Chapman's chest and said: "I don't like deputy sheriffs. They shouldn't be allowed at large. Get in the car."

As she spoke her companions also drew guns, which they trained on Chapman. Reluctantly, he got into the back seat of the car. Irene Schroeder stepped on the accelerator and the car roared westwards towards the Maricopa County border.

The abduction had been enacted before half a dozen eye-witnesses on the street. The local police were promptly notified and a telephone call was put through to the office of Sheriff Charles Wright in the town of Chandler in Maricopa County.

The sheriff detailed deputies Lee Wright, Shirley Butterfield and Joseph Smith to institute a road-block half a mile east of Chandler. Deputy Wright was the second officer to gaze upon the comely features of Irene Schroeder. He lived long enough to regret it. He didn't live much longer.

The deputies spotted the car at a mile distance and Lee Wright signalled it to stop. It bore down on the officers, weaving crazily from one side of the road to the other. Suddenly, there was a burst of revolver fire. Butterfield staggered, wounded in the leg. Lee Wright's gun fell from his hand as three bullets smashed the bones of his arm.

The abducted officer, Joseph Chapman, was hurled forcibly from the car. Glenn Dague shattered Chapman's elbow with a bullet as he hit the road. The car then roared on into Chandler, leaving three wounded men in its wake.

Chapman, it developed, had been right on one point. The Trigger Woman and Glenn Dague had been in the car, but the third occupant was not Tom Crawford. From the conversation in the car, Chapman gathered that Crawford had deserted a week before to strike out on his own. The new recruit had been picked up along the road in New Mexico.

Sheriff Charles Wright, with two of his best deputies injured, hurriedly organised a posse. Within the hour, more than 100 armed men had volunteered. On this occasion the trail of the Trigger Woman proved relatively easy to follow.

The fleeing car had broken down after travelling some 40 miles in the barren desert near the settlement of Laveen, directly south of Phoenix, Arizona.

On an Indian reservation nearby a gentleman named Lone Sun Dust had rented three horses to Irene Schroeder and her friends. They had paid cash in advance, left a handsome deposit and headed towards the Gila River.

An aeroplane which accompanied the posse soon spotted the trio barricaded in the lonely granite peaks of the Salt River Mountains, and pinpointed the hideout for the posse.

Sheriff Wright headed greatly superior forces, but he had no desire to suffer any more casualties. He split his posse in two. The main section advanced on the mountain hideout from the front. The rest deployed to the flank and climbed the peak from the rear.

The two groups toiled up the lonely crags of the mountains, guns ready for the inevitable battle. The rear group was able to make better time. Reaching a point a little above the lair where the fugitives were hiding, they let themselves down, hand over hand, to a point where they could rush the trio.

At that moment, however, the Trigger Woman spotted the advance of the front group, now scarcely 200 yards away. "Shoot the dogs, sweetheart!" her voice shrilled. "Let 'em have it, Red! Don't let 'em get us alive." A barrage of bullets punctuated her words.

Rifles from the posse in front answered in unison. But before the fugitives could fire again, a sound behind them made them turn. They saw themselves covered by the guns of the rear-guard.

The battle of the crags was over.

Waving a handkerchief, Irene stepped forward and surrendered to Sheriff Wright. Deputies hastily manacled the two men.

Irene's clothes were in tatters, her hands torn and bleeding from the sagebrush and mountain crags. Her shoes were ribbons of leather, her feet scratched and blistered, but there was still defiance in her face.

"Well, boy friends," she jeered at the posse, "you want me. Here I am — the nation's girl friend — the one they've been looking for. Here I am."

The two men had nothing to say. They spoke no words either as they were returned to Chandler.

Irene, however, had something on her mind. "Sheriff," she said during the drive back to Chandler, "I want you to do something for me." And now her voice was strangely soft. "I want you to wire home for me," she said. "I must know how little Donnie is. I love him." She added in a low voice: "He's all I have in the world — except Glenn."

A fingerprint check revealed the identity of the Trigger Woman's recruit. He was Tom "Red" Wells, recently released from a New Mexico prison, where he had served a term for armed robbery. Wells was charged with the shooting of Deputies Chapman, Butterfield and Lee Wright.

Irene and Dague were held to await the arrival of the Pennsylvania authorities and extradition.

At the time of the arrest Dague evinced some bitterness towards his mistress. "She caused all this trouble," he said. "And now I'm done with her."

But when he saw her again at the arraignment he had changed his mind. A female admirer of Irene in Phoenix had sent her a complete new outfit with which to face the judge. Clad in her new clothes, she entered the courtroom through a gauntlet of curious spectators.

The Trigger Woman scowled at them. "I ought," she said, "to charge all these people fifty cents a look."

But Dague, who 24 hours before had foresworn his love, saw her, smiled and said: "Hello, honey."

Irene Schroeder flashed him a tender smile. She noticed that he was unshaven and that he wore leg irons. She turned indignantly to the sheriff and demanded: "Why don't you let him shave? Why do you make him wear those irons? Do you think he'll run away?"

She threw her arms about Dague's neck and kissed him. Then she took a handkerchief from her pocket and carefully wiped the lipstick from his face. Then to everyone's amazement she denied that she was Irene Schroeder — a fact which both she and Dague had admitted before — and insisted that she was a a respectable woman whose name was Mildred Winthrop.

On January 24th the Pennsylvania officers who were to escort Irene and Dague back to New Castle arrived. In this party was Private Ernest Moore. He needed only a single look to identify Irene Schroeder positively as the woman who had wounded him and murdered Corporal Brady Paul.

"He's a liar!" Irene yelled. "I've never seen him before. Take him away!"

But during her trip across the country by train she not only admitted her identity, but gloried in it. It was in the nature of a triumphal tour. Huge crowds gathered as she passed through the intermediate stations. Irene waved to them regally and issued autographs which read: "Irene Schroeder, Trigger Woman."

As the train pulled into New Castle, Glenn Dague and Irene Schroeder kissed and vowed to love each other until the day they died. That day wasn't too far distant.

Shortly after Dague and Irene were lodged in the Lawrence County jail, Deputy Lee Wright died in Arizona of a gangrene infection from his bullet wounds. Tom Wells was promptly charged with murder. He was tried within the week, found guilty and sentenced to be hanged.

Sheriff Charles Wright announced that if Dague and Irene escaped with short sentences in Pennsylvania he would demand their return to Arizona to answer for Lee Wright's murder. However, it developed that his fears were unwarranted.

Irene Schroeder was brought to trial during the first week in March. Up to that time no woman had ever been executed in Pennsylvania. That tradition was seriously threatened when the foreman of the jury read the verdict: "Guilty of murder in the first degree, with the death penalty."

Irene Schroeder took the verdict with no more emotion than a block of granite. Her three sisters, who attended the trial, wept copiously.

Irene chided them. "Shut up, you sissies," she said. "I can take it."

Her cell was directly above that of Glenn Dague. She told him the news when she returned from the courtroom.

"I'm sorry," he said. "How do you feel?"

"I feel fine," she said. "They can't scare me." She added, laughing, "Come on up and see me some time."

Two days later Glenn Dague confronted another jury on the same charge as had been laid against his mistress. Though the jury was different the verdict was the same. Dague was found guilty of first-degree murder and sentenced to death in the electric chair.

The two killers were transferred from the jail at New Castle to Rockview Penitentiary, 180 miles away. They travelled together, holding hands in the car, murmuring words of love, exchanging kisses and still held by the bonds of their passion and their crimes.

At the death house a partition was erected at the end farthest from the death chamber to provide quarters for Irene. No woman had ever been incarcerated there before. A door in the partition led to the forward part, where Glenn Dague's cell was. In the death chamber itself a telephone was set up with a direct line to the state house in Harrisburg in case of a last-minute reprieve by the governor.

"If I do go to the hot seat," Irene said as they parted, "Glenn will want to go too. We will love each other always to the end."

The date of their execution had been set for February 23rd, 1931. The hour was 7 o'clock. There was no word from the governor to stay them from the last mile. Although justice is frequently tempered with mercy for a woman doomed to die, in the case of Irene Schroeder there was no executive clemency.

Directly or indirectly, the Trigger Woman was already responsible for three deaths. Lee Wright and Corporal Paul she had shot down with her own hand. Tom Wells had been hanged shortly after he had allied himself with her. Glenn Dague would be the fourth to die because of Irene Schroeder.

Officially, Tom Crawford was never found. Texas authorities, however, announced that a man answering his description had been killed during a one-man bank hold-up, although the identification was not positive.

The grey day dawned. At 5.30 the prisoners were awakened. Dague refused breakfast, but Irene ate grapefruit, toast and coffee. She inquired anxiously if Glenn seemed worried. She was told that he was calm, and that she would precede him to the chair. This meant that she would pass the cell where her lover awaited his final summons.

At 7 o'clock the death march began. Irene wore a dress of grey rayon with white collar and cuffs. Her stockings were beige silk, one of them rolled down to the ankle. At the back of her head was a bare spot where the hair had been shaved.

She was accompanied by a white-clad nurse and by two ministers. One of these was the prison chaplain, the Rev. C. F. Lauer. The other was the Rev. Harold Teagarden, pastor of the church in which Glenn Dague had once been an active worker. The voices of the two men mingled as they recited the 23rd Psalm.

A screen had been placed in front of the cell where Glenn waited so that the lovers might be spared the last painful glimpse of each other. As they neared the screen, Irene turned to the Rev. Teagarden. "Please stay with Glenn," she said. "He will need you now more than I do." The minister left the little procession to remain with Dague.

There were tears in the eyes of the nurse as they entered the death chamber, where the chair awaited its first woman occupant. There were no tears in the eyes of Irene Schroeder. She looked straight ahead as she seated herself, unaided, in the chair. She was young — she had become 22 only a few days before — but with death only a few seconds away her steely courage did not fail her. Although the prison chaplain stood close beside her as the straps and the mask were adjusted, she spoke no word.

The chaplain stepped back. The switch was thrown, and at 7.10 a.m. Irene Schroeder was pronounced dead.

As her body was lifted from the chair, placed on a stretcher and rolled into the autopsy room, the sound of voices chanting a prayer was heard outside the death chamber. Glenn Dague had begun his last mile.

Accompanied by the chaplain and the Rev. Teagarden, Dague entered the death chamber. Quickly, he seated himself in the chair. He closed his eyes as the straps and electrodes were adjusted.

A short time later two bodies lay side by side in the autopsy room. Glenn Dague, who had left home and family and an honourable profession to follow his sweetheart, had followed her once again — involuntarily, and for the last time.

8

THE COUNT OF GRAMERCY PARK

Edward DeBlasio

"Death itself isn't dreadful, but hanging seems an awkward way of ending the adventure." Gerald Chapman's remark to his lawyers, after sentence had been pronounced.

Let's call him Gerald Chapman, because that's the name history remembers him by. His real name was probably George Chartres, but nobody knows for sure. We'll call him Gerald Chapman and forget Chartres and the other names he called himself at one time or another, the names of the man who became America's first Public Enemy No. 1.

Chapman had one real love, and that was money. He loved to steal it and to spend it. He was born into a family which barely knew what the stuff looked like on Manhattan's lower East Side in 1892 or 1893, it's believed; *believed,* because in later years Chapman never talked about things like birth and family, whether through boredom, embarrassment or bitterness. Mr. Nobody from Nowhere later made up for those early years of poverty by living a life of which even the proverbial Reilly would have been jealous. It was, to be sure, a short life, but it had its moments.

The first of these was undoubtedly on the day in January, 1921, when Chapman walked into a rental agency in downtown Manhattan and told the man that his name was G. Vincent Colwell and that he'd come to inquire about an apartment.

It's certain that within a few minutes the rental agent was a much-impressed man. Chapman was rather impressive-looking. One description of him reads: "Standing about five feet eight inches and weighing ten stone, Chapman looks the part of 'The Professor' or 'The Count,' as he has been nicknamed. His features are thin, with high cheek-bones, and when he speaks he reveals a voice that is a joy to listen to. It is low-pitched and soft and he knows how to use it."

As soon as they were seated Chapman told the agent who he was — an oil man from the Middle West with a gushing desire to retire and settle in New York.

The agent lost no time signing up "Mr. Colwell." The next day Chapman moved into a large apartment at 12 Gramercy Park — then one of the better addresses in town. Moving in with him was his wife, young Betty, and his old friend and business partner George Brown.

For the record, however, Betty was really Chapman's naive mistress and George Brown was George "Dutch" Anderson, a convict friend he had known for years.

As the female of this trio, Betty should get a lot more attention than she's going to. But unfortunately there's very little known about her other than the fact that she came originally from Indiana and didn't know, or suspect, for a very long time that Chapman knew a lot more about hot water than he did about oil. It has never been made clear where she met Chapman, but wherever it was, the earth must have stood still for at least a full minute.

Dutch Anderson's first meeting with Chapman had a touch of the time-stood-still quality about it too. The two men had met in 1912 in a cell in Sing Sing. Anderson, in his late 30s at the time, was in for assault and robbery. Chapman, just turned 20, had been jailed for a 10-to-15 year sentence on the same charge.

The two men hit it off immediately. Chapman liked Anderson because the stocky older man (who taught Spanish in the prison's school) had a certain polished air about him; and Anderson liked Chapman because the young, skinny kid had a certain promising air.

Things went along beautifully and it was just like school for the two men. Anderson became the teacher and Chapman the pupil; Chapman following his maestro through the seven cell-blocks of learning in a course they hoped would pay off in easy living later on.

Chapman learned a lot from Anderson. It took him ages, but after a while it became clear that Anderson was succeeding in instilling in him some of the techniques which he himself had picked up over the years — although "picked up" is really not a fair way of putting it. Anderson was a genuinely intelligent man and had a sound knowledge of poetry, music, languages and, just as important to his purposes, disguises.

When, on March 20th, 1919, Chapman was released with a few years off for good behaviour, he was a far cry from the East Side kid who'd stopped going to school when he was eight and who'd gone straight to the poolrooms and into trouble.

His early record shows that he was the simultaneous head of two gangs, the West Side Mob and the Park Avenue Gang, by the time he was 15 and that he was picked up by the police and sent away at least three times by the time he was 18. Now, as he sat on the train that was taking him back to New York, he could think about nothing but the culture he'd picked up and about how he was going to get that knowledge to pay off.

Two months later Dutch Anderson was paroled and joined Chapman in New York. They took a room in a small downtown hotel and for days they planned and talked. Chapman undoubtedly made most of the plans and did most of the talking, because it was at this point that it became clear to both men that one of them would have to take over and that Chapman was the man for the job.

From May of that year to January, 1921, the two men spent most of their time in the Midwest mainly committing minor jobs here and there, picking up ready cash. Then they met somebody who introduced them to bootlegging — Prohibition was going strong — and things started picking up.

By January, 1921, things had picked up so well that they decided to return to New York. Between the two of them they had $200,000. They also had a yearning for some high living. And Betty, the brunette from Indiana whom Chapman had conquered by this time, didn't have any objection to either the money or the high living.

After Chapman had signed the lease for the Gramercy Park apartment he went out shopping for cars. He bought three — a Pierce-Arrow and two Packards — for $35,000.

The next item they required was a chauffeur. This, considering the plans the men had in mind, was a problem. It was solved easily, however, when Chapman, out walking one day, met a good friend of both his and Anderson's, a man named Charles Loerber. Loerber had been in prison with them, had just been paroled and was looking for something to do. Chapman asked him if he'd like to chauffeur for him, and half an hour later Loerber was being fitted for his uniform.

This, to repeat, was in January, 1921. From the middle of that month up until October 4th — the date of what has been called the Great Post Office Robbery — all parties concerned, Chapman especially, concentrated on having one hell of a good time.

For a while Chapman loved the lifestyle and the attention it brought him, but he realised that he was beginning to be seen around too much and that the business of being seen, while it was fun, might not turn out to be so good later on. So he changed his tactics — even buying a pair of glasses in an effort to change his appearance — and concentrated on that area of New York known as Greenwich Village, and on a restaurant in the village called Bertolotti's.

After a while Chapman and Betty dined at Bertolotti's as often as six nights a week. The routine, those who recall it have said, was most impressive. Chapman and Betty, dressed to the nines and reeking of expensive perfumes, would be driven to the restaurant in one of their cars by Charlie Loerber, ex-convict and chauffeur.

However, on October 1st Chapman sent Betty back to Indiana to visit her family for a few weeks. "I've got work to do," he said, and that was that.

Three nights later he went to work — he, Anderson and Loerber. Their job was to rob a United States Post Office truck. It was a success, a job well done. With the help of masks, a Studebaker car they'd stolen and a tip-off from a platform worker at the old City Hall Post Office, they held up a truck carrying more than $1,000,000 worth of cash and securities.

By midnight they were out of the city and on their way to a place on Long Island where they had rented a house for a month. They stayed there, hiding, eating, sleeping and counting and re-counting the money. They split something like $450,000 in cash three ways, with Chapman and Anderson getting a little more than Loerber. On the night of October 28th, they drove back to the city, dumped the stolen car in the Bronx and returned to 12 Gramercy Park — three criminals transformed into the oilman, his partner and their chauffeur.

On November 4th, Betty returned from Indiana. She asked Chapman how the business venture he'd talked about had gone while she was away, and he said that it had gone just fine. Then he told her they were going to celebrate by sailing for Europe the coming Saturday.

The trip was wonderful. Or at least Betty thought so. For Chapman it was a failure because he had gone abroad primarily to try to cash some of the hot securities from the post office robbery into cold cash, and he'd discovered that it wasn't as easy as he thought it would be.

So after less than a month he and Betty caught a ship back to the United States. They arrived in New York on December 22nd, and on the 23rd Chapman told Betty that she was going back to Indiana for the Christmas holidays. Betty objected a little, but Chapman said that another business matter had come up. That night she was on a train headed West.

An hour later Chapman and Anderson were on a train too, this one headed north. They travelled as far as Buffalo, and for the next few weeks they did nothing but pull off one robbery after another. They robbed five banks and a few big stores and made quite a tidy profit. Then, just before returning home, they decided to vary things a little and try their luck with the American Express company. They held up an American Express truck and found their luck was still with them. They got $70,000 in cash.

Chapman was all smiles at Bertolotti's restaurant the following night. A few weeks later, however, a private detective working for American Express traced Chapman and Anderson to New York and they were arrested.

It was while detectives were questioning the pair that the realisation dawned on them that these men were two of the three who had pulled off the post office job back in October.

The questioning went along very stuffily for the first 20 minutes or so. They sat in a large third-floor room — Chapman, Anderson, two detectives and three or four federal men. Anderson refused to say anything in answer to the questions, and Chapman wasn't much more helpful.

Chapman wasn't quite as grim-faced as his friend, but he did two things which annoyed his questioners very much: he insisted that he knew nothing about the post office robbery and he insisted on sitting back in his chair and constantly shifting his eyes around the room, looking up at the ceiling, then down at the floor, to a picture on the wall to his left, and over to his right at a large open window.

He was in the middle of a yawn when suddenly he shot up from his chair, said, "Sorry, gentlemen," made a swift turn, dashed towards the window, stepped on the sill and disappeared.

"He jumped!" somebody yelled, and with that everybody in the room — except Anderson and a detective who drew his gun and aimed it at Dutch's head — rushed to the window. They looked way out, over the edge of a yard-wide ledge, and then they looked down to the pavement 75 feet below. There was no Chapman lying there, sprawled out, bloody and dead. There was nothing but people walking by as if nothing had happened.

Then one of the detectives saw a woman standing in the window of an office building across the street. She was pointing to the right. The detective understood. He turned around and ran out into the corridor. He drew his gun, and one by one he opened the doors of every office along the corridor with windows facing Thirty-third Street. In the fourth office he found Chapman, who had dashed along the wide ledge running around the building and jumped into the first office with an open window he came to.

Within seconds there was more than one revolver staring Chapman in the face — and he gave up without a word. In fact, he went through most of the trial which followed without saying much. Both he and Anderson refused to confess to the post office or the American Express robberies, even though the evidence against them was overwhelming. On August 23rd, 1922, a jury found them both guilty and sentenced them to 25 years in the federal penitentiary at Atlanta, Georgia.

Chapman did express himself to at least one person during his trial. One of his lawyers, a woman named Grace Crampton, reported later that "Chapman's philosophy of life excused his crimes. He told me that he did not believe it as sinful to hold up a mail truck or rob a store as it was to speculate on Wall Street and probably steal money from widows and orphans and poorly paid teachers. 'At least we do not take money from poor people,' he said. 'What we steal hurts nobody. Everything that is sent by mail or express is fully insured and in the end the sender loses nothing. The man who comes out the winner on Wall Street is respected, and he is envied for his yachts and cars and homes, while we are hunted and despised. I think I am the more honourable of the two.' "

For Chapman it was now goodbye to Bertolotti's and to Broadway and to Betty — who finally realised what kind of business her boy friend had been engaged in. She went out of circulation, for a time at least.

Of course, Chapman had no intention of staying behind bars for anything like a quarter of a century. But he knew that it would take sound planning to break out of the prison, and he knew that the planning might take a long time.

In fact it took exactly seven months and four days: on March 27th, 1923, Chapman escaped from Atlanta.

At 4 o'clock that morning Chapman and a prisoner named Frank Gray, a forger, lay in the penitentiary's hospital ward. They had pretended to be sick to get into the ward. Now they pretended to be asleep.

At 4.05 a guard walked past Chapman's bed. Chapman sprang up, grabbed the man, and threw a towel over his face before he had a chance to cry out. Then he and Gray tied the squirming guard up with a cord and pushed him under one of the beds. From then on it was like clockwork.

Chapman lifted his mattress a few inches and pulled out a length of pipe about three feet long. He used the pipe to bend back a window bar which had already been half sawn through. He and Gray squeezed through the tiny opening and made their way down the outside wall, using that time-tested prop of cartoon characters, movie stars and, in some cases, real-life escapees — knotted sheets.

Down in the prison yard they got down on their knees and crawled through the shadows to a tree some 20 yards away. Chapman waited a minute. He could see the silhouettes of guards standing high in the turrets of the wall he was getting ready to climb. That was the trouble: he could see them, and they — even if they didn't try very hard — would be able to see him.

However, he had anticipated that. Chapman removed a rubber-handled knife from his waistband and sprinted to the tree. Somehow, probably by bribing one of the guards, he had learned that the wires which supplied the current to the prison yard's powerful lamps ran right past that tree.

Chapman pared several inches of insulation from the wires and, reaching into his waist again, pulled out a length of copper wire which he draped across the stripped lines.

The result was spectacular. First there was a brilliant flash of sparks and then every light in the prison yard went out.

Chapman and Gray made it over the wall a few minutes later. They were free men for little more than 48 hours.

Early on the third day they were tracked down by a posse of 200 men not far from Atlanta.

Gray gave up an instant after a bullet from one of the possemen's rifles whizzed over his head. Chapman had to be shot down, however. He was rushed back to the penitentiary from which he'd escaped, on a stretcher, with bullets in his arm, hip and back. The last bullet had gone through his kidney, and for a while it looked as if he'd had it.

Then, on April 4th, six days later, Chapman escaped again, and if anybody had had it, it was the officials of Atlanta penitentiary.

Although his body was bullet-riddled his brain was operating as soundly as ever. At 10.30 that night Chapman's nurse took his temperature. It was 102. "You'd probably like to sleep now," she remarked. "I would," Chapman answered.

The nurse thought for a minute. One of three around the-clock guards assigned to Chapman's private room was gone. She could wait for the guard to return, or she could turn out the light and get on with her own work. She decided to turn out the light. It was later estimated that the period of time from the nurse's departure until the guard's return was 22 minutes. At any rate, when the guard opened the door, Gerald Chapman was gone.

The prison was in a noisy panic for the next few hours. Then things calmed down to a period of silent panic, a panic that would remain until Chapman was found and this time tied to his bed.

A cutting from the *New York Herald-Tribune* of April 6th says that "officers believe Chapman is weak physically and is wandering or hiding in the hospital somewhere."

The officers were right. Chapman was *inside* the hospital. A nurse heard someone moving about in the basement at about 3 o'clock on the morning of the sixth. She didn't know it was Chapman at the time, but she'd heard a noise and she called a guard named Bishop to investigate.

Bishop looked around for a few minutes and then the nurse pointed to the door leading to the storage room. The guard opened the door. The nurse was right behind him and they both saw the man at the same time, in the shadows, lying on the floor, holding his side, groaning.

The guard reached for his gun. "Who are you?" he asked. "What are you doing here?" The man held up his hand. "Don't you know me, Mr. Bishop?" he asked. "Why, it's Chapman," the guard said. And with that the nurse, who was standing alongside him, let out a terrific scream and grabbed the guard's arm, the one holding the gun. "Don't let him get me," she yelled.

The guard must have been a pathetic figure at this point because even Chapman, it appears, felt sorry for him. Chapman, as legend has it, got up off the floor, approached the couple and said to the guard, "Come on, I'll help you take her upstairs."

The guard was stunned, the nurse was scared to death. She screamed again, even louder than before, and the guard turned around completely this time and tried to calm her. By the time he had calmed her sufficiently and had turned around again, Chapman had gone.

He got clean away this time — his second escape in a little over a week — and for days every newspaper in the country gave him more space than President Harding and Rudolph Valentino combined. Everybody knew about the man and his nerve and he gave the American public one of the biggest emotional kicks it had ever had.

On April 7th the *New York Times* ran an editorial titled *Something Almost Heroical*. It was most amazing for the *Times*, and it read:

"It is getting to be rather difficult to keep in mind the fact that Gerald Chapman is a thoroughly bad man, whose right place is in jail. The difficulty arises from the fact that in his battle with the law he shows qualities — courage, persistence, ingenuity and skill — which it is impossible not to admire.

"The result is that unless one is careful one finds one-self hoping that he isn't caught, and, so great are the odds against him, that the struggle seems somehow unfair.

"The temptation is strong to lament that such a man should make of his abilities and peculiarities such miserable employment as devoting them to theft. There must be some explanation of that, however, and the probability is that he is defective. But it does seem hard that his punishment for his crimes should be increased because of his attempts to evade it. That he hates imprisonment is only human, and that he takes desperate risks in his efforts to get out is rather to his credit than his discredit — from every standpoint except the safety of society."

George "Dutch" Anderson, meanwhile, lost little time following his friend out of Atlanta. On June 23rd of that year he got out too, without benefit of a parole board or the warden's permission. He was never quite the colourful figure that Chapman was, and the newspapers turned the escape into another excuse to fill their columns with a recapitulation of Chapman's career.

Gradually, however, the name Gerald Chapman started to lose some of its magic — although police throughout the country began to blame every unsolved crime in their books on him.

For over a year Chapman stayed out of the limelight. Then, on October 12th, 1924, in New Britain, Connecticut, Gerald Chapman became front-page news again. The big word in the headlines this time was murder.

At 7.30 a.m. that day two men held up the Davidson & Leventhal department store on New Britain's Main Street. A phone call sent five policemen hurrying to the building. One of the policemen — James Skelly, 56 years old, the father of three children and in the force for 22 years — was shot and killed by one of the bandits. This gunman then fled the store by way of the front door and escaped down an adjacent alley. The second bandit was caught after he'd fled through a back door and had run down an alley towards a car.

His name was Walter J. Shean. From Springfield, Massachusetts, he was head of the Shean Advertising Agency in that city, and was the black-sheep son of a wealthy hotel-owner. He was taken to police headquarters and asked to name his accomplice. He refused at first. Then he was told that he was the one who'd be charged with murder if he didn't talk.

"All right," he finally said. "I know my companion as Waldo Miller. But it's my opinion that he's really Gerald Chapman."

Three months later, on January 14th, 1925, Chapman was captured — in Muncie, Indiana. New Britain police had done some checking on "Waldo Miller" and they were convinced that he *was* Chapman, and that Chapman was their man. A tip and some good detective work located him in Muncie and the beginning of the end began.

Chapman, swearing that he was innocent, that he'd never heard of Walter Shean, that he'd never been in New Britain, especially not on the morning of October 12th, was returned to Atlanta in a heavily guarded train.

A *New York World* reporter who covered Chapman's arrival in Atlanta wrote:

"Chapman is much changed in appearance since he made his escape in March, 1923. The gay, debonair bandit, familiarly known in the past as 'The Count of Gramercy Park' is now a sick man, suffering with chronic diabetes, and he does not believe he will live to serve out more than a few years of his sentence . . .

"Arriving at the prison, Chapman was hustled off without ceremony to the Hole, as the dungeon, or isolation cell is known. There he will be kept for an indefinite period and then assigned to work in the tailor shop, where he will be under constant surveillance with no chance to escape."

There was some question for a while whether the state of Connecticut, which wanted to try Chapman for the murder of Patrolman Skelly, could get him. The federal government, insistent at first that the twice-escaped bandit finish out his 25-year sentence in Atlanta, thought the matter over and finally agreed that Connecticut could have him. So he was shipped off to Hartford — again under heavy guard — in the middle of March.

On March 30th, the trial began and two things were clear from the beginning: that millions of people throughout America were on Chapman's side; and that the 12 men serving on the jury would find him guilty of murder in the first degree.

The United States went potty over the trial. Chapman fan clubs were organised, and each member was responsible for writing to the accused man at least one encouraging letter.

Newsreels of the man were greeted by almost hysterical applause in theatres across the US, and at least four or five bouquets arrived at the front door of the prison every day of the trial — all of them for Chapman. Furthermore, the term Public Enemy No. 1, a new one, was bestowed on Chapman by a reporter.

All of this managed to disgust a few people, among them the editorial writers for the *New York Post*. One of them wrote:

"Mass psychology is making a hero out of a wastrel gunman and holding him up for the edification of his imitative kind in all crookdom. Humanity keeps the habit of making heroes, not of the sheriff, the policeman and the constable, but of the criminal.

"It sends him flowers and writes him letters. Having run itself out of breath catching him, it sits down, pats him on the head and admires his beautiful eyes. Shades of Robin Hood, Dick Turpin and Jesse James!"

The jury was even tougher than the *Post*. Of them it was written. "They seem solid, matter-of-fact men. Their eyes are clear and sharp. Their lips are thin lines of red, and their hands are rough where they have toiled to drag a bare living from a reluctant soil.

"Not all are farmers, but all are men of small property. Emotion lies deep down in them, and is not easily aroused. When it is, it does not carry with it the presumption of innocence for anyone."

The jury certainly carried no presumption of innocence for Gerald Chapman, and on April 4th — the last day of a

trial during which the defence maintained that Chapman
was completely innocent of the crime and the state produced several witnesses who swore that Chapman had
been in and around New Britain at the time of the murder
— he was found guilty.

It was a strange few minutes that followed. Spectators
who overflowed the courtroom sat and stood still, most of
them saying nothing. One or two women cried softly. The
gentlemen of the jury made a point of looking straight
ahead, as if suddenly entranced by a tree which could be
seen just outside a window directly opposite where they sat.

The late Edward Hickey, who was then a detective
instrumental in Chapman's capture in Muncie and who
later became head of the Connecticut State Police, was the
only person who seemed to get excited. He rushed from his
seat in the front section of the courtroom, walked rapidly
down the aisle and over to his wife who sat in a back row,
and gave her a triumphant hug.

Chapman himself bowed his head a little and at one
point he patted the arm of one of his lawyers. After he was
sentenced — "On the twenty-fifth day of June, 1925, you
shall be hanged by the neck until you are dead" — Chapman
returned to where his lawyers were sitting, straightened his
tie, smoothed back his hair, shook hands all around and
before he was led away, said: "It was only what I expected.
It was inevitable. The jury was prejudiced from the start.
They didn't convict the accused. They convicted a man
named Gerald Chapman . . . I had to combat the ambitions
of the state attorney, the wealth and influence of the Sheans
and the prejudice of the public mind. They were trying,
really, word pictures of Gerald Chapman, the terrible
figure. It was a supercrook built up by the newspapers that
this jury convicted. Death itself isn't dreadful but hanging
seems an awkward way of ending the adventure."

And awkward it would prove as the state prison at
Wethersfield employed a weird hanging contraption.

A weight at the end of a 50-foot length of rope was
suspended three feet above the floor. This weight was

connected by a steel rod to a lever close to the deputy warden's foot. Seconds after the noose was looped around the condemned man's neck, the deputy warden would press the lever.

With a click the mechanism released the weight and the victim shot 12 feet into the air.

Oddly enough, the hanging machine had been "improved" for Chapman's execution. Previously, it had been operated by buckshot. The prisoner was led to a small metal trap set in the floor. When he stepped on the trap his weight caused a container that held 50 pounds of buckshot to open. Released, the pellets rolled rapidly down an incline until their increasing weight pressed a trigger. The trigger in turn released a heavy weight suspended six feet above floor level. As the weight fell, it hoisted the prisoner six feet, fracturing his neck.

This device, first used in 1894, was the brainchild of a prisoner, who was given his freedom as a reward. After using it for more than 30 years, the state of Connetticut decided it was illegal because it forced the prisoner to commit suicide, an unlawful act.

Chapman's execution was postponed a couple of times and he spent most of his time between appeals reading poetry, writing some of his own and jotting down epigrams which he passed out to several of the guards.

However, at daybreak on the morning of April 6th, 1926, Gerald Chapman, slim and calm as ever, finally entered the execution chamber. He looked about with the brilliant eyes which had always detected some flaw in the forces arrayed against him, but this time he could find no way out.

The black cowl was slipped over his head, the signal was given, and the rope hissed over its pulleys. It took him nine minutes to die.

Four hours later his body was taken from the prison at Wethersfield to a funeral home in Hartford and held there until dawn and then rushed to Mt. St. Benedict Cemetery in nearby Blue Hills, where it was cremated.

The only persons present at the funeral were Chapman's lawyers, two mystery women wearing long black veils — one was believed to be a sister of Chapman's; the other Betty, the girl from Indiana — and about 30 photographers and reporters.

Newspapers throughout America were full of funeral pictures and stories the next day — a headline in *The World* read: "Tears of Bandit's Sister Provide the Requiem" — and millions of people devoured what they knew would be the last they would ever get to hear of a man who had given them more thrills than probably any other man of the time, a man they had come to know as America's first official Public Enemy No. 1.

Following Chapman's execution his mentor Dutch Anderson went berserk. Rampaging the country, he tried to wreak personal vengeance on everyone who contributed to Chapman's downfall. He murdered an Indiana farmer and his wife in the mistaken belief that they had turned Chapman in, and he tried to kill Walter Shean in jail but could not get to him.

In Muskegon, Michigan, a cop finally recognised him. The two men fired simultaneously, killing each other.

9

COP KILLER

Bryan Williams

"I am Jesus Christ." Aaron Mitchell's claim when carried into the death chamber.

The slender young man stood in the mid-morning sunshine. He lit a cigarette through a break in the line of tall buildings and stared at the blue expanse of San Francisco Bay. The buildings were an almost gay yellow-beige, but they were turned grim by rows of steel bars on the windows.

"I feel now that all the police officers in the state can feel safer," he said. "I have no regrets."

The speaker was 27-year-old Ronald Dean Shaw, patrolman in the Sacramento police department. He spoke on April 12th, 1967, at a historic moment in the history of California's penology.

Patrolman Shaw had just walked from the building in the compound of sprawling San Quentin Prison that housed California's gas chamber. He had just seen a man slump into the unconsciousness preceding death. The young patrolman had not waited for the official pronouncement of death. He had left the ring of 58 witnesses peering through the windows of the octagonal chamber to seek the privacy of the outdoors.

The 57 who remained were witnessing an event that had not occurred in California for the past four years. There had not been an execution since January 23rd, 1963, when James Abner Bentley, killer of a liquor-store owner in the community of Fresno, had died by order of the court and jury which found him guilty.

What had followed had been an unacknowledged moratorium on the use of the gas chamber. There had been an unsuccessful attempt before the legislature to abolish the death penalty, but the law stayed on the books.

The moratorium resulted from a combination of the state's political climate and the series of stays of executions ordered by courts and the then Governor Edmund "Pat" Brown. The governor had proved an opponent of the death penalty. Indeed, at the time of the resumption of the gas chamber on that sunny April morning in 1967, there were 52 men waiting on Death Row to pay the supreme penalty.

Nine Death Row inmates had taken the lives of California policemen, as had the man Patrolman Shaw had seen slump into unconsciousness in the gas chamber.

It had been a brutal crime and it had been witnessed by the patrolman who did not wait to witness the final struggles of the killing. It was a murder which occurred only 23 days after California began its moratorium following the execution of James Bentley.

It was February 15th, 1963, a crisp Friday evening in California's capital city of Sacramento, 100 miles to the north of San Quentin Prison and its gas chamber.

Shortly before 10.30 p.m., a hulking man parked an old Plymouth in an alleyway a short distance from Sacramento City College.

The man was attired in a dark brown check coat and he wore a dark blue knitted hat, similar to a Balaclava with slitted eye-holes.

The man peered about in the darkness through dark-rimmed spectacles. He reached into the car and drew forth a 12-gauge shotgun and slung it from his neck by a white plastic strap. The weapon's double barrels had been trimmed off with a saw to a point where the entire weapon extended to only ten and a half inches.

A few minutes later, Raul Bowen, pantryman and kitchen porter in the Stadium Club, dragged a tall can of kitchen grease waste through the club's rear door to the car park.

The Stadium Club is on Sacramento's broad thorough-fare of Sutterville Road and it takes its name from the concrete horseshoe of Hughes Stadium standing just across the avenue on the City College campus.

In the dim light of the car park, Raul Bowen saw a figure in a dark coat attempting to peer through an opaque window into a restaurant rest-room. The figure turned and the pantryman found himself staring into the barrels of a sawn-off shotgun. The gunman's head was sheathed in the dark woollen cap which he had pulled down to cover his face.

Bowen was prodded at gunpoint through the rear door into the club kitchen. Aldo Ricci, chef and co-owner of the club, was busily honing the grease-spattered top of the kitchen range with an emery stone. He saw the pantryman and the masked gunman march into the kitchen.

"I thought it was a farce," Ricci testified.

It was all too real, however, as he learned a moment later. The hooded man, his stubby weapon clutched in hands sheathed in rubber surgical gloves, ordered the chef and his three kitchen helpers into the big walk-in refrigerator nearby. It was a futile order. When the thick door was swung open, it was evident that the refrigerator could not have accommodated as much as another butter cube.

The masked man abandoned Ricci and his helpers and swept through the swinging doors separating the kitchen from the dining area. The dinner hour was over, but there was still about 20 customers in the front bar and lounge area.

In his first brief confrontation, Aldo Ricci had peered into the slitted eye holes in the mask and had seen that the gunman was wearing spectacles.

Ricci moved towards the telephone on the kitchen wall. He had immediate help in his daring move. His wife Carla had been behind the cash register counter in the front part of the restaurant and, with the appearance of the gunman, had moved to the rear. It was a point from which she could observe both her husband in the kitchen and the gunman.

She nodded and her husband picked the telephone from its cradle and dialled the operator. To the answering voice Ricci hurriedly explained that there was a gunman loose in the restaurant. The operator switched the call to the Sacramento police department, three miles to the north.

A short time later the voice of the radio dispatcher broadcast the news of the apparent hold-up to all cars.

In patrol car No. 4, Patrolmen Ronald Shaw and John Bibica heard the broadcast. In car No. 14, the same appeal was heard by Patrolmen Robert Reese and Arnold Gamble.

Although one of the officers was unaware of it at the time, the broadcast placed him on a collision course with death. He was going to be killed by a man he did not know — and never would.

In the Stadium Club, the wife of Aldo Ricci saw the masked gunman walk back towards the kitchen. She nodded again to her husband and Ricci hastily replaced the telephone in its cradle, then returned to honing the last traces of grease off the kitchen range.

The gunman entered the kitchen again and ordered Ricci and the kitchen workers into the dining and bar area. He brandished his sawn-off weapon at the customers and commanded them to move to an area across from the bar. The customers milled about, gawking at the hooded man, so he discharged a blast of pellets into a rafter. Frightened customers then rushed to the area designated by him.

In the car park, the intruder had questioned Raul Bowen as he struggled with the grease-container. A question asked and answered had been the names of owners of the Stadium Club. The pantryman had identified them as Aldo Ricci and his brother, Pietro.

The acrid fumes of gunpowder still hung in the club when the hooded man asked "Mr. Ricci" — he did not specify which one — "to step out." Pietro Ricci, who had been working in the bar, stepped forward.

"Have you made a phone call?" the gunman growled, indicating the extension suspended on a wall near the bar.

Ricci shook his head in denial. The masked man ripped the telephone from the wall.

He then performed a trick which the Ricci brothers and their customers would never forget. The masked man snatched the hem of a tablecloth covering a dining table. He gave a swift tug and the cloth zipped off, leaving salt and pepper shakers, sugar bowl, vase, ash tray and small lamp standing in place on the bare table. It was the legerdemain of a polished magician.

Grasping the tablecloth, the gunman moved Pietro Ricci towards the bar and its cash register. Ricci opened the register and the masked man scooped out $321 and 85 cents in cash and currency into the tablecloth.

The gunman asked Ricci the location of the restaurant safe and Ricci indicated a cloakroom adjacent to the dining and bar area. The restaurant-owner then knelt to open the small safe and the gunman rummaged through it and found it bare of valuables.

He motioned Ricci to rejoin the terrified people in the lounge.

When car No. 4 heard the armed robbery call, they were on patrol near a high school a mile from the Stadium Club. Car No. 14 was a quarter of a mile further away.

First to arrive at the Stadium Club car park was Bibica and Shaw. There was an unspoken plan of action. Young Shaw ran towards the club's rear door while Bibica moved to the front entrance.

Shaw moved quickly through the screen door of the service porch and pushed on past the solid door barring the porch from the kitchen. As he stepped into the kitchen he stared straight into the muzzle of the gunman's shotgun.

Shaw's .38 revolver was still in the holster at his right hip. It would have meant instant death for him to reach for it, so Shaw raised his hands and then, at the direction of the masked man, gingerly reached across his body with his left hand and placed the weapon on a kitchen table. The gunman picked up the pistol and ordered the officer to face the wall.

At the club's front door, Bibica glanced through a triangular glass panel set in the door. He had a fleeting vision of a hooded man moving towards the rear of the restaurant, where his partner waited. Bibica then moved swiftly around the side of the club to the rear door.

Car No. 14 had braked to a halt in the club's car park as Shaw was being disarmed in the kitchen. The crew of the second car was a combination of experience and youth. Patrolman Reese had served but five months; Gamble was a veteran of slightly more than 20 years service.

Before his car had come to a complete halt, Gamble had leaped from it. He ran to the rear door of the club and Reese followed him. The young officer placed himself just outside the screen door of the service porch and dropped to his knee in firing position, his revolver drawn.

Gamble moved into the service porch and took up a position at one side of the solid door barring off the kitchen. He stepped on a small box near the door. His .357 magnum pistol was in his hand.

The kitchen door swung outwards and young Shaw was prodded through the opening by the hooded man, a hard object pressed into his side.

Gamble stepped from his perch on the small box and moved towards the armed man and his hostage. Shaw, still a shield for the masked robber, felt the warmth of a gunflash at his side. There were other reports of gunfire and Gamble spun and fell face down on the floor. Shaw was also sprawled on the floor, a wound in his upper left thigh.

The masked man stepped over the fallen officers and sped through the rear door as Reese got off a shot. The man ran across the paved car park to an open field at the rear of the restaurant young Reese was in pursuit and he fired two more shots at the fleeing suspect.

Bibica was rounding the corner of the restaurant when the shots were fired in the service porch. He saw the running masked figure and also began firing. The fleeing figure dropped to the ground, but immediately bounced back to his feet. He sped through the field to a street, veered left and was at the entrance of another street. This was Attawa Street, a narrow, barely-paved lane in a neighbourhood of rundown housing.

The hooded figure lurched down the centre of Attawa Street. There was more police gunfire and the hulking man again dropped to the ground. He hauled himself slowly to his feet and the pursuing officers saw an unexpected spurt of flame at the lower part of his right leg.

The figure then turned left towards the driveway leading past a small house. The gunman made his way past a back garden garage and disappeared into the darkness at the rear of the property.

Flashing red lights and wailing sirens informed the pursuing officers that police help was moving to the Stadium Club. Moments later, Patrolman Jerry Finney joined Bibica and Reese in the pursuit.

The officers saw that an alley ran parallel with Attawa Street and passed the darkened back garden where the gunman was believed to have sought refuge. Taking advantage of the slight cover — a picket fence with many gaps and a lone telephone pole — they worked their way along the alley. Directly at the rear of the garage where the man had passed from view was a rusted metal shack.

Guns at the ready, Bibica and Finney kicked in the door of the shack. The probing beams of their torches told them that their search had ended. The masked man, barely conscious, was stretched out on the floor. The shotgun was beside him, still strung from his neck by the white plastic strap. In a slatted lettuce crate on the floor, the officers saw a crumpled wad of currency. It was the money from the Stadium Club cash register.

Bibica yanked the shotgun from the man. He glanced at the barrels and found the explanation for the firework-like explosion seen during the chase. When the man had fallen, the right gun barrel had become clogged with mud. The gun had gone off accidentally and had split the stubby barrel.

Five police bullets had struck the gunman. Three wounds

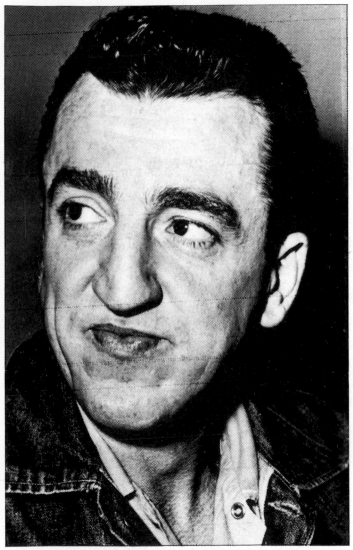

Caryl Chessman. Kidnapper who spent 12 years on Death Row

The Red Light Bandit: page 109

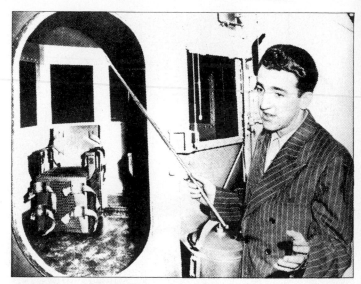

Montaged photographs of Caryl Chessman and California's lethal gas chamber, and the prisoner with the three best-sellers he wrote while on Death Row

Holding Father Richard's hand, Toni Jo calmly starts her walk to the electric chair. Her only complaint came when her head was shaved. "I want a scarf for my execution," she told them

The Cowboy and the Lady: page 208

"I've smiled twice, Mister. Have you any idea how much talent is being wasted here today?" Toni Jo told cameraman who snapped this death cell picture. Below, her body being removed minutes after her execution

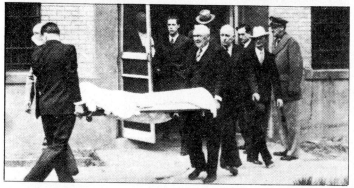

Aaron Mitchell: He was dragged screaming to the gas chamber

Cop Killer: page 180

Nineteen-year-old Frank DuPre was last man hanged in Georgia
The Deadly Diamonds: page 195

On his march to the gallows (arrowed)
in the Fulton Tower, young killer
Frank DuPre waved his farewell to the
large crowd below

Just as moths perish when their wings are burned so was Elmo Smith (above) singed to death by 2,000 volts

The Human Moth: page 237

were in his chest, a fourth in his abdomen and a fifth in his left elbow. The surgical glove on the left hand had filled with blood.

An ambulance was called and the mask was peeled from the wounded man's face. It was the face of a man in his early 30s, wearing spectacles.

In the service porch of the Stadium Club, Patrolman William Stenfeldt applied mouth-to-mouth resuscitation to Patrolman Gamble. But it was no use. Arnold Gamble was dead. There was a small hole ringed with powder burns on the right breast of his dark blue uniform.

Patrolman Shaw was sped to Sacramento County Hospital a mile to the north of the murder scene. Despite the serious wound in his left thigh, doctors said he would recover. It was later discovered that the bullet had come from the gun of Patrolman Gamble, possibly fired by a reflex action.

Meanwhile, in another emergency room of the hospital, doctors worked frantically to save the life of the gunman, who was heard to mutter, "How are the officers I shot — how are the officers I shot?"

At the edge of the paved car park behind the Stadium Club, metal glinted in the beam of the torch carried by Captain Albert White.

The captain retrieved the .38-calibre revolver which the masked man had taken from Patrolman Shaw. All six rounds in the cylinder had been fired.

A police criminologist would later testify that the bullet taken from the chest of the murdered Gamble had undeniably been fired from the revolver.

In hospital, the seriously-wounded gunman clung stubbornly to life. In a moment of consciousness he identified himself as Aaron Mitchell, 33.

Four days after the murder, Patrolman Gamble was buried, while Aaron Mitchell had passed the crisis point and was on the road to recovery.

As Aaron Mitchell's wounds healed, Sacramento police accumulated information on him.

Firstly, they looked no further than records in their own department. A file showed that Mitchell was accused of being the man who, on December 29th, 1962, just 18 days before the murder of Gamble, brandished a knife at Frank Miral, owner of a Sacramento laundry, and forced him to surrender $1,500 from his safe. Miral recalled that he had acted on the double persuasion of a pistol tucked in the robber's waistband.

Among the loot was a one-dollar bill with a cigarette hole burned in it, plus several coins which had been painted with nail polish. The coins were used as easily identifiable "testers" in the operation of Miral's washing machines.

A witness had taken down the licence number of the robber's getaway car and it was traced to Mitchell. When he was arrested, a cigarette-burned one-dollar bill was found in his pocket, plus several nail-polished coins.

At the time of the murder in the Stadium Club, Mitchell was free on $5,200 bail, an amount posted by his mother.

There were other records by which to chart the life of Aaron Mitchell. A birth certificate showed that he had been born in 1930 in Memphis, Tennessee. When he was 17, he had gone to Chicago to work as a car park attendant.

At this point he had his first recorded brush with the law. He stole a car and was arrested in Missouri. For that he served 14 months in an Illinois reformatory.

At 20 Mitchell was in Memphis and yearned to return to Chicago. So he took another car without permission and was arrested in Chicago. He was returned south and sentenced to serve three years on a chain gang. Ten days after sentencing he escaped from the rural road gang. He was arrested several months later in Chicago and was returned to serve 31 months of the chain gang sentence.

On November 16th, 1954, the gates of Colorado state penitentiary at Canon City swung open to receive Mitchell following his conviction for assault with intent to commit robbery. The assault was an incident with near-national complications.

On the night of September 29th, 1954, Fred Trembley,

general manager of the exclusive Cherry Hills Country Club on the outskirts of Denver, got home to his apartment after a hectic day at work. Trembley had been completing preparations for the impending visit of no less a personality than Dwight D. Eisenhower, President of the U.S.A.

The visitor to Trembley's apartment that night was not of the calibre of a head of state. He was a muscular young fellow who slipped out of the shadows in the apartment. The club manager struggled with the man although the assailant carried a pistol and was struck on the head and suffered the loss of his wrist-watch. It also took several stitches to close the wound on his head.

Aaron Mitchell was arrested for the crime and he served time from 1954 to 1961 in Canon City.

After his release, Mitchell followed his mother to California, where she worked in the laundry of the giant Mather Air Force Base on the outskirts of Sacramento. The mother secured a job for her son in the same laundry.

Somewhere along the line Aaron Mitchell acquired and divorced a wife and fathered a son, 15 years old at the time of Patrolman Gamble's slaying.

Mitchell had switched from his laundry job and at the time of the murder was a $62-a-week presser in a Sacramento dry cleaning shop.

On March 8th, Mitchell used his long-necked metal toilet bowl to knock his hospital guard unconscious. He could not escape, however, because one ankle was still manacled to the foot of the bed and the guard's key fell out of his reach.

On May 8th, almost four months after the murder, Mitchell went on trial before a jury of five men and seven women. He did not deny the club robbery; he pleaded guilty to that offence, choosing only to defend himself on the murder charge. Through his court-appointed lawyer he contended that the killing of Patrolman Gamble had been more by mistake than by malice.

After 13 days, however, the jury found him guilty. Then, as required by California law, the same jury sat through six more days of sentence hearing to determine what penalty fitted the crime. On the sixth day the jury voted again and fixed Mitchell's sentence as death in San Quentin's gas chamber.

He joined the prison's Death Row population on June 2nd, 1963. It had now been five months since the gas chamber had last been used. Mitchell's appeal went automatically to the state Supreme Court for review. There, Mitchell found he was to be the oblique recipient of benefits aimed initially at another killer.

This man was 20-year-old Joseph Bernard Morse, who had been given a life sentence for beating his mother to death with a rock and killing his 12-year-old sister with a baseball bat. However, in the penalty phase of his trial, the judge had commented that there was the possibility of parole during a life sentence. The California Supreme Court ruled that this was a violation of Morse's constitutional rights and ordered a new penalty trial.

The decision occurred in January, 1964, about the time Mitchell's appeal was being reviewed. The record of his trial showed that the judge had also commented on the possibilities of parole. So a new trial was ordered for Mitchell, but only with regard to the death penalty.

After one year and four days on Death Row, Aaron Mitchell was brought back to Sacramento for his partial new trial. Again the tragic and bloody events of the February night in the Stadium Club were relived, and again through the many witnesses. Aaron Mitchell gave evidence in the hope of convincing a second jury that a death sentence was a terrible mistake.

"Well," he informed the jurors, "it happened like this. I was sort of pressed for money. I admit that and I went there to commit a robbery."

Mitchell told of "running around" most of the day of the murder trying to borrow money for lawyer fees to defend himself from the charge of robbing the laundry. He said he was unsuccessful and added that his bank account then stood at $15. He told of cashing a cheque to buy a box of shotgun shells, vodka and orange juice. He also told of sawing off the shotgun barrels.

Asked why he had endangered lives in the Stadium Club by firing at the ceiling, he said, "I shot into the ceiling for the sole purpose of — it actually was done to keep anybody from getting hurt. You can't commit a robbery if you — if you — the people think you are playing.

"When I saw this officer with the gun [a reference to Patrolman Shaw], I said, 'You got me' and all this shooting — looked like — I don't know what happened. Everybody — the shooting started and that's about all I remember…"

Of one thing Mitchell said he was certain. He said he had not fired the first shot.

Then for a second time a President of the United States played a personal part in the life of Aaron Mitchell. His testimony was interrupted so that the court could be adjourned to allow jurors to join the throng welcoming a campaigning President Lyndon Johnson.

The next day, Mitchell resumed his denial of intent to murder a policeman. That same day the jury again fixed his penalty at death in San Quentin's gas chamber.

But death was not immediate for Mitchell. His case assumed the antics of a ping-pong ball as it bounced on appeal from a lower, to high, to higher, to highest court and back down to starting point to bounce again, and yet again.

With some show of finality his execution date was set for May 11th, 1966. At that point, Mitchell would have been on Death Row for almost three years: a relatively short time when one considers the Chessman case.

Twenty-four days before the scheduled execution, U.S. Supreme Court Justice William Douglas stayed the order while he examined the well-worn record. On May 3rd, California's Governor Edmund Brown held a clemency hearing in his office, a scant two miles from the murder scene.

"If ever there was a first-degree murder case, this is it," said the governor. "Don't count on us," he added in denying clemency and advising that the murderer's attorneys return to the courts for relief.

Six days before the gas chamber date, Justice Douglas refused to halt the execution any longer. The next day, Mitchell's attorneys urged the California Supreme Court to issue a stay. The court said "no" three days later.

On May 10th, the eve of execution, Mitchell went through the formality of ordering a last meal. It was never prepared. Federal District Judge Alphonso Zirpoli ordered a stay of execution on the grounds that he needed time to look into Mitchell's latest point of appeal. This was that the condemned man testified in his trial only because he thought the prosecuting district attorney or the trial judge might have commented on the absence of himself from the witness stand. Mitchell said through his attorneys that in a sense he felt compelled to testify against himself.

Fifty-nine days later, Mitchell again left Death Row to appear in court, this time before Judge Zirpoli. He listened to the condemned man's testimony that the jury might have been prejudiced by his failure to testify. Mitchell returned to Death Row, and six months later, on November 23rd, Judge Zirpoli ruled that there was no merit to Mitchell's plea.

The year 1967 was ushered in by the setting of another execution date for Mitchell. It would be April 12th, slightly more than 90 days hence.

The appellate manoeuvrings took on brisk staccato tempo. Justice Douglas again said no to a stay of execution. Seven days before the scheduled death, Zirpoli did the same. Two days later, Mitchell's attorneys argued before the United States Court of Appeals in San Francisco that Mitchell had been unfairly treated by Judge Zirpoli. The Appellate Court upheld Judge Zirpoli's ruling.

Six days remained until the execution. An appeal was dispatched to the United States Supreme Court. The court replied that no stay of execution would be forthcoming.

Again it was the eve of execution. A second clemency hearing was held in the office of Governor Ronald Reagan, an outspoken proponent of capital punishment, who had been elected just six months before by a 1,000,000-vote majority. Reagan took no part in the hearing, but was represented by his clemency secretary. Through that secretary the governor's office announced that there could be no clemency.

In his cell in San Quentin, Aaron Mitchell made the most desperate appeal possible. He wielded a contraband razor blade to slash the inside flesh of his left elbow. The suicidal wounds were near the spot where he had been wounded in fleeing from the scene of Patrolman Gamble's murder. However, his suicidal wounds proved superficial.

"I was making my peace with Jesus," said the now 37-year-old condemned killer.

At five p.m. on execution eve, Aaron Mitchell left the Death Row cell which had been his home for so many years. He was taken to a small holding cell just a few yards away from and out of sight of the gas chamber.

One hour later he was served the condemned man's privilege — the meal of his choice. Mitchell chose Southern fried chicken, bread, butter and milk.

Throughout the night he dozed fitfully and awoke to discuss religion with the prison chaplain. At six a.m. he refused a truly last meal of scrambled eggs.

Even doomsday brought no halt to appeals. Ninety minutes before the time of execution, one of Mitchell's attorneys asked Justice Douglas by telegram to halt the execution because the lawyer believed that his client was under sedation. The telegram was referred to the entire U.S. Supreme Court, which assembled, considered the petition, and denied it.

Ten minutes before the scheduled execution another attorney appealed to a superior court judge in the nearby city of San Rafael for a delay on the grounds that Mitchell's attempted suicide indicated that he had become insane, and insane persons cannot be executed in California. The judge rejected the appeal.

It was 10 a.m., the time set for the execution. The many

witnesses clustered around the octagonal apple-green hut that is the gas chamber in San Quentin suddenly turned to peer down a nearby corridor in alarm.

There had been a series of screams emanating from the small holding cell where Aaron Mitchell had waited throughout the night. The cell was barred from the view of witnesses by a slatted screen. The shrieks died away, to be followed by a low moan.

A prison telephone line was opened in direct connection to Governor Ronald Reagan's office in Sacramento. Meanwhile, the door was swung aside and hulking Aaron Mitchell, bearded and wild-eyed, was literally carried screaming and yelling into the death chamber by two guards.

There are two metal chairs in the chamber. One is designated chair "A," the other "B". Five glass panels in the steel walls afford the witnesses a view of the chairs. The fear-stricken man was placed in chair "A."

"I am Jesus Christ!" he shrilled.

Swiftly the guards dragged him into the chair, secured the straps to his chest and arms. There was no ceremonial pat on the shoulder for good luck. The guards withdrew and the steel door clanged shut.

The phone line to the governor's office remained silent. At a signal from Warden Lawrence Wilson, a guard — his identity is never disclosed — pulled a lever. A gelatin capsule of cyanide the size of a goose egg dropped into the vat of hydrochloric acid beneath the execution chair.

Eyes glazed, Mitchell scanned the windows in the death chamber. His head dropped to his chest and his body convulsed against the straps.

Patrolman Shaw, who had witnessed the murder of Arnold Gamble so many months before that April day, broke away from the ranks of witnesses and sought the sunshine-filled prison compound.

It was not over at that moment. It was 10.14 a.m., and 1,516 days after the murder in the Stadium Club, before Aaron Mitchell was officially pronounced dead by the prison doctor.

10

THE DEADLY DIAMONDS

Lieutenant Olin Sturdivant, as told to
James Belflower

"The police are dumb. They couldn't catch a cold." Extract from Frank DuPre's letter to an Atlanta newspaper.

It was a coincidence that the chain of events which eventually led to the abolition of the gallows in Georgia had its inception at a time when peace and good will reigned on earth — Christmas Eve, 1921. And the first link in that chain was murder — a murder that rocked a city, a state and an entire nation.

Picture the scene — the late afternoon before Christmas, when Atlanta's Peachtree Street was thronged with shoppers. There was a bite in the air, and lights were beginning to gleam in gaily decorated windows.

None of the crowd that flowed down Peachtree Street had time to study others. But if any had noticed they would have seen in front of number three — before the ornate windows of Atlanta's leading jewellery shop — a well-dressed young man studying the display of diamonds that sparkled in the lights. This man stood just in front of the prize exhibit of the display, a beautiful ring beneath which was the price tag of $2,500.

After a moment's hesitation, the man turned and walked into the shop. At that precise moment the place was bare of customers. An assistant stood near the entrance, another was behind the counter. A young woman was busily at work in the shop's office.

As the youth stepped into the bright interior he was

subjected to a close inspection by Irby Walker, the "assistant" by the door; in reality a Pinkerton detective stationed there to guard the shop. Apparently he saw nothing about the youth to arouse his suspicions.

The assistant behind the counter — who subsequently became president of the company — inquired how he might serve the young customer.

"I'd like to see that ring in the window — the one with the twenty-five-hundred dollar tag on it," the youth said.

The assistant came from behind the counter, crossed over to the windows, opened the sliding panel and removed the ring. He handed it to the young customer, who turned it around in the light.

"The price is pretty steep, isn't it?" he asked.

"It's an expensive stone," replied the assistant, "but it's a bargain. It is absolutely without a flaw."

Holding the ring close to his eyes, the young man walked over to the door as if to study it in a better light. As he did so, the Pinkerton detective — as a matter of routine — moved close to the door to intercept him in the event he tried to dash out.

Almost without warning the youth pulled out a gun from his right overcoat pocket and darted for the door. But the alert Detective Walker leapt to head him off. The bandit's gun roared once and Walker crumpled forward, dead before he hit the floor.

Instantly the shop was in uproar. The assistant shouted the alarm and the girl accountant screamed. Before they could leave their places, the gunman had rushed out into the teeming mass of Christmas shoppers.

Consternation reigned as he smashed his way through the crowds, pistol in hand. Only one person sought to stop him. That was Graham West. He was emerging from the door of Kimball House as the gunman dashed in, and he rushed at the youth, but he was shot in the face and neck for his pains.

Kimball House is a hotel that occupies an entire block with entrances on four streets. The gunman evidently knew this, for he ran down the narrow passageway towards the lobby. Midway down the passage he darted into a pool-room.

A policeman on the beat had heard the shots and saw the confusion. He was stationed only a short distance away and had given chase at the first alarm, but he had not noticed the gunman enter the pool-room. However, seeing no fleeing figure when he ran into the long passageway, the policeman dashed into the pool-room as it was the first door in the passage, shouting to the startled players, "Did a man with a gun in his hand run in here?"

The bewildered pool-players only stared at him. They didn't know what he was talking about. No one had run in! The trail ended as abruptly as the life of Detective Walker had been snuffed out!

This was the situation when I reached the scene, having been assigned the case within a few minutes of the alarm being flashed to the police station. Meanwhile, Mr. West was taken to hospital, where grave doubts were expressed as to his recovery.

Hastily, I talked to the uniformed men, and finding that the gunman's escape was complete, I knew that I must begin at the beginning. I interviewed the assistants in the shop, but all they could furnish was a description. The assistant who had waited on him described the bandit as being about 18 years old. He had worn a cap, a brown suit, a grey overcoat and a flashy multi-coloured tie. And oh, yes, there was something odd about one of the gunman's eyes — some sort of variance.

I then followed the trail down Peachtree Street, past the scene of the second shooting, and into the pool-room. Inside the trail came to an end. So I began to question the men in the pool-room one by one. To each I repeated the detailed description and asked if he had seen such a person. At last I found one who had.

"I saw the man come in," the witness said, "but he didn't have a gun and he didn't wear a cap. He carried an overcoat over his arm, but it was folded back and I didn't see the colour."

"Where did he go?"

"Just after that policeman ran out he went out of the door that leads into the main lobby."

We hurried to the lobby. Sure enough several people had seen the youth with an overcoat on his arm pass through; but there was nothing outward in his manner that indicated he was in any trouble. He had quietly left by the Wall Street entrance.

Out on Wall Street there was a street-medicine hawker selling his wares, putting on a little show to attract customers. A crowd had gathered about him, so we sifted through them, asking the same questions over and over again. No one had seen our man. The trail had grown cold again.

I next rushed a description of the robber to the police station, and it was sent to all patrolmen on the beat. I then settled down to a careful search of the neighbourhood. Someone must know something, and it was to be my luck to find him.

Working carefully from shop to shop, I came at last to a small business trading in ready-to-wear men's clothing. I repeated the same old questions, giving the gunman's description.

"Sure I saw the man," the assistant answered. "I sold him a black tie. He took off his own one in here and changed to the new one."

Hours passed in fruitless searching while we watched railway stations, hotel lobbies and boarding houses. Late that night we received an astounding piece of information. It came from Frank Foster, then a barber, who later joined the Atlanta police force and then became a detective.

"I saw that fellow," he told me. "He came in my shop and asked for a haircut and shampoo. I know he's the one. He was bareheaded, but he had a cap stuffed in the pocket of his overcoat — and he wore a black tie."

The information Foster gave us was the last direct tip we got. From then on, as the hours drifted by and no new clue came in, the case looked hopeless. We had sent out the usual description to the police departments of nearby cities, giving details about the ring and asking them to watch all pawnshops and fences.

Meanwhile, eye-witnesses had viewed the pictures in our rogues' gallery without any luck. Fingerprint expert J. M. Wright reported that he had been unable to find any prints in the jewellery shop, men's wear shop or the barber shop.

That night I sorted through the facts in my mind in order to draw some definite conclusions, and what I decided was this: when a young fellow of about 18 steals a ring, particularly on Christmas Eve, he wants it for a girl. Furthermore, such a person would rarely try to get away by train.

With this in mind I set men watching hotels and boarding houses. I hoped, though the chances were slim, that I would find the girl. Finding the man would then be easier. My second thought led to a thorough check of taxi companies.

Detective Stone was assigned to interview every taxi-driver in town if necessary, and he did a thorough job. In short order we established that there was only one taxi-driver who might have aided the gunman in his getaway. That man was already several hours overdue in checking in after his night's business. I gave orders for him to be questioned as soon as he showed up, then turned in another direction.

The bullet taken from Walker's body was passed over to me, together with the one surgeons had removed from Graham West, who was showing signs of recovering after a delicate operation.

Now, Atlanta was not blessed with a scientific laboratory for the detection of crime, so the test I made to establish the markings and grooves of the firearm used in this slaying were extremely simple and "home-made." I rolled the bullets over a piece of smooth tinfoil that I had taken from a packet of cigarettes, laying the tinfoil carefully on a piece of smooth leather stretched tightly over a smooth surface and rolling with just enough pressure to get a definite impression.

I studied these bullets and the markings on the tinfoil under a powerful glass, and with the aid of a local amateur firearms expert, I came to the conclusion that these bullets were fired from a .38-calibre automatic made by a certain widely known firearms manufacturer.

I then put the bullets carefully aside until such time as we might have a pistol to check them against. However, at that time I knew the chances of finding the pistol were remote.

I got in touch with Detective Stone and learned that the missing taxi driver had not returned. We took his licence number and a description of his cab and wired it to nearby cities. Early the following morning he called from Rome, Georgia, about 70 miles to the north, and said he had taken a fare to Chattanooga and was on his way back. He would arrive in a few hours, he said. Stone went to the taxi office to wait for him.

Meanwhile, a development came from another source. I had spent the night previously — along with a number of my men — circulating hotel lobbies and boarding houses on the hunch that a woman was mixed up in this in some way. My men were instructed to keep their eyes open, start conversations and see what they could pick up. Just about everybody was talking about the hold-up and shooting, and if anyone had any information they were going to say something to someone sooner or later.

One of my men, not a full-time detective, but one who did some special work for me, met a girl in a hotel coffee-room. During their chat she told him that her girl friend was the sweetheart of the jewellery-shop killer. She was quite excited about it, he said. He didn't ask too many questions, but instead he sent for me.

I picked the girl up and asked her to repeat her story. "It's true," she said. "The girl's registered at the Childs Hotel under the name of Mrs. E. J. Anderson. She's very pretty. That's all I know."

The receptionist on duty at the hotel admitted that the

woman was there, and led us to her room.

The girl who answered our knock was a brunette of striking beauty, with dark, piercing eyes. Only 19 years of age, she initially denied knowing anything about the slaying. Then the truth came out:

"But my sweetheart promised to get me a present," she said, "and I haven't seen him since Christmas Eve — and I've read the descriptions of the killer in the papers —" She broke down and wept. "I love him so much," she sobbed.

Later we were to discover that her sweetheart kept a rendezvous with her just after the shooting, and that her real name was Betty Andrews.

After she had become calmer I asked who her sweetheart was. "Frank DuPre," she said. She told us all she knew about him, which wasn't much.

. When I got back to the police station with my attractive prisoner there was another person waiting there — C. R. Buckley, the taxi driver who had just been picked up by Detective Stone.

"I picked up a fare on Peachtree Street just before midnight on Christmas Eve," he told us, "and he wanted me to take him to Chattanooga — had very important business there, he said."

"Who was he?"

"I don't know his name. I didn't ask him. I make it a rule not to bother my fares. I just take them where they want to go."

We questioned Buckley for more than an hour, but that was all we could get out of him. After a while I left the other men and went out to where his cab was parked. I got in the back and closed the doors. The pocket in the left hand door bulged. I put my hand in it and pulled out a .38-calibre pistol of the same make that I believed the death weapon to be.

Hastily I examined the other pocket, and there I found a roll of money.

Before announcing my find, and to determine if it was the death weapon, I went to the police shooting range and fired it several times. I procured the discharged bullets and again employed my "home-made" tinfoil ballistics test on them. I compared them with the bullets that had killed Detective Irby Walker and wounded Graham West. My tests showed that all the bullets had been fired from this gun.

In a few minutes I was back in the room with my men and Buckley.

"What about this?" I asked, thrusting out the pistol.

"I never saw it before," the taxi driver replied.

"I don't believe you!" I shouted at him. Then I pulled out the roll of bills.

"What about this? It's yours, is it? Then where did you get it?"

Buckley changed his story then. The money was his, he admitted, but he knew nothing about the pistol. His passenger must have left it without his knowledge.

I exhibited the discharged bullets to him, and pointed out in detail the markings on each that proved that they had been fired from the same gun, the weapon that had slain Detective Walker.

"Wasn't his name Frank DuPre?" I asked. He had not been informed of the girl's detention, or that I had already wired Chattanooga with the new information obtained from her.

"Yes, his name was DuPre — Frank DuPre."

This time the taxi driver told an amazing story — one that convinced me that DuPre had the most astounding luck.

Buckley said he had picked up DuPre a short distance from the scene of the killing and was told to drive to Marietta, 20 miles away. There, he said, DuPre had displayed his pistol, and by threats and intimidation had forced him to drive on to Chattanooga.

During the long-night ride to the Tennessee city, DuPre had taken the taxi driver partially into his confidence, announcing his intention of pawning a valuable ring as soon as he reached Chattanooga and giving him a nice tip.

Buckley said at this point that he didn't know the man had killed anybody.

When they came to the business section of the town, Buckley had followed DuPre's directions and driven to a certain pawnshop DuPre said he knew would be open for a short time that morning, and shown the pawnbroker the ring.

"It's a nice piece of jewellery — worth two and a half grand," DuPre said.

"Sure. It's the goods," the pawnbroker replied, "but I ain't doing business today. It's Christmas Day and I haven't got much money. How much did you want?"

"Six hundred — outright sale," said DuPre.

"It's worth it, but I haven't that much money on me. I'll make you a proposition. I'll give you three hundred and a pawn ticket. Any time you want you can get the other three hundred. If you are not here just mail your ticket, giving me your address, and I'll send the other three hundred."

"Okay," said DuPre. "I need the money — now."

While they were talking, two Chattanooga plainclothes detectives walked towards the door. The pawnbroker hastily motioned DuPre and Buckley into a small back room. While crouched there, Buckley said they heard the conversation between the men in the shop:

"We've got a wire from Atlanta," one of the detectives announced. "They're expecting a man to pawn a hot diamond. There's a murder charge in it. Have you seen anything suspicious?"

"Not a thing," the pawnbroker replied.

The detectives walked out and passed within two feet of the taxi bearing a Georgia licence number parked right outside the door!

That's the story that Buckley told, and it was checked later in every detail. The pawnbroker waited until the detectives had gone and then motioned the pair out of the back room. He gave DuPre 300 dollars — in 50-dollar bills — and a pawn ticket.

"When you get where you are going write to me and send

the ticket. I'll send you the balance," the pawnbroker promised.

They shook hands on it and Buckley drove DuPre to the railway station, where DuPre paid him the amount of the meter reading, tipping him 25 dollars.

"It was to keep my mouth shut," Buckley said, and he smiled grimly at the ring of detectives that sat around him.

Buckley said that DuPre gave him Betty's address, saying: "When I get to my destination I'm going to wire you to put Betty on the train, and I want you to do it." He promised he would.

We finally had a trail now. Hastily, I made preparations to get to Chattanooga. Meanwhile, some of the officers following Betty Andrews's directions had unearthed an old group of photographs of DuPre. I ordered one of them enlarged and widely distributed.

F. E. Fenn of the Pinkerton Detective Agency accompanied me to the Tennessee city. We went directly to the pawnbroker, telling him what we knew about his stalling of the Chattanooga detectives, and threatening to hold him for aiding the slayer's escape. He turned the ring over to me. We then hurried to the railway station, where the clerk on duty remembered DuPre after I had shown him one of our enlarged photographs.

The ticket clerk said that he had sold DuPre a ticket to Norfolk, Virginia. Our man had gone — and he was 36 hours ahead of us. The gap was widening, and with the slayer getting all the breaks, it began to look hopeless.

Meanwhile, I communicated with Atlanta and learned that one of the daily newspapers had received a letter from Norfolk signed "DuPre." In substance it read:

"The police are dumb. They couldn't catch a cold. Why, after the shooting, I walked the streets and elbowed with the crowd at the scene for fully forty minutes.

"I'm sorry I had to kill Mr. Walker, but I'm glad I shot Mr. West. He should have had better sense than to get in my way."

While waiting for the next train to Virginia there came the second amazing development in which DuPre's unbelievable luck was mingled with stupidity on the part of others.

It seemed that when DuPre arrived in Norfolk he had wired Buckley — the taxi driver — as promised. The message was for him to pick up Betty Andrews, put her on a train for Norfolk, and wire "F. B. Parker" at the Norfolk telegraph office when to expect her.

Buckley being in custody the telegram naturally fell into our hands, and a decoy was sent. At the same time the Norfolk police were notified of the situation and instructed to post detectives at the receiving counter in the telegraph office. Feeling certain then that our man would be taken easily, my chief ordered me back to Atlanta.

I was confounded upon my arrival to hear the following story from the Norfolk police:

Two detectives had been sent to the designated station and took up an unobtrusive position after informing the employee behind the delivery counter as to their business. After several hours' wait, a young man walked past the officers to the desk where the delivery girl was on duty.

"Have you a telegram for F. B. Parker?" he inquired.

"Yes, I have," she replied, "but there are a couple of gentlemen seated over there who want to see you first."

DuPre looked calmly at the two officers without betraying his nervousness.

"Those two there?" he asked, pointing to the detectives.

"Yes, sir," the girl said.

"Thanks." He tipped his cap and strolled casually towards the detectives. There was a sudden flurry of customers, and in the confusion DuPre slipped past the waiting officers and escaped.

There was nothing to do now but again resume the tangled trail ourselves.

We spent several days in Norfolk. During that time we had Betty parade the downtown streets in the hope that she would recognise DuPre or be recognised, but we failed to uncover a single lead. Once more our quarry had flown. Disappointed and baffled, we returned to Atlanta to await further developments.

The next came swiftly, and proves human nature is a strange thing. DuPre — just as he had trusted the taxi driver — showed he had a similar faith in the pawnbroker. He wrote to him in Chattanooga, enclosing the pawn ticket, and directed him to send the 300 dollars to "F. B. Parker, General Delivery, Detroit, Michigan." DuPre never stopped to think that the name which he had used at Norfolk was in the hands of every police official in the country.

Although the pawnbroker was not in custody — as was the taxi driver — he took the message to the Chattanooga police. They promptly communicated with us. A decoy letter was sent and Detroit detectives posted at the general delivery window of the post office there.

This time there was no slip-up. DuPre walked up to the general delivery window through a screen of detectives and asked for mail for F. B. Parker.

"I'm looking for a letter. It's pretty important," said the killer, "it's got some money in it!"

The hands of the officers quickly fell upon his shoulders.

DuPre smiled and shrugged his shoulders. "Oh, well, my name isn't Parker at all, but I guess I'm your man anyway. I guess luck isn't with me today."

Meanwhile, at the first word of the decoy plan, I had boarded a train for Detroit, having taken the precaution to secure a murder warrant and extradition papers.

DuPre was turned over to me and the Pinkerton man, and we took him back to Fulton Tower, the historic county jail at Atlanta.

West was recovering. But public sentiment over his injury — coupled with the death of Walker — was aroused, and DuPre was quickly tried, found guilty and sentenced to hang. He had waged a stiff fight for his life, pleading not guilty to the charges. In this trial my home-made test of the bullets and death weapon played a large part, and the jewellery shop assistant positively identified him.

C. R. Buckley, the taxi driver, received a short sentence as an accessory. Betty Andrews was also given a short sentence. She was eventually paroled to the Rev. G. W. Gasque, an Episcopal clergyman, who sent her west to a boarding school after she had taken on an assumed name.

In the year during which DuPre's appeal for a new trial was pending in the state supreme court, public sentiment took a strange turn and flowed back in his favour.

The killing of Detective Walker was forgotten in pity for the youth who was about to die. Clubs and groups were organised in an effort to save him because of his age, and the movement for the abolition of the gallows in Georgia gained nation-wide proportions. In the archives of the Georgia Prison Board today are thousands of letters written on behalf of the youth, including many from the killer's father.

But they were all in vain. Both the Prison Board and the state governor declined to interfere, and on August 25th, 1922, Frank DuPre went to his death on the gallows.

An immense crowd gathered about Fulton Tower standing high above Atlanta. For a while it was feared that some demonstration might break out. Police were sprinkled throughout the crowd, but no trouble developed.

Only when DuPre, on his march to the gallows, looked down on the crowd from two windows and waved his handkerchief at them was there a moan of horror.

He died like a man in the prescribed manner, paying the penalty for a cold-blooded murder.

Nevertheless, horror at the hanging of one so young crystallised into a definite sentiment against the gallows in Georgia. Men and women marched upon the legislature at its next session. They demanded that the gallows be abolished and some other more humane means for legally taking life be substituted.

And their will was done. The next person put to death in Georgia was murderer Howard Henson. He was executed on September 13th, 1924.

The method — electrocution...

11

THE COWBOY AND THE LADY

J. E. Griffin

*"Get rid of that prison suit and go out the
front door. Go straight and try to make
something of your life. So long, honey."
Toni Jo's last words to her lover.*

Known as Toni Jo, she was small and slim, with lustrous
black hair worn in a shoulder-length bob. She was 24, but
looked younger, despite the hardness in her too-knowing
eyes. He was 27, tall, burly and dark. Known as "Cowboy"
in the boxing ring, he was a tough nut, out of funds and in
bad trouble. The shuttered dwelling from which they
emerged had been the girl's place of employment from
childhood. It was, in fact, the town's whorehouse.

"I'm going for a walk," Toni Jo told the henna-haired
madam who stopped her as she approached the door.

The woman's lips tightened. Then, unexpectedly, she
capitulated. "Well, for an hour, maybe," she conceded.
"But don't be late. This will be a big night after the football
game."

"I'll be back," Toni Jo promised lightly. She flung a light
topcoat over her slim shoulders, though it failed to conceal
the alluring figure outlined by a clinging sweater and a too-
tight skirt. "Come on, Cowboy."

"What's your real name, honey?" Cowboy asked, as they
walked hand in hand along the San Antonio street.

"You first," she retorted pertly. "What's behind Cowboy?"

"Claude Henry," he told her. "Henry's the family name.
Believe it or not, I once had a family and a home."

"Sure you did. So did I." Toni Jo sighed with sympathetic understanding. As they strolled along in the gathering dusk, she told him that she had once been known as Annie Brown, but her real name was Annie Beatrice McQuiston. She was born in Louisiana, where the McQuistons were of some consequence. One relative of hers was a nurse. Another was a the high-ranking officer in the Louisiana state police.

"For crying out loud, honey!" Cowboy blurted. "Don't you go messing me in with any cops!"

The girl's eyes clouded. "Look, Cowboy," she began. "Are you in some kind of trouble?"

He saw the fear and appeal in her eyes and, though he had been on the point of confiding in her, he just shrugged. That could come later. Right now, there was another truth to be faced.

"Getting late," he said. "I got to be getting you back — you promised." He added bitterly: "If I only had the right kind of dough —"

"Nuts to that!" Toni Jo snorted. "I had this figured. We got dough, right here in the first national bank." She patted her leg. "I didn't dare come out carrying a handbag, or that old hag would have squawked. But I could tell you're not in the chips right now and I knew we'd need —"

She saw the white line around his mouth, the slow mounting flush. For a moment, she thought he was going to walk away from her. "Don't be like that!" she pleaded. "We're friends, aren't we? Anybody can help a friend. You'll pay me back, Cowboy — every nickel."

The folding money from the top of Toni Jo's stocking amounted to a very considerable sum of nickels, for Toni Jo had not meant to keep her promise to return that night. And for the next 72 hours, the couple spent it freely, with no thought for the future, no idea of accounting. They were together every minute and were deliriously happy.

Late in the afternoon of the third day, Toni Jo returned to the shuttered house to collect some of her things and some money due her — and to resign her post as the most popular inmate of that lush establishment. "He wants me," she explained briefly to the hard-eyed madam. "This is for keeps. And, know what? Cowboy's going to take me off the dope."

"He is, is he?" the woman sneered. "Well, while you've been AWOL, I've been checking up on your Cowboy Henry. Did he tell you how many fights he ever won? He can count 'em on one hand. And did he tell you he's lugging around a bail bond heavier on the back than that monkey you're carrying?"

Toni Jo recalled Cowboy's reference to "messing with cops," but she did not blink. "Sure, he told me," she lied.

"So you know you've picked yourself a cowboy the courts ride herd on!" the woman snorted. "This guy's been tried for murder!"

"As if I didn't know that!" And Toni Jo stalked out of the house and hurried back to the furnished room she now occupied with Claude Henry. She at once demanded that Cowboy give her the facts and give them to her straight.

It was true, he admitted. He had stood trial on a charge of homicide, and a jury in Bexar County, Texas, had found him guilty. He was free now only because his attorneys had appealed the verdict and got him out under heavy bail.

"What's the story?" Toni Jo demanded.

He slowly related the facts of the case. It had begun on an autumn night, November 16th, 1939, more than 22 months ago ...

Cowboy Henry and an acquaintance of his, Arthur Sinclair, a special policeman, had escorted two girls to a tavern. The older man — Sinclair was 34 — had grown surly and said something about the girl with Cowboy, which provoked an ugly argument. At length, Sinclair stepped outside. Cowboy promptly followed him.

Right after that came the sound of a shot. A bullet whined past Cowboy's ear, fired from ambush. Cowboy then rushed at his lurking adversary, wrestling Sinclair for the gun and disarming him.

There was a second shot. Arthur Sinclair died that night

from a bullet fired by his own gun. Cowboy Henry was accused of murder.

Testifying during the trial held the following January, the accused boxer stuck to his story of the attempted ambush. He insisted that he had only taken the gun away from Sinclair and fired in self-defence, convinced that the policeman would get another weapon and try again to shoot him from behind.

This defence failed to impress the jury, which voted unanimously for conviction. But Claude Henry's lawyers were granted a new trial for their client by the appeal court. The justices ruled that the trial judge had "inadequately instructed the jury". As a result, Cowboy was out on bail.

His second trial was to come up next winter, he told Toni Jo. His attorneys had won their argument in favour of a change of venue.

"Whatever that is," said Toni Jo unhappily.

"It's a cinch, honey," said Cowboy. "You tell 'em you feel you never can get a square shake in the court you been in and you petition that they hold your next trial in another county, where nobody knows you. Mine, they say, would be shifted maybe to Hondo."

His optimism irritated the girl. "You could have told me all this before," she complained. "Took me for a quitter, didn't you? Thought maybe I wouldn't stick if the going looked rough?"

"It can get plenty rough. And expensive," he admitted. "And I already owe you —"

"So now I'm a tightwad!" she rasped.

Her tension increased. And both knew what lay behind it — an overpowering hunger for narcotics. Finally, Toni Jo said she was sorry, he would have to excuse her — but she just couldn't go on without a last fix.

Nothing doing, Cowboy told her. And when she raged at him, a wily tigress with unsheathed claws, he threw into the struggle his whole strength and the strategy of the prize ring.

It got so bad, however, that he had to take the girl to a

doctor he knew. Cowboy was inflicting — and Toni Jo was suffering — what the initiated call the "cold turkey" cure. The worst kind. You just quit drugs entirely, sweat out the torment, with no sort of tapering off at all.

The physician, a knowing man with half his practice on the fringes of the underworld, warned them both that they had better not go through with it. But Cowboy, a hard driver, and Toni Jo, his voluntary if rebellious slave, went through with it.

The girl's cure resulted. It was signalised on November 25th — an amazingly short time since that early autumn Saturday when Cowboy had called and she had walked away with him from the whorehouse. They borrowed a car from one of his pugilistic pals and drove to a little town in her native state.

In Sulphur, Louisiana, a justice of the peace married them — Claude Henry and his big bail bond taking for life Annie Beatrice McQuiston and her heavy past as Toni Jo. For the first time in over five years, the girl used her right name when signing the marriage register. After Cowboy's trial and acquittal, young Mr. and Mrs. Henry were "going legitimate," they agreed.

With the monkey of dope addiction off her back, the mental burden of his approaching second trial could be thrust aside. They set out on a honeymoon trip. As a reward for her gameness in submitting to the "cold turkey" cure, Cowboy Henry, as he had promised, took his bride on a trip to southern California.

However, he had to keep in touch with his attorneys and his bail bondsmen. The former might use the police to trace and overtake him. The latter had "connections" and were tough-minded individuals, certain to get after him, should he switch from honeymooning tourist to fugitive and try to jump his bail.

The crisis came when Cowboy opened a lawyer's telegram and learned that, in 10 days' time, he must appear in Hondo, Medina County, Texas, on trial for his life.

When he told her, Toni Jo exploded: "You won't go! It

was self-defence. Trying you again is just a frame-up, Cowboy! Now you're out here, they can't —"

"Extradite me? You bet they can! The lawyers wised me up to that before we left."

"Then we'll hide. Change our looks. I'd be a cute blonde — guys have often told me."

"This guy likes you just the way you are. But never mind. I ain't aiming to leave my bondsmen holding the bag."

"But we'd pay 'em back. We could get the dough, lots of ways. Like, well, for instance, me," she went on recklessly, assuming an inviting pose.

"Skip it! That's *out*. We got married, remember? I'll go back," he decided, speaking with unaccustomed gravity. "This change of venue, they say, is a break. I tell my side of it, get acquitted — and the Henrys are in business for life. We'll find some decent, legitimate way to set us up in comfort."

"Yeah? Name one," Toni Jo said bitterly.

All the same, they *did* return to Texas and to the county seat of Medina County. It would have been a foolish mistake for Cowboy to try to dodge the law, or run out on his bondsmen. But his arrival in Hondo soon began to look like another mistake. And a fatal one.

On the witness-stand, he was quiet and confident. Sitting down front in the courtroom was his bride of two months — such a different Toni Jo, tense but smiling, a faithful wife, working on the sympathies of the court and jury every step of the way.

Unfortunately, the steps were few and all in favour of the prosecution, all harmful to Cowboy's defence. The jury foreman, a sandy-haired, weatherbeaten man, stood up and replied to the judge's formal question: "Yes, your honour. We have reached a verdict. We find the defendant guilty of murder."

This darkest of days in the rarely roseate life of Toni Jo was Saturday, January 27th, 1940. She heard the judge pass sentence. He had, like the jury, seemed little impressed with Cowboy's plea of self-defence. And he now showed that he thought the boxer's punishment had been delayed quite long enough. The sentence was 50 years in the Texas state penitentiary at Huntsville.

Toni Jo had listened to the verdict with some degree of composure. Perhaps she had been half expecting and bracing herself for that harsh pronouncement of guilt? But the greater harshness of the 50-year term detonated something inside her.

On her feet, swift and frantic, she climbed over the low railing to evade a bailiff at the gate, swept aside the deputies surrounding the prisoner and, on tiptoe, clasped him against her pounding heart.

"You can't do this, ma'am!" a bailiff protested.

The girl ignored him.

"Cowboy! Oh, Cowboy!" she cried. Her eyes shone with the fire of a fierce resolve. "Don't you worry, Cowboy, I'll get you out! I swear it, boy! I'll get you out!"

Sheriff's deputies intervened. "You can visit him, ma'am, just as soon as the law allows," she was told.

That same day, Toni Jo conferred with her husband's attorneys. These had proved themselves loyal and persistent, but they now told her frankly that the appeal court, having once before set aside Cowboy's penalty, would be far less receptive to renewed petitions, in as much as the Hondo trial had been conducted with impeccable fairness.

"Furthermore," one of them added, "appeal is expensive. Any further action initiated by you is going to run into money."

"Don't I know! But I can get any amount," Toni Jo bragged recklessly.

In jail, having also conferred with his lawyers, Cowboy reached a decision. The convicted boxer threw in the towel. No use gambling on another appeal. And on February 8th, 1940, he entrained for Huntsville to begin serving his term of 50 long years.

Toni Jo left Hondo the same day and went to Beaumont, which was fairly convenient to the prison. From there, she would be able to visit Cowboy regularly, she reasoned. But she also nurtured far more dangerous plans.

For she had contacts in Beaumont. Beginning in 1933, when she was but 17, she had worked the circuit, so she knew madams and girls who had been through every mill that warps and toughens humankind. In a frenzy of longing for her Cowboy, the killer's bride turned to several of these seasoned campaigners to ask what she should do.

"Don't do nothing, kid. Not right away," one advised her. "You only hurt your guy's chances if you try to spring him too soon. Let the dust settle. Wait a year at least. Visit him regular and always beg him to obey the rules, give no trouble and keep his nose clean. Then, for his good conduct, they'll move Cowboy to a prison farm. From there, you'll be better able to spring him."

Toni Jo promised to be cautious and wait. But she never meant to wait a year. And it was around that time that she met a young ex-convict of several aliases, who was introduced to her as "Arkinsaw."

At that moment, he seemed eager to head back to Arkansas, for he was being compelled to lie low in Beaumont. Although only 23 years old, he had already served a term in Huntsville. Released from the penitentiary, he had enlisted in the army, another error in judgment which he had recently undertaken to correct. The day Toni Jo met Arkinsaw, he was AWOL from Fort Sam Houston in San Antonio.

His having been imprisoned at Huntsville made him seem a practically perfect foil to the girl determined to liberate her Cowboy. He claimed to know the Texas prison inside out. What was more, he was broke, on the run, in need of transport and looking for more profitable adventure. So Toni Jo proceeded to sell him on her hope for an early reunion with her husband.

"O.K. I'd say we could spring your guy," he assured her. "But you'll need some things. You need dough — a big fat roll of it. And, of course, we've got to have a good fast car."

He and Toni Jo were soon plotting seriously. Arkinsaw came quickly to the meat of his proposition. Up in his native

Arkansas was a little hick town near Camden, with a small but well-heeled bank, just begging to be robbed. The exburglar, ex-convict and ex-soldier had stopped to case the institution on the one occasion he had gone home on leave.

"So there's our dough. And the fast car's a cinch," Toni Jo said. "But, Arky, you can't afford to buzz around Beaumont. The M.P.'s might spot you. But me, I'm in the clear. So I get us our guns."

And she got the guns that very night. For two agile teenagers, recommended to her by another underworld acquaintance, listened to her problem, then named their price — five dollars. For this handsome sum, the pair broke into a hardware store and came out with an assortment of guns. There were .32 revolvers and .38 automatic pistols, together with a quantity of cartridges of both calibres.

The youthful Arkinsaw exulted over them when he called next day at the house where Toni Jo was staying. "All this for five bucks? For fifty, maybe, those kids would go and get your husband out!"

He laughed. But Toni Jo didn't. Her eyes were glinting wickedly. Arkinsaw stopped laughing. He concluded that this confederate of his might turn out harder than any girl with her curves was entitled to be.

The guns were stolen on Monday, February 12th. On the 14th, St. Valentine's Day, the pair were set to pull out of Beaumont. When Arkinsaw slipped around cautiously to pick up his companion, he found her wearing bright red slacks and a green jacket.

"How come?" he objected. "We'll be spotted for sure, with you in duds so easy to remember."

"You sure smartened up in the army!" Toni Jo jeered. "In that small bundle there, I got a plain little dress. After we hijack the car, I change into it. When the guy whose car we take squawks to the cops, he remembers this red and green outfit and they broadcast my description. But by then, I'm dressed differently. Get it, stupid?"

Arkinsaw *did*. It was her plan — and she could be the leader, he agreed, at least until they got into Arkansas and were ready to rob the bank. The fact was, in setting out on their excursion into violent crime — the car, the bank, the prison break — each felt lucky in teaming up with the other, though from different motives. Toni Jo was bossy and uncompromising — and few men would willingly subordinate themselves to her. Arkinsaw, however, was easy-going, his main object being to get back to Arkansas and hide there, the US Army permitting.

The one motive he and Toni Jo shared was larceny. And to this end, he took care of loading the guns — two of the .38 automatics for himself, a nickel-plated .32 for the girl. Having various other guns and plenty of ammunition left over, a burden neither of them wished to carry, Toni Jo made up a neat parcel, tiptoed up to the attic of the boarding-house and hid it where she might find it again, should her plan for breaking out her husband require more weapons.

Proceeding late that February afternoon to the outskirts of Beaumont, they posted themselves on the New Orleans highway, Route 90, known locally as the Old Spanish Trail. Almost immediately, a friendly motorist pulled up to offer the dashing-looking girl and the inoffensive young man a lift.

"Not his car," Toni Jo murmured. "Too old. No speed."

Arkinsaw agreed with a nod, yet they smiled and accepted the ride. They told the driver that they were newlyweds, on their way to New Orleans. Rolling into Orange, the Texas town on the Sabine River across from Vinton, Louisiana, Toni Jo thanked the driver with a radiant smile. Would he kindly drop them now at the bus station? He would and did, waving and tipping his hat as he drove off — one good-natured Texan who wouldn't realise his own immense luck until he read about it in the papers.

Dusk had fallen and it was beginning to rain when Toni Jo and Arkinsaw again stood at the edge of Route 90, signalling to eastbound motorists from the side of the highway. "There — that one's for us!" the girl suddenly exclaimed.

A new, dark green Ford coupé had slowed and stopped some 20 feet beyond where they were standing. Its driver was well dressed, genial-looking, a rather thick-set man of about 40. He swung the door open and, as the pair climbed in beside him, said something about the rain and its being a mean night to wait by the roadside.

Having asked and been told their imaginary destination, New Orleans, he said he could take them as far as Jennings, Louisiana. He was doing a favour for a friend in delivering this coupé to a dealer in Jennings, he revealed.

The Ford V-8 was brand-new, a good speedy car, he said. Once, since passing through Beaumont, he'd had it up to 90 mph, he said. Hearing this, Toni Jo gave her accomplice a light nudge in the ribs. She was sitting on the outside with Arkinsaw between her and their chosen dupe.

"Not many heaps around these parts could pass a new coupé doing ninety," Arkinsaw commented admiringly.

After leaving Vinton, they sped through several small Louisiana towns. One of these was Sulphur where, only 11 weeks and four days ago, Toni Jo and Cowboy had been wed. Making fine time, despite the weather, the Ford reached Lake Charles and took the winding highway route through that city. And now they were gliding away from habitations again, speeding along through open country.

Toni Jo's elbow gave Arkinsaw a harder nudge. This was it! She drew her shiny .32 from where she had kept it hidden. Leaning forward, she pointed the gun so that their driver could see it clearly defined in the light from his dashboard instrument panel.

"Say, what's the idea?" he began, instinctively applying the brakes.

Toni Jo rasped: "None of that! Keep going, you, till I tell you where to stop. Turn left here," she ordered, as they drew near to a crossroads.

Shocked and unnerved, the driver obeyed. They rode on in wary silence for another 10 minutes. Suddenly, the girl called a halt. With the coupé parked on a lonely side road, she scrambled out. Arkinsaw, who had drawn one of his two automatic pistols, kept the driver covered.

"Look, I have only fifteen dollars on me," the man said. "Oh, yes — and this wrist watch. You're welcome to them —"

"Thanks!" the girl jeered. "We're taking 'em. This is a stick-up, mister. We want the car, your dough — and your clothes."

"My clothes?" he quavered.

"You heard me! Out of that car and out of that suit! Unless you want the top of your head blown off!" she snapped.

The big man again obeyed. Shivering in the night air, he stood before the flint-eyed girl, hesitant to undress under her shameless gaze. "I can't see what you want my suit for," he ventured. "It's sizes too big for your husband."

"A fat lot you know about my husband!" the girl blurted. "He's as big as you and, right now, he's wearing a prison suit. I need yours for him when we spring him —"

From the car, her confederate gave a meaningful snort. Toni Jo wheeled and Arkinsaw hurriedly directed her attention towards some nearby towering oil derricks, visible in the light of sundry gas flares.

Their victim now had his suit off and stood shaking in his underwear. He handed Toni Jo his wallet and the watch which he had unstrapped and taken from his wrist. She made sure there was 15 dollars in the wallet, then slipped it into a side pocket of her slacks. The watch she handed to Arkinsaw. Then she snatched up their victim's clothing and tossed it into the car.

She had been pointing the .32 at him, intending to send him loping off into the dark, but now she didn't dare. He could quickly raise an alarm. For men worked at the oil derricks, tended those spurting gas flares.

She motioned irritably with the revolver, ordering him into the boot of the coupé. When she slammed the lid down, it caught his hand, crushing it cruelly. But when he cried out in protest and pain, the girl only cursed him for being so awkward.

"What you gonna do with him?" Arkinsaw asked Toni Jo as he took the wheel.

Toni Jo slid in beside him. "You drive. I'll think of something," she ordered.

Arkinsaw drove, picking up speed. They were soon crossing the federal highway again, their direction now bearing south-east towards the Gulf of Mexico. After almost 40 minutes, Arkinsaw braked the coupé and asked her: "Well, kid — how 'bout it?"

"Him? O.K., one of those haystacks'll make as good a spot as any," the girl answered. "After I get him out of the boot, Arky, turn the car around for a fast take-off."

"Look, baby — you ain't?"

"Just do as I say. I'll attend to this!" Toni Jo snapped at him.

She got their victim out and had to hold him up until he overcame the numbness brought on by his cramped quarters. She looked with unconcern at the injury to his hand.

"Strip off that underwear, too — I might need it for Cowboy. And don't get blood on it," she warned him.

"I'll be naked —" the shivering man protested faintly, but with little hope.

"You'll be walking in front of this gun, so you won't see me blush!" she snapped.

Once he had stripped to the skin, she marched him ahead of her across a field, well beyond the small area reached by the glow of the car lights.

When she halted him, he gripped his throbbing hand and forced his voice to sound steady. "I suppose you know you'll go to the penitentiary for a thing like this?" he reminded her.

"Seeing where I'm sending you, mister, you better kneel down. You don't have a wish, but you still have a prayer."

The doomed motorist sank to his knees. "I won't pray for myself," he said simply. "I'll pray for us —"

Toni Jo stood straight and aimed the gun downwards. The first crashing .32 bullet tore into the praying stranger's skull and killed him instantly.

Further back, on the byroad he had chosen, Arkinsaw was turning around the stolen coupé. At this moment, he wanted most of all to get out of this mess, leave Toni Jo flat. Let her figure some other way, find some other sucker to help her snatch Cowboy from the Huntsville pen.

He was, in fact, just about to take off at high speed when Toni Jo, the nickel-plated gun in her hand, appeared at the car door. If he tried to bolt now, Arkinsaw knew, five .32 bullets would stop him.

So he swung the coupé's door open. "So that's that," he said.

"Get going, Arky!"

He drove fast and by a circuitous route, heading for Arkansas. He drove all night, stopping twice to buy petrol. Toni Jo paid for it, disbursing the murder money — that pitiful 15 dollars — grudgingly. It was nearly sunrise on February 15th before she consented to halt a third time and get themselves something to eat.

The town of Camden, county seat of Ouachita County, was their immediate destination. From here, it had been agreed, their planned assault upon the neighbouring small-town bank would be scouted and set in motion.

Only once did the worried Arkinsaw venture to refer to the deadly night, now breaking into day. "Why did you want his suit and stuff?" he asked.

"Makes it hard to identify him," she answered. "Could be maybe a week before an alarm for this car goes out. Besides, I want 'em for Cowboy. He won't dare shop for new clothes after we get him sprung."

Arriving in Camden around 8 a.m., they parked the coupé and entered a small hotel on the main street. They registered as Mr. and Mrs. Ray Johnson and, because they were without baggage, paid in advance. The exhausted couple went straight up to their second-floor room.

Toni Jo still carried her small parcel. She hadn't changed from the vivid red and green outfit, since no description of her conspicuous slacks and jacket would ever be given by the man whose car they had hijacked. Now she said curtly:

"Go look out the window."

Arkinsaw took the hint. Looking down onto the main street gave him an idea, too. Toni Jo had nipped out of her clothing and was in bed, covered to the shoulders and dragging on a cigarette. Arkinsaw cast a longing glance at the other twin bed. He was so tired, he could barely keep his eyes open. But he had a plan of his own now.

"Y'know, there might be an alarm already out for that car, since the guy didn't own it. It was maybe a bum idea, parking it down there, so close to where we are. It could lead trouble to us." He stretched and yawned. "Looks like I better go down and move it a block or two away."

Toni Jo flipped ash from her cigarette. "Your tough luck, Arky," she said, with a mocking grin. "If I went down to move it like I am, it could sure lead to something."

Arkinsaw unlocked the door and went out quickly. The girl luxuriated upon the bed. Crushing out her cigarette, she dozed. When she roused herself later with an effort, she was still alone in the room.

She swung her feet out and leaned over to reach the doorknob. Arkinsaw had left it unlocked, the key in the lock.

"The sneaking yellow rat!" she raged. "He ran out on me!" But how far would he run? To the Camden cops? Toni Jo, now wide and viciously awake, jumped up and dressed. She changed her appearance as much as she could, putting on the mousy outfit which she had brought.

She walked down through the lobby, looking along the street for the green coupé. She explored side streets, walking faster, growing angrier. But she knew that it was precious time wasted. Arkinsaw had fled with the car and that big guy's wrist-watch and clothes, leaving her only what was left out of the 15 dollars.

Seeing a bus terminus across the street gave Toni Jo an idea. It was sheer impulse and a complete change from her original plan to rob a bank for big money, big money, use it and the stolen fast car to spring Cowboy. She now plunked down most of the money she had left and bought a one-way bus ticket from Camden to Shreveport, Louisiana. In want and distress, she was heading home.

It was dusk when she climbed stiffly from the bus in busy Shreveport. Everything looked familiar. She headed for Hattie's place. As a very young girl, just making the grade in a highly competitive profession, she had been allowed to "work" for Hattie. In the seven years since then, she had not forgotten the woman's shrewd firmness, or her many little kindnesses. Hattie would want her back. Hattie would provide shelter and an immediate income. Hattie would know what she ought to do.

The madam received her with outstretched hands and a warm welcome. "Lordie, child, what we been hearing about you!" she cried. She observed Toni Jo's startled reaction. There were no sharper eyes than Hattie's anywhere in Shreveport.

"How you been getting married to a handsome young fighter," she went on. "And how he took you off a big habit. Oh, we hear the gossip." Hattie smiled contentedly, noting the girl's undisguised relief. What ailed her, anyway?

While Toni Jo was using Hattie's bathroom to clean up, Hattie glanced into the girl's handbag. Almost no money, but a new-looking .32 revolver! She sniffed the muzzle, examined the cylinder — five live cartridges, one empty shell.

Later, she offered warm food and steaming hot coffee. "Could it be you are in some trouble?" Hattie asked.

"I'm broke," the girl confessed. "Put me to work, Hattie. I need to start right away. Tonight."

"Got to see a doctor first. Any new girl. You know my rule."

"But I'm married. Though Cowboy's in the pen —"

"Hadn't you better tell Hattie all about it?"

Toni Jo nodded. She brazenly answered Hattie's questions. It was an even worse story than the exploded cartridge in the nickel-plated .32 had led the older woman to expect.

"My girls live here. They don't hide here," Hattie said

sharply. "Look, kid, I barely got pull enough to keep this house open. But you come from nice people in these parts. They can help you. There's your uncle. And your aunt, a fine, respected woman. You're going to her."

"When I haven't been near her for over four years?"

It took Hattie almost two hours to overcome Toni Jo's loud objections and defiance. However, Hattie would have been out of business years ago if she hadn't known how to win arguments with shrill and impudent females. Thus, at length, Toni Jo was bundled off to the residence of her aunt, where she was received with the generous show of affection that Hattie had predicted.

It was late and the aunt obtained only a vague and more garbled account of the girl's St. Valentine's Day adventure than the probing, blunt-speaking Hattie had got out of her. But early next morning, she felt so disturbed by the hints and intimations in her niece's story that she decided to consult her brother, an officer of the Louisiana state police.

Hurrying to the state police post in Shreveport, she was told that her brother was away on an important assignment. She hesitated, then decided to reveal her misgivings to the officer in charge, Sergeant Dave Walker. He consulted the inquiries and alarms that had recently come over the teletype. There was one in particular which might be pertinent.

The day before — February 15th — Eileen Calloway had appealed to police in Houston, Texas, on account of her husband. It seemed that he had set off to accommodate a friend and deliver a new Ford coupé to a firm in Jennings, Louisiana. At his home, it had been understood that he would phone from Jennings upon his arrival. He expected to be in Houston on Saturday, February 17th — his 42nd birthday. Mrs. Calloway and their daughter were preparing for the birthday festivities.

Joseph Calloway, a valued employee at a department store in Houston, had neither phoned nor returned. The firm in Jennings stated that the new Ford coupé had not been received by them. Calloway would have travelled over the familiar Route 90 and Houston police had checked with communities along that highway between his home and Jennings.

He had stopped in Beaumont long enough to call upon a friend. A service station attendant whom he knew in Orange, Texas, remembered having served and spoken to the motorist before he drove on into Louisiana. They had discussed the new Ford and Calloway had said that, despite the bad weather that Wednesday evening, he ought to reach his destination within two hours.

Then he had driven on, presumably crossing the Sabine River into Louisiana — and had vanished. An interstate alarm was out for him now and the authorities in Shreveport had received it, as had every other police post and sheriff's office in the state.

"I'll come with you, ma'am. I'd like a talk to this young woman," Sergeant Walker said.

Toni Jo candidly told the Louisiana officer about her life — of her drug addiction, her cure and her marriage, of her husband's "unjust" conviction and imprisonment and her determination to set him free. When she came to the hitch-hiking episode with her confederate and the shooting of the kneeling, naked motorist, a man who had befriended them on a rainy night, her manner was so composed and casual that Walker wondered if what she said could possibly be true.

"Where did you get rid of the gun?" he asked.

"I didn't. I've got it here," Toni Jo said. She reached into her handbag and brought out the snub-nosed revolver.

Walker took the gun from her and spun the cylinder. Sure enough, one .32 cartridge had been fired. "Tell me about this fellow 'Arkinsaw.' What is his real name?" he asked.

"I don't know! And I don't want to know!" Toni Jo rasped, displaying more emotion than she had when describing the murder she had committed. "He was as yellow as they make 'em, Sergeant. And when he showed his true colour, I slugged him with that gun there. Knocked him

225

cold and left him." She insisted that she had abandoned her unconscious accomplice in the car, on the road between Camden and El Dorado, Arkansas.

When Toni Jo's state policeman uncle reported back to Shreveport, he found his niece in police custody. She repeated her incredible story to him with the same eerie composure. He phoned the police in Lake Charles and learned that no murder victim had been found in that area. Arkansas police, similarly contacted, replied that the Camden-El Dorado highway was regularly patrolled and that no unconscious or injured man in a green Ford coupé had been found thereabouts.

Upon her uncle fell the harsh duty of having Toni Jo handed over to his colleagues in the state police at Lake Charles. Captain John Jones, the commander there, asked her: "Why did you do all this you claim to have done?"

"I did it for Cowboy. I'd do it again. I'd hang four times to get him out," she told him.

On the drive from Shreveport to Lake Charles, she tried to direct her captors to the scene of the murder, but wasn't able to pick it out. Now, early on the morning of the 17th, she drove with Captain Jones and Trooper Fremont LeBleu as they covered miles of country roads outside Lake Charles. The girl assured them that, in daylight, she would soon spot that haystack towards which she had prodded her shivering, defenceless victim.

It began to rain hard. Wet, these back roads were no bargain. Visibility was reduced to a few yards. Jones and LeBleu began to suspect that they were victims of a crazy hoax. They often had to leave the car and get soaked exploring fields. Toni Jo didn't seem to relish this much, either.

Once, returning to the car over sodden, squelching terrain, she snarled: "Damn that crummy fool! I ought to have put a couple more bullets in him, if he was going to make us all this trouble!"

LeBleu glanced over the top of her shining head. Jones nodded. Anybody expressing thoughts as callous as hers was probably not faking.

By early afternoon, the searching party had looked everywhere, except in a region known as Plateau Petit Bois, some 12 miles south-east of Lake Charles. Here were more watery rural lanes. But Toni Jo seemed excited as she peered from the car window.

Suddenly, she exclaimed: "There — that could be it! Yeah, that's right where I made Arkinsaw turn the coupé around!" And, as the police car crept forward, she pointed to a rice-chaff stack nearly 100 yards from the road. "There's that old haystack!" she exulted.

The officers left the car and hurried across the field with her. "What did I tell you? And you chumps thought I was kidding!" Toni Jo sneered.

The dim figure of a naked man lay in front of the stack, his knees still bent, exactly as the girl had described the death scene. The man had been shot once between the eyes, the bullet ranging downwards through the skull to the back of the neck. It was obvious to the officers that the man had been on his knees and below the gun muzzle when shot. His left hand, crusted with blood, appeared to have been badly crushed.

While being escorted back to Lake Charles, Toni Jo rummaged irritably in her handbag for a cigarette. "Gee, look — I forgot this!" she cried. "I got it from that guy's wallet when I took out his measly fifteen bucks." She handed Jones a driving licence. It bore the name of Joseph Calloway from Houston, Texas — the man whose wife had reported him missing.

Jones had already summoned the owner of the field to stand guard over the murder victim's body. And now the coroner, Dr. E. L. Clement, and District Attorney C. V. Pattison, together with other officials, arrived to relieve him of his grim responsibility and to study the scene of the crime.

The body was removed to Lake Charles, where a post-mortem was held. Close relatives of the victim hurried from Houston and made a conclusive identification. A ballistics expert established that the bullet taken from the back of Calloway's neck had been fired by the .32 revolver taken from Toni Jo Henry.

Meanwhile, a complete description of the stolen Ford coupé had been teletyped to police all over the South and South-west. The licence number on its Texas plates was given as N-10-754. Within a few hours, Sheriff A. M. Shaw, of Clark County, Arkansas, reported that the green coupé had been found abandoned in the county seat, Arkadelphia.

Examined for fingerprints, the vehicle showed none, Shaw explained. But in the ashtray were several cigarette butts showing lipstick. There were bloodstains in the car's boot. A bundle of clothing, suit and underwear to fit a fairly large man had been found rolled up on the shelf behind the seat. In the suit was the label of a Houston clothier.

Townspeople said that they had noticed the green Ford coupé parked in Arkadelphia for some days. But the sheriff had been unable to find anyone who remembered seeing the driver.

Toni Jo, detained in Lake Charles since the finding of Calloway's body, had become uncommunicative and venomous. She refused to reveal her confederate's name, or describe him, or discuss their activities further. She kicked out at the cameras of newspaper photographers sent to get her picture. Finally, a deputy sheriff held her head, so that one glowering photograph might be snapped. And while Toni Jo sulked in jail, insulting questioners, flatly refusing to identify Arkinsaw, police were securing all possible information about her ...

She was born on January 3rd, 1916, in the small community of Mooringsport, some eight miles north of Shreveport.

Her mother, always ailing, had finally succumbed to tuberculosis when the child Annie Beatrice was eight years old. Her father had been a railway employee, but had left that job to become a foreman with an oil company. He had lost this more promising job because of habitual drunkenness. Even so, he had acquired a second wife — and a new brood of children added to the poverty and discomfort felt by the girl's own brothers and sisters.

Annie Beatrice ran away from home at the age of 14, blaming this on poverty and the crowded home. She hadn't liked school and had found jobs and the discipline of steady work "no better than school". In spite of her tender years, she was soon well known in Shreveport's nightlife. She became an inmate of a house of prostitution well before her 16th birthday.

Marijuana and then drug addiction had been her next backward steps. For four years, she had lived with a succession of boxers and had been involved in the narcotics racket with a bantamweight. Her police record in several states, when the Louisiana officers finished assembling it, was a significant one. As Annie Brown, then as Toni Jo, the girl had been in trouble eight times.

Her first arrest occurred on August 6th, 1933, when she was 17. With two other prostitutes, she was charged with "assault with a dangerous weapon" — the weapon a broken bottle — and with "wounding less than mayhem". But the girl (then selling her juvenile body under the name of Annie Brown) had been spared any punishment because of her youth.

During the next four years, she had been arrested on six different occasions, with the charges against her ranging from vagrancy, drunkenness and disorderly conduct to assault. Her drug addiction had grown so serious that she was finally placed under a peace bond, at the request of another prostitute with whom she had been fighting. The complaining trollop swore that she had been threatened repeatedly and had good cause to fear for her life. Evidence given in court indicated that men too feared the girl now known as Toni Jo.

Late in 1937 occurred her last serious brush with the law, so far as the record showed. She had sold a quantity of mortgaged furniture in her possession, taken the money and headed south-west with her then favourite boxer. In the autumn of 1939, she had only recently ventured back into her former haunts when she met Cowboy Henry.

DA Pattison and Captain Jones studied the record. "She looks a bad one, through and through," Pattison commented. "But this convicted murderer Claude Henry seems to have been the one big thing in her life."

It was Captain Jones who hit upon a clever use of this one moving influence in Toni Jo's sordid and turbulent life — her love for her husband. It might get her to talk. And so, after a complicated manoeuvre, she was extradited to Beaumont, Texas, for an unexpected reunion with Cowboy. He had been interviewed by officials and had promised them that, if he were taken from Huntsville and allowed to see his wife alone, he would persuade her to do the right thing and tell the whole truth.

The meeting in Beaumont of the young man serving a 50-year sentence in Texas and the young woman jailed on a murder charge in Louisiana occurred in a private room of a city structure so heavily guarded that neither prisoner had the slightest chance of making a break. After the agreed-upon interval, officers entered. They found Toni Jo crying.

"Cowboy says I got to tell you!" she sobbed.

And she proceeded to identify Arkinsaw, her hitch-hiking accomplice, as an army deserter and former convicted burglar whose real name was Harold Finnon Burks. He had, she said, served his term in Huntsville in 1938.

The Texas and Louisiana officers confirmed these details immediately. Since the stolen Ford car had been transported across state lines, the FBI now entered the case. They traced him to Warren, Arkansas, and to the home of a sister, where they made the arrest.

Burks was unarmed and offered no resistance. He told the FBI agents that he had sold the two .38 automatics in Texarkana, Arkansas, after fleeing from Camden and Toni Jo. He then drove on to Arkadelphia, abandoned the green coupé and found a buyer for Calloway's wrist-watch. Thus provided with funds, he took a bus to Warren, where he went immediately to his sister's home.

Burks did not hesitate to admit that he had been afraid of Toni Jo. But he denied that she had ever struck him, let alone left him insensible in the hijacked Ford. He confessed that he had been fooling Toni Jo, even before he learned to be afraid of her. He had never intended to help her with any jailbreak, he declared.

When they met in Beaumont for the first time on February 10th, the army deserter was flat broke. He wanted to get home, and saw a better chance of getting a lift with this flashy girl along. So he deliberately encouraged Toni Jo with his "inside knowledge" of the Huntsville prison, brief though his stay there had been. Then he had induced her to direct their course towards Arkansas, with the concocted story of the bank he claimed to have cased.

"That dame is just nuts," he said. "But she sure is one dangerous nut!"

Back in Lake Charles, Captain Jones asked Toni Jo why she claimed to have knocked out Arkansaw, or Burks, then left him unconscious in the stolen car. The girl conceded blandly that she had not done that.

"And there's another thing I faked —" she jolted her interrogators — "I didn't shoot that guy Calloway, either. It was Burks that took him to the haystack and plugged him. I couldn't help seeing it. But I never got out of the car."

Toni Jo Henry and Harold Finnon Burks were both indicted for the first-degree murder of Joseph Calloway. The court appointed Norman Anderson and Clement Moss to defend Toni Jo. These attorneys, hitherto special-ising only in civil cases, launched a truly heroic campaign for their 24-year-old client. It couldn't have been more intensive or devoted if she had been a respected and wrongly suspected person and their fee astronomic.

They first obtained a severance, so that Toni Jo was tried before Burks. To the mass of reporters covering the sensa-tional trial that began on March 27th, 1940, the defendant was a "sultry brunette". She was also a pitiless perjurer, for she took the witness-stand to shift all the blame and swear Burks's life away. He was the killer. She had suggested stripping their victim naked, she said, only in order to prevent pursuit.

Judge John Hood declined to allow Toni Jo to sob over or act out the story of her "abused" childhood and girlish induction into brothels. This, the judge ruled, had nothing to do with the murder.

The jury deliberated nearly seven hours, then found Toni Jo Henry guilty. She was sentenced to death. Burks, in his subsequent trial, was convicted as quickly and was also sentenced to be executed.

However, on November 4th, 1940, the state supreme court granted Toni Jo a new trial, on the grounds that Judge Hood had permitted prejudicial conduct in the courtroom. At the same time, the execution of Burks was stayed, to permit him to testify against Toni Jo.

Her second trial began on February 3rd, 1941, with Judge Mark Pickrel presiding. Burks was the prosecution's star witness. And this jury's deliberation consumed but 60 minutes. Toni Jo was again found guilty. But her attorneys, fighting ever harder, appealed against the death sentence on 19 counts — and won.

Still another trial was granted to her, on the grounds that DA Pattison had subjected prospective jurors to improper questioning. Judge Pickrel was again on the bench when, on January 20th, 1942, Toni Jo faced her third set of jurors. And, for the third time, she heard the death sentence solemnly pronounced, the only difference now being that the supreme court of Louisiana upheld the conviction and the sentence.

But Attorneys Anderson and Moss were not done for yet. They found an obscure loophole for appeal in the wording of the 1940 state law which had changed Louisiana's executions from hanging to death in the electric chair. While this was being weighed and decided, Toni Jo remained in her cell in the Lake Charles jail, where she was permitted to have a pet, a small black-and-white dog.

The high court ruled that the electric chair in Louisiana was constitutional, whereupon Governor Sam Jones let it be known that he would refuse any clemency plea made to him on Toni Jo's behalf. The date for her execution was set for Saturday, November 28th, 1942.

Having abandoned hope of further reprieve, she granted reporters a rather flamboyant interview, in which she tried to explain her feeling for her husband. She gushed: "That guy is king of my heart. Nobody ever really cared about me until he came along. Every man wants a passionate woman, but few are willing to risk marrying them — and Cowboy did that. He took the monkey off my back — and I'll always be grateful to him. Most folks wonder what goes on in the mind of a condemned person. In the first place, the victim doesn't return to haunt me. I never think of him. I've known all along it would be my life for his. I believe mine is worth as much to me as his was to him.

"Sometimes," she went on, "I wonder why I didn't just knock Calloway unconscious. But it was like being drunk, real drunk. Ever pull something when you were drunk — and that something seemed the cutest, smartest thing in the world, but it was really the awfullest? Well, me, I was drunk with pressure."

Toni Jo also attempted to offset two years of perjury and prevent the execution of Harold Burks. At each of her three trials, she had declared under oath that he was the real killer. But eight days before her scheduled date of execution, she dictated and signed this statement:

"I, Annie Beatrice Henry, fired the shot that killed J. P. Calloway. It is my hope that Harold Finnon Burks will not have to suffer the death penalty."

Just three days later, on November 23rd, came a spectacular development. Cowboy Henry had been transferred from Huntsville to the Central Prison Farm No. 2, near Sugar Land, Texas, where he was assigned to work in the laundry. When a small truck pulled up in front of the laundry building at around 11 a.m. that day, Henry and another prisoner named Clyde Byers clubbed the driver and made off in his truck, sending it smashing through the prison-farm gate and speeding in the direction of Houston,

25 miles distant.

A general alarm describing the escapees was immediately sent out. By questioning other convicts, prison officials learned that Cowboy had become unnerved after reading Toni Jo's farewell interview. He remarked to several of them that she was only in this trouble on his account, so he'd have to break out and try to save her from execution.

Following the escape from Sugar Land farm, authorities in Lake Charles were notified. And a special guard was thrown about the jail there, where Toni Jo waited in the death cell. That night, floodlights were set up to focus upon the jail and crack marksmen were placed where they could survey every foot of the structure.

Over in Texas, the hunt for Henry and Byers was being pressed in Houston and in San Antonio. When Toni Jo learned of all this, she exclaimed: "Cowboy's crazy if he thinks he can get me out of here!"

All that night, like the marksmen manning the floodlit walls, the condemned girl kept vigil at the window of her cell, ready to yell a warning to Cowboy, should he rashly try any storming operation.

In Houston that afternoon, police received a reliable tip. Cowboy Henry had been there and he was saying that, if Toni Jo died, he'd kill the judge who'd sentenced her. It seemed that Cowboy was on his way to Lake Charles to try to kidnap either Judge Pickerel or Judge Hood. So guards were placed around the homes of both jurists, while members of their families were forbidden to go out without police escorts. By Tuesday night, Lake Charles and the vicinity resembled an armed camp.

On Wednesday, police in Beaumont heard that Cowboy Henry had been seen there. If true, this meant that he had closed the gap between himself and Toni Jo from over 200 miles to a mere 66 miles. No mean feat, with a large segment of eastern Texas hunting him.

Beaumont police and detectives began covering every cheap hotel and boarding-house in the community. They eventually came to a shabby hotel near the railway station.

The sleepy-eyed porter snapped awake when they asked him to study a photograph of Cowboy Henry.

"Say, that looks like a guy we got registered tonight!" he exclaimed. "He came in after dark and —"

Radio calls were already bringing reinforcements. Men armed with sub machine-guns stood ready to cut down resistance. But when a detective rapped on the suspect's door, it opened and he came out, both hands raised.

It was Cowboy. "Don't shoot," he begged. "I haven't got a gun." He said that he had separated from Byers in Houston and admitted that he had been aiming for Lake Charles, intending to aid his condemned wife as best he could.

All the way back to Huntsville — a maximum-security prison to which any prison farm escapee would be re-committed — Cowboy pleaded for a chance just to say goodbye to Toni Jo. At Lake Charles, she was begging for at least a telephone farewell. The sentimental South couldn't refuse this last brief boon to the recaptured Romeo and his doomed Juliet.

On Friday, November 27th, Cowboy waited in the warden's office at Huntsville. The phone rang. Toni Jo, from the chief jailer's office in Lake Charles, was being permitted to call and say goodbye.

Her husband sobbed throughout the exchange. But Toni Jo, bright and encouraging, chided him for his foolish escape and begged him: "Get rid of that prison suit and go out the front door. Go straight and try to make something of your life. So long, honey," she ended.

She was still trying to help Harold Burks too, again protesting his innocence. But this was to no avail. Four months later, on March 23rd, 1943, Burks was executed for the murder he had sat by and seen committed.

Toni Jo amazed her guards by her cheerfulness after that farewell call to Huntsville. On November 28th, 1943, her only complaint came when her head had to be shaved. "I want a scarf for my execution," she told them. And she was indeed permitted to cover up this unsightliness to the last moment with a gay bandana.

She had asked for — and received — the continuity of the radio serial Abie's Irish Rose, to which she had been an avid listener. In this way, she could know what would happen next.

"I'm scared," she said. "Because I don't know where I'll be. But it's good to know what 'Rose' and the rest will be doing after this is over."

At the end, Toni Jo was praying, just as the unlucky motorist she murdered had done. Then, at 12.12 p.m., the big lightning bolt of the law in Louisiana struck and ended her life for a senseless and horrid crime.

12

THE HUMAN MOTH

Hal White

"Oh, let's not go into that right now. You've heard the expression, 'Curiosity killed the cat'? Well, let's not kill the cat yet."
Elmo Smith's reply when asked how he felt about going to the chair.

Whoever heard of a human moth? Pennsylvania did. It had one. Residents in the south of the state had only to switch on a light, it seemed, and he'd be there. Looking through the window. And then coming in ...

It was on October 23rd, 1947, that the district first realised it had a problem. Later, the "moth" himself was to describe what happened.

He was driving at night through Hughes Park on the outskirts of Philadelphia, he said, when he saw two lights. "So I stopped near the corner leading to one of the houses. I walked over and the front door was ajar. I went inside and there was a lamp burning.

"I saw two black purses on one of the tables. I looked into them and there was no money there. I seen the phone over on the corner table and there was a pair of scissors laying there and I cut the wires and went upstairs.

"I looked in one room and all I seen was a lot of clothes on the bed and there was a crib in there. I looked in the room next to it and I see this old lady with a night table and a lot of medicines on it and this other girl was on the other bed. There were twin beds. This girl was in the bed next to the window.

"I went back downstairs and then I saw this rolling-pin laying on the sink in the kitchen, so I got that and went back upstairs and I hit her a couple of times with it, and about that time someone behind me said, 'Who is there?'

"I turned real quick and bumped into her with my arm, which knocked her down. I ran down the steps and out of the house. I still had the rolling-pin in my hand and before I got back in the car I threw it in the bushes ... To tell the truth, I don't know why I went in. I didn't know who lived there or anything."

The girl he'd attacked was rushed to hospital with a fractured skull, together with her grandmother, who was also injured. Then, as she recovered in hospital, the girl had a surprise visitor, who was leaving the ward as Police Sergeant William Bradley arrived.

"What a terrible thing!" said the neatly dressed young man. "The beast who did it should be lynched."

A week later, an elderly woman was asleep in her ground-floor bedroom in Hamilton, Pennsylvania, when she was woken by her cat jumping on her bed.

"She looked over towards the window and started screaming," the "moth" later related. "Her husband jumped out of bed and hollered, 'Who is there?' I ran and jumped in the car and drove down to Stanridge Street, where I entered a home through a window. As I went in the window this girl woke up. She screamed and I ran back out again and got in the car and went home."

Police responded with additional patrols at night in residential areas. Scores of known sex offenders were called in for questioning.

A month later, the moth took another flutter ... this time in broad daylight. It was 8.30 a.m. when, driving along Powell Street, Norristown, he passed a woman pedestrian.

"I went up the road and turned back," he later told the police. "When she came up to me I had the lower part of my body exposed. She stopped and stared, and then started running. I threw my trousers at her. I didn't say anything, just threw my trousers. That was the first time I ever exposed myself to anyone."

Less than a week later, he was driving to his parents'

home in Bridgeport at 2.30 a.m. when he saw a light on at a house in Green Street.

"I went over and looked in the window and this girl was lying asleep on the couch," he later admitted. "I knocked on the window, trying to attract her attention, but I couldn't awaken her. I tried the doors, and they were locked — but one window was unlatched and I pushed it open.

"I started into the front room and I saw a frying pan and took it with me. I made one swing and I think I hit the studio couch and the pan broke. I scuffled with the girl for a few minutes and she started screaming, and her mother hollered from upstairs, 'What is wrong?' So I ran out the back door and I went home."

He never admitted striking this victim, another teenage schoolgirl, with the cast-iron frying pan. She too was taken to hospital with a fractured skull.

Less than an hour before this incident, another lit window at a house in a nearby village had caught his eye. "I stopped because there was a light in the window and there was a young couple in the living-room," he said later. "I watched them. When he left, I tried the front door. It was locked. I went around the back and the screen door was unlatched and the kitchen door was standing open.

"I walked into the house and the telephone was there and I cut the wires. I went upstairs. I flashed a light in a bedroom. There were two little children sleeping. When I flashed the light one little girl cried out and the dog downstairs started barking. I figured it was time to leave and I ran outside and got in the car and started for my mother's place. But on the way I stopped at that other place in Bridgeport."

Ten days after that, he entered another house at night after seeing a girl through the window. He fled when other occupants were aroused.

On the evening of January 4th, 1948 — three weeks later — he put chains on his car wheels to cope with a snowfall. The first lit window to attract him proved a disappointment. Someone switched the light off, so he moved on, to a house in Norristown.

"I tried the front door and it was locked, and the back door was locked but the screen door was open," he said later. "The window on the right opened easily and I pushed it up and went in. Before going upstairs I cut the telephone wires with a pair of scissors I found laying on the desk in the front room, which I later threw over into the next yard. I started up the steps, and saw a lady in a room. She hollered, 'Who is making all the noise?' or something like that. I flashed the light on her and I ran out and back to the car where I had left it."

Minutes later, Detective Sergeant Edward Carrigan and Detective Jeremiah Delaney arrived in response to a call from neighbours who heard the woman's screams.

"He ran out to the alley!" an elderly woman cried. "I heard his car drive off. He must have parked it out there."

There was only one set of tyre tracks in the snow. They showed that the rear wheels of the car that had been parked were equipped with chains of the emergency type, which buckled on to provide a quick grip.

Returning to their patrol car, the two officers followed the tracks to a lock-up garage behind a house on Cherry Street.

There was a heavy padlock on the garage door. The officers went to the house and Carrigan rang the doorbell. Moments later, an elderly, greying man with sleep-drugged eyes stood before them.

"We're police officers and we'd like to take a look in the garage behind your place," said the detective-sergeant.

The householder explained that he rented the garage out and did not believe he had the right to open it for inspection.

"Then we'll have to break in the doors," Carrigan warned.

"No, I'll get the key," the pyjama-clad man said reluctantly. "But you'll have to answer to my tenant."

Moments later, the trio entered the garage. In the beams of their torches, the officers observed the emergency chains on the rear wheels of the dark green Mercury parked inside.

They also noted that the car's engine was still warm.

Going to the car-owner's address, the detectives found this was a ground-floor flat.

The door was opened by a pale, thin-faced man with strangely expressionless blue-grey eyes. Although his light brown hair was rumpled, and he was in his underwear, he did not look as though he had been suddenly roused from sleep.

The man identified himself as Elmo Lee Smith, 26. He admitted ownership of the Mercury in the garage down the street. But he denied having used the car since early the day before. He was unable to account for the engine being warm and the fresh snow on the tyres.

Back at headquarters, Sergeant Bradley was on duty when the two plainclothes men entered with Elmo Smith. Recognising the prisoner as the man he had seen leaving the hospital ward of the bludgeoned teenager six weeks earlier, Bradley called the detectives aside for a whispered conversation.

Elmo Smith never revealed whether he in turn recognised the police officer. But when Sergeant Bradley disclosed that he remembered him as the man who had suggested lynching for the girl's assailant, Elmo cracked and started talking.

After he pleaded guilty to five counts each of burglary and attempted criminal assault, he was sentenced to serve from 10 to 20 years in prison.

Elmo Smith's attractive, dark-haired young wife visited him on the day before he was taken to the state penitentiary. With her, she brought the son who had been born while Elmo was in jail awaiting trial.

While being brought down from his cell to the reception room where he was to say goodbye to his wife and the child he had never seen before, Elmo was observed slipping something from the pocket of his sweater. This proved to be a letter he had written in his cell shortly before he decided to plead guilty.

He later admitted that he had hoped to slip it unseen to

his wife, who until that time had stood staunchly by him.

"My Beloved Wife & Son," he had written, "I love you both with all my heart and soul. And I always shall till my dying day. If for some reason I get the limit for my wrong doing … and may not ever be able to see you two again, please try hard to forgive a fool for his mistakes and do your best to bring our son up to be a nice young Man and Friend of every one.

"I know that deep down inside you are wondering just what the outcome will be. I am too. But I promise you this, Darling. If I am able to return to you after all this is over I'll do everything I can to make this hurt and misery up to you. I am only sorry all this had to happen. But honestly, Darling, I'll never really know just what caused me to do these things.

"I am willing to confess to all the things I have done in this place. And vow to pay my debt to society. And return home to you all after it is over. And make you a good Husband and our son a Father. How long I will be gone I do not know …

"I only wish there was some way I could [tell] all these people I have hurt how sorry I really am. I have so much I would like to say to you to comfort you and help you. But I don't know just the words to say and use.

"I know I should have confided in you before this all happened. Now I realise it, where at the time I didn't for fear of hurting you. I only hope and pray to our Father above that He will help me and that these Doctors here can cure me so I will be fit to live once more again a Free man…"

Blaming his actions on his over-warm nature, he said this got the better of him when he saw women undressing or nude at a window, and he tried to get them to satisfy his desire.

"Please be careful and try to forgive me, Darling," he concluded. "I will close for now with love and kisses to you both and hope to see you all someday soon.

 Love yours alone,
  Hubby."

But Elmo never saw his wife or son again.

Examined by a prison psychiatrist, he was found to show "sexual psychopathic trends, with sudden impulses which lead to caveman tactics." Nevertheless, on completing his minimum term in 1958, he was released on parole.

He remained at liberty for less than four months. Always addicted to cars, he attempted to obtain a driving licence, in violation of the terms of his parole. Exposed when he signed a false name on the application, he was sent back to prison.

On at least three separate occasions after this, doctors who examined Elmo Smith pronounced him "dangerous to society." Judge William Dannehower, in returning him to prison after the parole violation, had recommended that he be forced to serve out his full 20-year term.

Yet in October, 1959, Elmo Smith was again released on parole. Once more he returned to his parents' home in Bridgeport.

Less than three months later, on December 28th, 1959, 16-year-old Maryann Mitchell failed to return to her home in Manayunk after going to a cinema with three girl friends.

Described by her mother as "a good girl who didn't chase around with boys," she had promised to be home by 10.30 p.m. Her father telephoned the Philadelphia police and an immediate search was begun after Maryann's friends told of leaving her at a bus stop about a mile and a half from her home.

Two days later, a couple of highway maintenance workers found her horribly mutilated body five miles away, in a roadside ditch. Maryann was lying on her back, her dress pulled up over her waist.

One of the first police officers on the scene reported: "Her head was a bloody mass. Her clothing had been ripped and disarranged. Strange markings were scrawled across her stomach. Her arm was extended upwards as though she'd tried to ward off a blow just before she died."

A pathologist who conducted an autopsy concluded that

she had been struck five or six times with a heavy blunt instrument. The injuries were consistent with blows from a car jack.

The pathologist believed that Maryann was alive when she was dumped in the shallow, water-filled ditch, and that she had lain there for several hours before she succumbed to her injuries.

The girl's abdomen bore markings which her killer had apparently made with her lipstick. There were the letters T B, a number symbol and the numerals 101. In addition, there was a semi-circle with the convexity pointing downwards. From the top of this semi-circle, there were radiating streaks of red pigment between four and six inches long. The markings had a scriptural significance, it was later believed. It was suggested that they constituted the symbol for St. Elmo.

Meanwhile, Elmo Smith had been picked up for questioning soon after the discovery of Maryann's body beside the road over which he drove to his job as a handyman at a suburban motel. But the ex-convict had been released after detectives corroborated his alibi that he was at home at the time of the murder.

Then, two days later, a stolen car with bloodsoaked upholstery and a bloodstained tyre jack in the boot was found near the home of the suspect's parents in Bridgeport. A licence plate stolen near Lancaster, Pennsylvania, had been substituted for the owner's.

Elmo Smith was rearrested. Some of his clothing, stained with Type-A blood, the same as that of the victim had been found in Room 101 at the motel where he was employed.

The owner of the car in which it was believed Maryann was attacked was a Bridgeport businessman. His two-tone 1958 Chevrolet had been stolen from the street in front of his home on the night of December 12th, 1959.

He and his wife had been attending a party that evening. Shortly before midnight, they learned that a fire had broken out in their home. Later, police reported that a burglar had broken into the apartment, stolen an expensive gold wrist-watch and other articles, and then started four fires in an attempt to cover his trail.

The burglar had also taken the Chevrolet that was parked outside. When the car was subsequently recovered, Maryann's bloodstained garter belt was found a few hundred feet away.

Charged with the murder of Maryann, Elmo Smith was confronted at his trial by another woman in his life. Into the witness box stepped an attractive blonde, Mrs. Jeanne Bormann.

Earlier in the proceedings, Prosecutor Vincent Cirillo had produced the gold wrist-watch which had been stolen from the home of the owner of the Chevrolet. Now Cirillo showed the watch to Mrs. Bormann, asking her if she could identify it.

Yes, she could, said Mrs. Bormann. It had been given to her by her old friend Elmo Smith on Christmas Day.

What, asked Cirillo, was her husband's name?

"Tracy Bormann," she replied.

"What are his initials?"

"T.B."

For weeks there had been speculation about the two initials lettered on the body of the young victim. Here, it seemed, was the answer to the enigma.

The next witness, identifying himself as "the husband of Jeanne Bormann's cousin," told how Elmo had visited him during the third week in December, 1959.

A fortnight passed before the witness noticed that the licence plate on his Plymouth car had been changed. In its place was another ... which turned out to belong to the stolen Chevrolet, which upon recovery was found to be displaying the Plymouth's licence plate.

Detective Samuel Hammes told the court of Elmo Smith's response to questioning. "He told us that he left his parents' home at six p.m. on the night of the murder. He said he was in the car he had stolen two weeks before. He said he drove around in that car for several hours, trying to pick up a girl, before finding Maryann Mitchell."

The officer said that Smith called her "Honey" and asked if she wanted to go for a ride. He insisted that the girl got into his car of her own free will.

On retiring to consider their verdict, the jury took with them a transcript of questions which had been put to Elmo Smith, and the answers he had given. They read the following dialogue:

Q. Did you stop during your ride?

A. Yes, about 10.30 on a back street.

Q. Did you remain seated in the car?

A. We sat in the front seat for a few minutes and next thing we were in the back seat making love.

Q. Tell us what you did while you were on the back seat?

A. We went in the back seat and we had a love affair and … She had a lipstick in her pocket and I took it … and then I was marking her stomach up with letters and numbers.

Q. What did you put on her stomach?

A. I marked a "T" and a "B" and a number sign and "101" and a few marks with lines with the lipstick.

Q. Then you did what?

A. She was giggling and then when I wanted her again she didn't like the idea and she wanted to go home … she started struggling. I guess I got mad and I reached over on the floor and my hand touched something and I found it was a tyre jack and I picked up the jack and hit her over the head and she was squirming. She was partially on her side and when I hit her I would say it was back of her ear or the back of her head.

Q. Did she say anything?

A. She said, "Don't hit me any more. Just take me home." I threw the jack on the floor and started back where I had picked her up.

Q. What route did you take?

A. The same route I came over previous but I pulled up alongside a fence and I told her to get out and walk and she didn't say anything, just groaned, so I opened the door and grabbed hold of her dress and it came up above her shoulders at the time and I rolled her out of the car. I think she rolled down the bank.

Q. Was she still living?

A. She was living because she was moving and the things she said she must have been living.

Q. What did she say?

A. Just take me home.

Q. Did you expect anybody to find her?

A. I expected the people in the house to find her or else her crawl up to the house. [The closest residence was four hundred and sixty feet from the spot where the body was found two days later.]

Q. Then what did you do?

A. I got in the car and came back to Bridgeport.

Q. Do the letters T and B have any significance?

A. At the time I didn't know.

Q. Do you know anybody with the initials, T.B.?

A. Tracy Bormann.

Q. Is his wife's name Jeanne?

A. Yes, sir.

Q. Is she your girl friend?

A. Yes, ever since childhood.

Q. The symbol and No. 101? Does that have any significance?

A. No.

Q. The aurora that was painted around her — does that have any significance?

A. No, sir. It is some lines that came up and I marked them all down, not knowing what it meant.

Asked about the stolen car, Elmo Smith denied having robbed and torched its owner's apartment. He took the car from in front of a theatre in Norristown "about a couple of weeks before the murder." He claimed that he found the wrist-watch in a handbag in the car.

Taking the stand during the closing days of his trial, Elmo Smith denied murdering Maryann Mitchell, and claimed that his confessions had been made under duress.

The jury were not impressed. On September 2nd, 1960, they found Elmo Smith guilty and recommended the death

penalty. Five months later, he was sentenced to be executed
… but his case was far from being ended.

On his way back to a jail cell to await further moves by
his lawyers, Smith was asked, "How do you feel about going
to the chair?"

"Oh, let's not go into that right now," he replied.
"You've heard the expression, 'Curiosity killed the cat'?
Well, let's not kill the cat yet."

Pressing for a new trial, the defence argued that Maryann
Mitchell would still be alive if the State of Pennsylvania had
not freed a proven psychopath.

Elmo's lawyers pointed to his history as a molester of
girls and women, to the reports of several psychiatrists who
had pronounced him dangerous, and to the irrationality of
his conduct. In an effort to prove that their client suffered
from a split personality, they quoted his own words. In the
letter to his wife and child, he had spoken with tenderness
and compassion; in the description of his crime which he
gave after his arrest, he showed himself a psychopath with
violent and sadistic compulsions.

Prosecutor Cirillo countered that the condemned man's
sanity had been clearly established by the evidence of
experts. And the fact that Elmo had been freed before
serving out his maximum 20-year term for the earlier
offences did not mean that the state had given him a licence
to go out and murder an innocent girl.

The defence responded by pointing again to the moral
responsibility of the state, which had freed Elmo after he
had repeatedly been pronounced dangerous, and which
had overruled the objections of the judge who first sent him
to prison.

The State Board of Pardons, however, refused to recom-
mend clemency, and on April 2nd, 1962, Elmo Smith was
taken to the death house at Rockview Penitentiary. His
head was shaved and he was issued with the black trousers,
open-neck white shirt and black bedroom slippers in which
he was to die.

At 9 p.m. he walked calmly to the electric chair, where

guards placed heavy leather straps around his abdomen and chest. Electrodes were fixed to his head, and to both wrists and both ankles.

The condemned man's problems had begun with his moth-like fascination with illuminated windows. Now, just as moths perish when their wings are burned, so was Elmo Smith singed to death by the 2,000 volts which passed through his body.

TRUE CRIME LIBRARY SERIES

1 A CENTURY OF SEX KILLERS
Brian Marriner

This book confirms Brian Marriner as the leading authority in his field. From Jack the Ripper to the Serial Killers, the most comprehensive work available on sex murderers.

£4.99

2 FATAL ATTRACTION
When Love Turns to Murder
Mike James

Twenty incredible stories make up this enthralling volume of murder at its most passionate. It will root you to the spot. Compulsive reading for all fans of the true crime genre.

£3.99

3 A DATE WITH THE HANGMAN
T. J. Leech

This is an outstanding volume of British murder cases, uncanny and strange. The killers are an odd mix — robbers and rapists, cop-killers and con-men, jealous lovers, paedophiles, madmen and ruthless women. But all had one thing in common … a date with the hangman.

£3.99

4 MURDER WITH VENOM
Brian Marriner

"These sixteen celebrated murder cases coupled with an absorbing study of the poisons used reinforces Brian Marriner's claim to be one of the most distinguished living crime writers"

£4.99

5 BRITAIN'S GODFATHER
Edward T. Hart

Rave reviews include:

"A best-seller in the making"

"It is one of those un-put-downable books. Once started, I just had to keep on until I reached the final page"

"An incredible story written by a craftsman"

"A captivating story that could be the perfect format for a film"

£4.99